Communist Indochina and
U.S. Foreign Policy

Westview Special Studies in International Relations

Communist Indochina and U.S. Foreign Policy:
Postwar Realities
Joseph J. Zasloff and MacAlister Brown

This study examines the important political and economic developments in Vietnam, Laos, and Cambodia since the Communist victories in 1975 and analyzes the critical policy issues facing the Carter administration in dealing with these states. Summarizing the major options immediately available to U.S. policymakers who confronted the new regimes in Indochina as "wait and see," "neocontainment," and "rapid reconciliation," the authors assess such persisting issues as Vietnam's admission to the United Nations; Americans missing in action in Indochina; the normalization of relations; and reconstruction aid to Indochina. They trace developments within the Indochina states and deal with leadership, political doctrine, party and government organization, economic problems and prospects, and external relations; in so doing, they demonstrate that the revolutions in Indochina were fundamental social revolutions, conclusive and irreversible. They make clear that, although the new Indochina regimes came to power in rapid succession—the results of three closely intertwined revolutions—there are distinct differences among them in their internal revolutionary activities and their foreign policies.

In preparing their study, Professors Brown and Zasloff have examined translations of Vietnamese, Laotian, and Cambodian daily radio broadcasts and newspapers; conducted interviews with members of the U.S. Congress and the executive branch; and drawn on insights gained during trips to Japan and Southeast Asia.

Joseph J. Zasloff is professor of political science at the University of Pittsburgh. MacAlister Brown is professor of political science and chairman of the Political Economy Program at Williams College.

Communist Indochina and
U.S. Foreign Policy:
Postwar Realities

Joseph J. Zasloff and MacAlister Brown

Westview Press / Boulder, Colorado

Westview Special Studies in International Relations

This book has been expanded by the authors from a report originally prepared under the auspices of The Asia Society, a not-for-profit, nonpolitical, educational organization dedicated to deepening American understanding of Asia and promoting thoughtful trans-Pacific intellectual exchange. The report served as the basis for a discussion of United States Indochina policy by a distinguished panel of experts meeting at Asia House in New York in April 1977.

While the Society attempts to stimulate discussion of the important questions involved in America's relations with Asia, it takes no stand on any public policy issues. The opinions expressed in this volume are thus those of the authors and do not necessarily represent the views of The Asia Society.

Copyright © 1978 by Westview Press, Inc.

Published in 1978 in the United States of America by
    Westview Press, Inc.
    5500 Central Avenue
    Boulder, Colorado 80301
    Frederick A. Praeger, Publisher

Library of Congress Cataloging in Publication Data
Zasloff, Joseph Jeremiah.
    Communist Indochina and U.S. foreign policy.
    (Westview special studies on international relations)
    Includes index.
    1. Indochina—Foreign relations—United States. 2. United States—Foreign relations
—Indochina. 3. Indochina—Politics and government. 4. Indochina—Economic conditions.
I. Brown, MacAlister, joint author. II. Title. III. Series.
DS546.Z37   327.73'0597   77-28462
ISBN 0-89158-150-2

Printed and bound in the United States of America

Contents

Figures

Abbreviations

ADB	Asian Development Bank
ARVN	Army of the Republic of Vietnam
ASEAN	Association of Southeast Asian Nations
CMEA	Council for Mutual Economic Assistance
COSVN	Central Office for South Vietnam
DRV	Democratic Republic of Vietnam
ESCAP	Economic and Social Commission for Asia and the Pacific
FEOF	Foreign Exchange Operations Fund
FPJMT	Four-Party Joint Military Team
FRETILIN	Revolutionary Front for an Independent East Timor
FUNK	Front unifié nationale de Kampuchéa
GRUNK	Gouvernement royale d'union nationale de Kampuchéa
ICP	Indochinese Communist Party
IDA	International Development Association
IMF	International Monetary Fund
JEC	Joint Economic Commission
LPDR	Lao People's Democratic Republic
LPF	Lao Patriotic Front
LPP	Lao People's Party
LPRP	Lao People's Revolutionary Party
MIA	missing in action
NLF	National Liberation Front
NSC	National Security Council
PAFNLK	People's Armed Forces for National Liberation of Kampuchea

PAVN	People's Army of Vietnam
PGNU	Provisional Government of National Union
PL	Pathet Lao
PNF	Patriotic Neutralist Front
POW	prisoner of war
PPL	People's Party of Laos
PRA	People's Representative Assembly
PRC	People's Republic of China
PRG	Provisional Revolutionary Government of South Vietnam
RLG	Royal Lao Government
SEATO	Southeast Asia Treaty Organization
SPC	Supreme People's Council
SRV	Socialist Republic of Vietnam
UNDP	United Nations Development Program
UNHCR	United Nations High Commissioner for Refugees
UNICEF	United Nations International Children's Emergency Fund
U.S. AID	United States Agency for International Development
VCP	Vietnam Communist Party
VWP	Vietnamese Workers' Party
WHO	World Health Organization

Preface

Indochina has consistently confounded Americans. Official policy toward the area has veered from Franklin Roosevelt's disapproval of French colonialism during World War II to the American replacement of the French in Vietnam in 1954, and from critical support of President Diem's government in South Vietnam to complicity in removing him in 1963, followed by U.S. assumption of the major burden of war for seven years. Throughout this prolonged and intimate involvement, illusion after illusion about Indochina has been shattered in the public and official mind. Today Americans find themselves confronted by an area that persists in contradicting expectations bred by wartime perspectives. Even discounting the rhetoric and rationales of U.S. policymakers during the 1960s, the region manifests internal conflicts and foreign policy tactics almost unimaginable five years ago. Yet no Western journalists reside in the three new communist states to report on their internal development. Formal diplomatic relations between Washington and Vietnam have remained broken since April 1975, and each side charges the other with failing to fulfill obligations under the Paris cease-fire agreement. Laos only tolerates a residual American Mission and charges bad faith over the promise of reconstruction aid. Cambodia has scornfully turned its back on diplomatic relations with most of the world.

One need not fully catalog the false assumptions that Americans have made about Indochina to make it clear that caution is required in examining the present situation and future U.S. relations in the area. The notion that the Viet Minh represented a struggle between "world communism" and the "free world," or that the revolutionaries acted on orders from Moscow or Peking, gradually eroded as the cold war itself receded. The idea that U.S. military and political mentorship could decisively determine the outcome of the revolutionary struggle in the area—though some cling to it—was contradicted by events. The notion that "Vietnamization" of the American role would be sufficient to stem the revolution or provide a "decent interval" after the U.S. departure is clearly discredited. Predictions that the fall of the Saigon government would be followed by a "bloodbath," or that communist takeovers in Indochina would lead to "falling dominoes" in Southeast Asia, remain unfulfilled. The hypothesis that the Vietnamese communists, if victorious, would impose a Vietnamese-dominated federation upon their Lao and Cambodian comrades has not materialized, but Cambodia and Vietnam are engaged in border hostilities which might well be labeled the third Indochina war. The internal social and economic policies of the new communist regimes have ranged from economically constrained and ideologically pragmatic in Vietnam and Laos to radical beyond historical record in supposedly gentle, slumbering Cambodia. In their foreign relations, Vietnam and Laos have tilted toward Moscow, while Cambodia has aligned itself with Peking. Vietnam's vast windfall of arms and mobilized manpower has not been used to menace Thailand, and economic reconstruction problems have all but overwhelmed the victorious revolutionaries.

Given such past misjudgments about Indochina, and the political polarization that the United States suffered in debating the morality and legitimacy of its participation in the Indochina war, it is not surprising that Americans today seem either to ignore the area or to lash out in anger at the Indochina states' failure to account for all the Americans listed as missing in action. The neighbors of these three new communist states, who could not afford simply to let the dust settle in Indochina, attempted to improve relations wherever possible; but the United States at first pursued an essentially wait-and-see policy after May 1975. Recognizing that such a policy runs the risk of hardening into intractability after several years, the Carter administration responded to the need for reassessment and initiated negotiations with Vietnam to explore prospects for the normalization of relations. However, when Congress vigorously opposed the allocation of funds, direct or indirect, for reconstruction aid to Vietnam, which the Vietnamese had been demanding, the administration slowed down on normalization and gave priority to other pending foreign policy issues.

Meanwhile, war-bred expectations regarding the nature of communist rule in the Indochina states have not been thoroughly reexamined in the absence of U.S. diplomatic, journalistic, or scholarly access to these countries. Notwithstanding this lack of access, this book presents a report on the nature and policies of the new communist regimes of Indochina since 1975 and an examination of U.S. policy options in dealing with them. Three years after the communist takeovers, new patterns of foreign relations are being tested in Southeast Asia, and the United States must be prepared to move forward realistically in recognition of new conditions. To facilitate such a new departure, an informed public perspective on Indochina is needed.

An effort in this direction was undertaken by a panel discussion at The Asia Society in New York City on April 28, 1977, entitled "U.S. Policy Toward Indochina," for which we prepared a working paper. Herbert D. Spivack, who organized the meeting, encouraged us to expand our paper into a book-length study, and the idea was supported by our publisher. We are grateful for their inspiration and backing, as well as for the advice and assistance of many friends and consultants.

The foundation of our study lies in the years of teaching, research, and writing of Joseph J. Zasloff in and about Vietnam and Laos since 1959, and the collaborative efforts of both of us in writing about the Indochina war since 1971. In July 1974, we conducted extensive interviews in Saigon and Laos, with side trips to Phnom Penh and Bangkok. Since 1973, we have written annual reports on the year in Laos for the *Asian Survey.* In the spring of 1977, while engaged in a speaking tour sponsored by the Department of State, we conducted interviews with officials in four ASEAN countries. Although unable to obtain visas for entry into Laos, we visited the refugee camp at Ngong Khai, Thailand, across the Mekong River from Vientiane. In Paris we interviewed former officials of the Laotian government and French specialists on the region.

As primary source material we have relied on translations of daily radio transmissions from Vietnam, Laos, and Cambodia published by the Foreign Broadcast Information Service (FBIS). We have also extensively consulted the journalistic and scholarly writing about postwar Indochina, in English and French. The weekly reportage of the *Far Eastern Economic Review* has been particularly helpful. Numerous American specialists in Indochina affairs, both in and out of government, have shared their insights with us and given generously of their time. We shall not attempt to name them all, since the list is lengthy and we would risk inadvertent omissions.

We are particularly indebted to Timothy Carney, Allan Goodman, Michael McPherson, Thomas Miller, and William Turley for reviewing chapters in draft. Their generosity should in no way associate them with any omissions or faults in our work. We have also received able research assistance from Lewis Stern and Chris Broda of the University of Pittsburgh and Williams College, respectively. Timothy Carney, Judith Johnson, Thomas Miller, and John J. Pavone of the Department of State were generous in supplying information and insights. Tela Zasloff has contributed a surgeon's skill as editorial advisor.

Finally, we express our appreciation to our respective academic institutions for supplying research facilities and funds through the University of Pittsburgh's Asian Studies Program, its Research Development Fund, a John G. Bowman Faculty Grant, and the Williams College Faculty Research Fund.

The United States and Indochina: Postwar Relations

Impact of the War on U.S. Policy

The great American frustration in Vietnam has left its mark on the institutions and future direction of U.S. foreign policy. Even though the nation moved abruptly from obsession to amnesia with regard to Indochina, the aftereffects of the lost war penetrate the public consciousness from time to time. The bitter feelings of the wounded veterans, of draft evaders and deserters, and of families of fallen servicemen or those missing in action will not quickly disappear. Nor will the problems of Indochina refugees trying to fit into a very un-Asian society simply go away. Even the U.S. military services are suffering through a readjustment, after a period in which conscription was discredited and there was a serious loss of morale and discipline in the field.

The least tangible legacy of the U.S. failure in Indochina will be the "lessons" that policymakers will learn. The succession of rationales set forth by U.S. presidents to justify their policy in Indochina is best left to historians. The important point here is simply that the cold war outlook as applied to Asia, and awkwardly adapted to changing circumstances, is now recognized as wholly outdated. The most significant act of the Nixon administration was not the "peace with honor" arranged in Paris, but the opening of relations with China. The policy of dealing with China as a major power quite separate from the Soviet Union underscored the secondary importance of Vietnam and the fact that the Indochina revolutions were not inspired by either the Soviet Politburo or Chairman Mao. Obviously, the outcomes of people's liberation wars still matter to the United States, but the U.S. government now recognizes both the importance of nationalism to communist states and movements and the possibility of working with this force to reduce the pressure on U.S. interests. By the same token, the misadventure in Vietnam has invited the conclusion that U.S. arms and technical advisers cannot in themselves provide national cohesion or build a nation, even in opposition to an externally assisted guerrilla enemy, and that without such cohesion U.S. efforts may prove futile and debilitating both at home and abroad. This conclusion was implicitly expressed in both the Nixon Doctrine and President Ford's Pacific Doctrine.

Closer to home, the war severely chastened, even discredited the U.S. armed services, covert operations, the presidency, the departments of State and Defense, and the Congress. The scrutiny focused on these institutions by the press and by Congress itself, in the wake of mounting resistance to the war, uncovered deficiencies and deceits that have profoundly shaken public confidence. Because of this and the deceptions associated with Watergate, Americans' trust in their leaders in Washington suffered a serious decline. All the assaults on traditional American values need not be cataloged here, but there are more than enough to spread through the government. Such notorious terms as My Lai, Operation Phoenix, the "Secret War," Special Forces, "Cambodian incursion," Washington Special Action Group (WASAG), the Tonkin Resolution, "protective reaction strikes," defoliation, Public Safety Division assistance, Program Requirements Office, "guns and butter budget"—all bring to mind the incredible poses and roles assumed by Americans during the Indochina nightmare. Individual careers were blunted as public scrutiny of the conduct of the war revealed questionable behavior; and the armed services, the CIA, and the aid agencies have been obliged to accept safeguards against future loss of balance.

These restrictions on secrecy and executive discretion are significant for future U.S. policy toward Indochina insofar as they might narrow the options. Congress has asserted its authority in the realm of national security policy as a result of the national debate over how to end the war. Having voted for military aid in Vietnam since 1950 and having passed the Tonkin Gulf Resolution with but two dissenting votes in 1964, it had a long road to travel before breaking with executive policy and forcing the president to end U.S. bombing in Cambodia in August 1973. That path of retrenchment included belated committee probes into such questions as U.S. commitments abroad, the rationale of the war, the Tonkin Gulf incidents, the weapons procurement budget, the uses of U.S. aid, the role of the CIA, and the whole record of executive decision making revealed in the Pentagon Papers. Out of this discomforting scrutiny emerged congressional enactments of more than momentary impact.

The War Powers Act of 1973, passed over Nixon's veto, requires the president to report promptly to Congress any introduction of U.S. forces into ongoing or imminent hostilities and obliges the Congress to decide whether military action should be sustained beyond sixty days. The president is also now required to report an executive agreement (for example, in acquiring bases abroad) to the Congress within sixty days. As a result of recent revelations about CIA activities, activities only partly related to the Indochina war, the Senate set up a separate Committee on Intelligence, which appears ready to play a more active role in monitoring clandestine operations abroad than did the previous group of elders from the Appropriations and Armed Services committees. Congress has also recognized the compromising path that U.S. aid-giving relationships have sometimes taken. Greater restrictions on executive discretion have been written into recent foreign economic and military assistance appropriations, and military aid has also been declining. Not only have specific controversies, such as the Greek-Turkish war over Cyprus, been affected by such strictures on the U.S. executive branch, but economic aid to countries that abuse human rights has also been brought under congressional limitation.

Within the military services, the retrenchment of the U.S. presence in Asia did not create any publicized resistance for many months after the fall of Saigon. The U.S. military apparently accepted the negotiated abandonment of U.S. air bases in Thailand as cost-effective in the broadest sense, given the end of the Indochina war. Nor were there attempts to breathe life back into the Southeast Asia Treaty Organization. The policy of reducing U.S. forces stationed in South Korea, however, has not been implemented without misgivings within the U.S. Army, misgivings expressed in the summer of 1977.

The bite of new legislative requirements and the temper of

Congress itself were felt by Secretary of State Kissinger in 1976, when he requested congressional support for covert U.S. aid to the faction he favored in the struggle for power in newly independent Angola. His plea that the United States could not afford to let the Soviet-backed and Cuban-backed group prevail was rejected in Congress with resounding incantations of the Vietnam analogy. One case does not make an orthodoxy, but the Vietnam lesson on intervention may prove to be as easy to invoke as the Munich lesson on appeasement. Ironically, a year later, when the Mobutu government in Zaire seemed threatened by Cuban-trained rebel forces in Katanga, the Carter administration lay low, and the Mobutu government recovered its position with the aid of France and its African neighbor Morocco.

Immediate Postwar Policy Options: 1975

In the aftermath of the inglorious U.S. retirement from Saigon, Phnom Penh, and all but the embassy compound in Vientiane, the United States government had to choose policies for dealing with the victorious revolutionary governments throughout Indochina. We do not know how thoroughly the Ford administration debated the question, but several major options were available. Secretary of State Kissinger and his chief advisers chose essentially to "wait and see," looking to the future rather than the past, gearing U.S. actions to the behavior of the Indochina states, particularly to their relations with their neighbors, and also stressing the U.S. desire to obtain an accounting of its servicemen missing in action.[1]

A second option, which could be called "neocontainment," might have been to pursue a more vindictive or aggressive policy against the military power and revolutionary aspirations of Vietnam. Under such a policy, the United States might have actively encouraged ASEAN (Association of Southeast Asian Nations— Indonesia, the Philippines, Thailand, Malaysia, Singapore) to develop thorough coordination of military planning and training (especially in counterinsurgency) and procurement of equipment. Covert assistance might have been provided for insurgent or resistance groups in the three Indochina states, groups whose base of supply and control would have been in Thailand. This policy would have urged the retention of some U.S. base rights in Thailand and perhaps the assurance of easy U.S. reoccupation of air bases upon mutual agreement. The United States might have publicly supported Thailand and the Philippines in their maritime territorial claims—which conflict with those of Vietnam and Cambodia— thus demonstrating U.S. solidarity with Southeast Asian states that feel threatened by the new Indochina. The United States not only would have imposed a full embargo on trade by Americans with the Indochina states but also would have withheld any eco- nomic assistance and would have discouraged other states from trading with or aiding the revolutionary regimes. At the same time, the United States would have used its position in international institutions such as the World Bank and the World Health Organiza- tion to block or discourage programs destined to assist the new people's republics. The entry of Vietnam into the United Nations would have been blocked—by a U.S. veto in the Security Council, if necessary—with the argument that this revolutionary state must first demonstrate willingness to fulfill the UN Charter's require- ment of being "peace-loving" and other obligations of member- ship. To underline its adverse position, the United States would have highlighted the harsh treatment of dissidents in Vietnam. It might also have relentlessly condemned the death and dislocation imposed upon Cambodia by its new rulers.

Would such a cold war–like policy have benefited the United States? In some respects it might have. The withholding of eco- nomic assistance might well have delayed the reconstruction and development of these states, holding back their achievement of a higher living standard and diminishing their political attraction as a model of national development. The bolstering of ASEAN solidarity and cooperation in countering any communist-inspired insurgencies would have helped restore confidence within that organization, which the frenzied U.S. exit from Indochina shat- tered. The United States itself would have refused to deal with the new regimes, even though some Americans might suffer from uncertainty over the missing in action, and it would thereby have demonstrated its steadfast disapproval and rejection of communist political systems.

On the other hand, the costs of such implacable hostility would have been considerable. Not only would the tension between the Indochina states and their neighbors have remained high, but the socialist states would have been enhanced as the champions and providers for their comrades in a situation they would interpret as provocative and vindictive. A siege mentality might have developed within Indochina, which would perhaps have diverted energies from economic development and encouraged government repression, hurting particularly those who had placed their faith in the United States and old regimes. ASEAN states might not have readily maintained the breach between themselves and Indochina, especially in the light of ASEAN's support since 1971 for the idea of neutralization of Southeast Asia. The U.S. Congress might have been reluctant to authorize military assistance that Thailand or Malaysia might request for counterinsurgency training and equipment, since such aid might reinvolve U.S. forces on the Asian mainland. A contradiction between U.S. verbal policy and congressional implementation would have further weakened U.S. credibility. In May 1975 there were probably few serious advocates of this containment policy within the U.S. government.

A diametrically opposite policy to neocontainment might have been "rapid reconciliation." Such a stance was hardly conceivable in the summer of 1975. The airlift of Vietnamese orphans and frantic scramble to the helicopters on the U.S. embassy roof in Saigon and to U.S. Navy pick-up vessels offshore still preyed on American minds. After years of talk in Washington of a communist "bloodbath" if Saigon should fall, and with some accounts available of the Draconian Khmer Rouge evacuation of Phnom Penh, the American public was in no mood to forgive and forget or to press for normal diplomatic or economic relations with the triumphant communist regimes. Instead, Americans seemed inclined to repress the memory of the unsuccessful war and to avoid ugly questions about how to live with the results. Any U.S. effort actively to promote normal relations with Vietnam and Cambodia in 1975 would probably have been rebuffed and would have made the United States seem hapless and irresolute.

Between the extremes of sustained hostility and rapid reconciliation lay the policy of eventual rapprochement. The critical dimensions would be timing and conditions. The "wait and see" policy chosen by Kissinger and Ford seems to have rested on the assumption that "they need us more than we need them." Indeed,

Secretary of State Kissinger reportedly so testified to Congress some months later.[2] However, although on the one hand Indochina did badly "need" U.S. reconstruction assistance, on the other hand, the U.S. government itself came under political pressure from American families to obtain information on the missing in action (MIAs). U.S. policymakers assumed that this pressure would not reach intolerable levels in Washington, and many argued that the United States should not submit to "blackmail" in order to obtain confirmation of the fate of its servicemen. Yet the issue remained highly emotional, and the families were well organized. The attitude might become not "wait and see" but rather "how long must we wait?"

Another element pushing for renewed relations with Indochina was the interest of U.S. businesses in retrieving assets and contractual privileges abandoned in South Vietnam. However, this group could be expected to remain quiescent for a few years. Another factor to be considered by U.S. policymakers was the tiny group of religious and humanitarian organizations that was anxious to assuage a sense of national guilt by donations of supplies and, if possible, services to the war-torn nations. These humanitarian groups were not politically strong, and they could carry out their activities in the absence of U.S. recognition of the revolutionary governments. Nonetheless, their voices were heard, and they found a few friends in Congress.

On balance, the "wait and see" approach of insisting on proper behavior and letting the new states come to the United States seemed a reasonable policy. It withheld U.S. legitimization of the communist takeovers as well as U.S. aid in building the new communist societies. At the same time, it spoke of putting the past behind us, and it steered clear of involvement in sponsoring insurgent activities against the new regimes. It would require the Vietnamese to approach the United States for the economic benefits they would so obviously wish to receive. It would avoid, or at least delay, resentment on the part of other Southeast Asian states, which would compare their U.S. aid with what a former enemy in Indochina might be offered.

On the other hand, this policy did not give the United States any leverage over how long it might have to wait in Indochina, especially with regard to the missing-in-action question. In addition,

the Soviet Union, China, and other socialist states would build up
a substantial economic foundation in Indochina, a foundation that
might make American ideas or equipment less sought after in the
future, especially if industrial countries such as France and Japan,
and international organizations such as the World Bank, actively
entered the scene. Furthermore, it would be difficult to defend
the principle that Vietnam's entry into the United Nations should
depend simply upon its behavior toward the United States. Eventually, the passivity of the Kissinger-Ford policy, with its lack of
leverage within Vietnam, and the lack of allied support created
strains that the Carter administration sought to resolve by solicit-
ing an opening of discussions on the MIA question with a view
toward early normalization of relations with Hanoi. In doing so,
however, the administration seemed to precipitate new dissension,
in which the Congress resurrected elements of the neocontainment
approach; e.g., it placed a total ban on economic assistance and
publicized the political transgressions of the Indochina governments.

Notwithstanding the differences in emphasis between administrations, and between the executive and legislative branches of
government, the pursuit of a prudent postwar policy toward
Indochina has obliged U.S. policymakers to confront certain major
issues.

Major Postwar Issues Confronting the United States

At the end of the war, four major questions were at issue
between the United States and the states of Indochina. The first—
discussed below—has since been resolved, but the remaining three
still await solutions.

The Admission of Vietnam to the United Nations

In August 1975 both the Democratic Republic of Vietnam and
the Provisional Revolutionary Government of the Republic of
South Vietnam (PRG) sought to join the United Nations.[3] The
Republic of Korea was also applying, but the Korean People's
Democratic Republic had made it clear that it opposed any
Korean membership before unification of the nation. A majority
of the Security Council members, therefore, voted to drop the

South Korean application from the provisional agenda. On August 11, 1975, the United States cast a solitary veto against the pending Vietnamese applications, because their sponsors had "refused to act equitably toward the application of another nation." Ambassador Moynihan declared that his country "would have voted for the admission" of all three applicants, and for North Korea as well, but it would "have nothing to do with a selective universality."

A year later, following the formal unification of Vietnam, the Socialist Republic of Vietnam (SRV) applied for admission, and on September 13, 1976, U.S. Ambassador Scranton, after conferring at the White House, announced that he would veto the application in the Security Council because of Vietnamese failure to provide a full accounting of the Americans missing in action in the war. A day later, the Security Council, upon the initiative of the French delegation, postponed consideration of the issue until November (after the U.S. presidential election). Apparently Secretary Kissinger had worked out this arrangement a week earlier in Paris, and France had obtained Vietnam's agreement to the postponement. Following the election, however, the United States cast its veto against the SRV application on the grounds that the SRV had failed to meet the charter's standard as a "peace-loving state" by not satisfactorily accounting for the MIAs of the Vietnam war.[4] A subsequent UN General Assembly resolution, opposed only by the United States, recommended (without legal effect) a favorable reconsideration of Vietnam's request for admission.

President-elect Carter's ambassador-designate to the United Nations, Andrew Young, was quick to announce his view that relations between the United States and Vietnam should be repaired. At his confirmation hearing before the Senate Foreign Relations Committee on January 26, 1977, he expressed his hope that the United States would permit Vietnam's entry into the UN at its next application and indicated that the administration intended to move forthrightly toward normalization of relations through reopening bilateral talks within ninety days. The State Department clarified this intention the next day, saying it was ready to work toward normalization but without any fixed time frame.

The Carter administration moved definitively to abandon the

UN membership question as an issue between the United States and Vietnam when it opened formal talks in Paris on May 3–4, 1977. The U.S. negotiators pledged that the United States would no longer veto a Vietnamese application for UN membership. The Vietnamese had earlier described the question—in talks with President Carter's emissaries on the MIA question—as an "erroneous policy" rather than an issue for discussion between governments. A U.S. holdout on this question would have antagonized the Vietnamese and much of the Third World, but an early abandonment of the veto policy could be used as an opening gesture of goodwill. The latter course was adopted, and on July 20, 1977, the UN Security Council, after a two-day debate, approved the admission of Vietnam, without a formal vote. The final vote of admission by the General Assembly awaited its reconvening in September.

Thus the UN admission issue had involved the United States in an inconsistency, one in which it departed from its long-standing advocacy of universal membership. No other member state supported the U.S. stand, and the new U.S. ambassador was eager to abandon it. The use of a U.S. veto as a bargaining device to pry out information about MIAs began to look like a policy of spite, and the Carter administration easily chose to make an opening concession to Vietnam on this question in the hope of stimulating reciprocal gestures.

Americans Missing in Action in Indochina

A year and a half after the fall of Saigon, 786 American servicemen and civilians were officially listed as "missing" or prisoners as a result of the Indochina war.[5] The governments of Indochina could still provide information on the fate and burial place of some of them and could still return some human remains. The House Select Committee on Missing Persons in Southeast Asia, which investigated this problem from September 1975 to December 1976, agreed with the national intelligence community's conclusion that there was no reliable evidence that any American was still being held captive as a result of the war. The committee, chaired by Congressman G. V. "Sonny" Montgomery, pointed out that the MIA category had been inflated during the war by "many questionable classifications." They regretted that a temporary court injunction in a class action suit and a Defense Department moratorium on unsolicited case reviews had created "an unrealistic situation in which the administrative status of a missing American" —whose pay and allowances are continued to his beneficiaries— "depended primarily on the desires and actions of his primary next of kin." The National League of Families of prisoners of war and missing servicemen—which the Nixon administration encouraged to "go public" with demands for proper treatment of captured Americans in 1969—has continued after the war to harry the government for not giving a "satisfactory" classification of cases and for not obtaining a full accounting from the enemy.

An unanticipated by-product of the popular attention focused on this question was the Vietnamese revelation to the Montgomery Select Committee in Hanoi, in December 1975, that President Nixon had sent a letter to the prime minister of the Democratic Republic of Vietnam (DRV) within five days of the signing of the Paris Agreement. According to Vietnamese sources, the president wrote that "the USA will contribute to postwar reconstruction in North Vietnam without any political conditions." The letter further identified a preliminary U.S. planning figure of "$3.25 billion of grant aid over 5 years."[6] The Ford administration declined to produce the secret Nixon letter of February 1973, citing executive privilege. Secretary of State Kissinger, however, insisted that no unconditional commitments had been made to the Vietnamese. Under Secretary of State for Political Affairs Philip C. Habib also insisted before the committee that "there was no agreement" with the Vietnamese, though he also testified that he had not known of the letter at all until it was revealed in Hanoi in December 1975.[7]

The DRV's early cease-fire proposals at Paris had put together two responsibilities under one point: the release of prisoners of war and "U.S. responsibility for war damage." Eventually, however, the Paris Agreement had separated these issues. Article 8 dealt with the return of prisoners and detainees, calling for the parties to "help each other to get information about those personnel and foreign civilians missing in action" and "to facilitate the exhumation and repatriation of remains." Article 21 stipulated that "the United States will contribute to healing the wounds of war and to postwar reconstruction of the Democratic Republic of Vietnam and throughout Indochina."

The implementation of both articles floundered after apparently genuine starts in the Four-Party Joint Military Team (FPJMT), which visited grave sites in North Vietnam in May 1973, and in the Joint Economic Commission (JEC), which met in Paris in March-April and June-July 1973. At meetings of the FPJMT, the PRG made efforts to tie repatriation of remains to recognition of the PRG as a legitimate government. In addition, the DRV demanded the return of political prisoners from the South—which the agreement stipulated was to be regulated by the two South Vietnam parties (PRG and Republic of Vietnam) alone. These demands, which the United States considered "unrelated" and unwarranted, were attempts, but not the only ones, to link the fulfillment of one provision of the Paris Agreement to the fulfillment of others, or to additional goals.

The United States suspended JEC talks in April, stating that they could not continue in view of cease-fire violations by the DRV. After a renewal of talks of June 19, they were recessed again on July 23, 1973 (permanently, as it turned out), with the United States insisting that there must be a cessation of war in Cambodia. The DRV, however, disavowed any responsibility for the existence of hostilities in Cambodia. Two months later, a U.S. statement specifically linked the U.S. unwillingness to move forward with an assistance program for North Vietnam to that country's failure "to live up to a number of important terms of the Paris Agreement, including those provisions relating to the accounting of our missing in action."[8] Only later, after the final military victory of April 1975, however, did the DRV begin to use the same argument in reverse, by insisting that the fulfillment of Article 8(b) on MIA information and repatriation was no more binding than the fulfillment of Article 21 on reconstruction aid. Having given up the American POWs as a bargaining element in 1973, the DRV came to recognize the growing importance to the United States of information on MIAs, however minor its significance in Vietnam.

In March 1976, after being pressed by the Montgomery Committee to renew contact with the Vietnamese in the interest of resolving the MIA question and by pending congressional legislation to lift part of the U.S. trade embargo on Vietnam as an inducement to Hanoi, Secretary of State Kissinger sent a note to his North Vietnamese counterpart inviting discussions "looking toward eventual normalization of relations." A leisurely exchange of six notes from March 26 to August 27, 1976, led to formal talks at the embassy level in Paris, on November 12, after the U.S. election. The U.S. side reported that the MIA issue had been its primary concern at the meeting, and the SRV's communiqué said it was "disposed toward an exchange of views on the problems which preoccupy the American side and to meet fully its obligations under Article 8B." No date for a second meeting was set, nor was one expected until after the Carter administration settled in.[9]

Thus the Ford administration, which had insisted upon a "complete accounting" of MIAs as "an absolute precondition" to normalizing relations,[10] left office with the ice at least broken on the diplomatic freeze that had followed the U.S. evacuation of Saigon in 1975.

A critical question attending any further talks with the SRV was what would constitute a wholly satisfactory accounting. The SRV leaders could not be certain of satisfying U.S. demands for information even after releasing all that they knew, and they did not appear willing to accept U.S. search parties on their territory. The periodic release of information and remains by the DRV preceding votes on embargo legislation or UN resolutions was interpreted by Washington as a cynical, macabre exploitation of political opportunities. The remains of twenty-three Americans had been returned through the FPJMT in March 1974, three more through the Montgomery Select Committee in December 1975, and two more to Senator Edward Kennedy in February 1976. In September 1976, when the UN General Assembly convened, the SRV simply announced the names of twelve U.S. airmen who had died attacking North Vietnam, without acknowledging that it must have known some of these names since the time of death.[11]

The Montgomery Committee contributed immensely to resolving the accounting problem by concluding in its final report that *no* unaccounted-for POW/MIAs remained in Indochina and that only a partial accounting was possible by the Indochina governments. After hearing the most expert testimony, it estimated that the Indochina governments might be capable of returning the remains of about 150 Americans and of providing some information on other individuals.[12] The remaining deaths would be forever obscured by physical inaccessibility or the ravages of climate and time. A decisive endorsement by the president and the Department of Defense would be necessary to legitimize, in American eyes, such a partial accounting by the Indochina governments.

On October 6, 1976, during the second debate of the presidential election, candidate Jimmy Carter scored a point or two by asserting that his opponent had not pursued the MIA question in Indochina aggressively enough. The challenger pledged that if elected, he would actively seek out information from the Indochina states and implied that he was ready to bargain on the question. True to his campaign promise, President Carter, one month after his inauguration, dispatched a presidential commission headed by Leonard Woodcock, head of the United Auto Workers, to Southeast Asia to help obtain an accounting of MIAs in the region. The commission also included former Senator Mike Mansfield, former Ambassador Charles W. Yost, Congressman G. V. Montgomery, and Mrs. Marian W. Edelman, director of the Children's Defense League. These five members and an experienced staff were briefed in Washington by the departments of State and Defense and by members of groups representing MIAs and humanitarian assistance interests. The president directed them not to apologize for past relations, but to emphasize his "desire for a new beginning with these governments on the basis of equality and mutual respect."[13] Laos agreed to receive the commission only one day (March 12, 1977) before its departure from Washington, but Cambodia refused the U.S. request (delivered to the Cambodian embassy in Peking) to arrange a meeting with the commission. The atmosphere for the reception of the commission was brightened by the president's announcement on March 10, 1977, of a lifting of the U.S. restrictions (largely unenforceable) on its citizens' travel to Vietnam and some other countries with which the United States had no diplomatic relations.

The commission's three-day visit in Hanoi, March 16–19, 1977, was later reported as cordial and indicative of "a genuine desire for a new and improved relationship with the United States." The commission delivered an exchange of personal letters between the two chiefs of government. The Vietnamese announced a "formal undertaking to give the U.S. all available information on the missing men as it is found and to return remains as they are recovered and exhumed." They also announced the establishment of a special office for this purpose and released the remains of twelve servicemen killed in action, whose fate had been made public in September 1976.[14] All living U.S. military POWs had returned, the SRV declared, and all U.S. civilians registered in South Vietnam after the capture of Saigon had left the country. The SRV would gratefully receive medical and transportation equipment for aiding the search process.

Although President Carter could hail the commission for its "complete success" and welcome the "good faith" attitude of the Vietnamese government on the MIA question, little was achieved that could put the issue finally to rest, and there were subtle indications that the Vietnamese and Lao were still linking MIA information to the matter of reconstruction aid. In Vientiane, on March 19–20, 1977, after an initially cool beginning, the commission received the same assurances as in Hanoi concerning POWs, but there was no symbolic gesture such as turning over new information or remains. The Lao seemed to stress the great difficulties of searching for remains in their rugged terrain, and they stated even more explicitly than the Vietnamese that they "connected the MIA problem with that of U.S. assistance to 'heal the wounds of war' and rebuild their country."[15] The Laotian government's delayed response to the U.S. request that the commission be received, the cool reception on the first day, the lack of a symbolic gesture, and the explicit linkage of the MIA and reconstruction aid question—all this contrasted with the Vietnamese performance. It raises the intriguing speculation as to whether the Lao were acting quite independently, or in tardy coordination with Vietnam, or simply as the hard-line spokesmen of a two-country team.

The more subtle Vietnamese approach had pointed to three key areas of discussion with the United States: the MIAs, normalization of relations, and aid. No one issue need be settled as a precondition to the others, they noted, but the issues were "interrelated." When discussing reconstruction aid, which they referred to as an American "obligation" and "responsibility" in both a legal and humanitarian sense, they also spoke of reciprocity, suggesting that each side must address the concerns of the other, in a two-way transaction. The Vietnamese have in fact provided new information on missing Americans, thus highlighting their "good-will and serious attitude." Twenty additional confirmed deaths and remains were offered as a token of their attitude at the second round of talks with the United States in Paris on June 2–3, 1977. Such intermittent revelations, however, suggest to some observers a cynical bargaining strategy rather than genuine discovery of new information, and the "goodwill" tends to be discounted. The Vietnamese may come to realize this and present their future MIA information in a manner that Americans can view as orderly and systematic rather than as tied to bargaining situations.

Normalization of Relations

After the communist seizure of power in Indochina, the United States maintained its mission in Laos (eventually reduced to twelve persons by order of the Laotian government) but did not recognize the revolutionary governments of Vietnam or Cambodia. A total trade embargo, under the Trading with the Enemy Act, category 2, was extended by President Ford on May 16, 1975, from the "Communist-controlled area" of Vietnam (imposed in 1958) to the entire country and to Cambodia. Since that time, Cambodia, although it has established relations with more than twenty countries, has shown no interest in reopening relations with the United States. The SRV, on the other hand, has, as it wrote in response to Secretary Kissinger on April 10, 1976, "re-peatedly declared its willingness to discuss" outstanding problems and to normalize relations with the United States provided it obtains satisfaction on the question of reconstruction aid.

The break in relations between the United States and Vietnam and Cambodia led the State Department to put restrictions on the travel of Americans to those states and on the entry of their citizens to the United States. This policy not only inhibited the exchange of information between the countries, but also pre-cluded any easy arrangement for the return home of some Viet-namese refugees who decided they would like to leave the United States. Despite the embargo on trade, a limited number of "chari-table humanitarian exports" from the United States to Vietnam were licensed each year under pressure from humanitarian assis-tance groups and a few members of Congress.[16] The Bingham Amendment to the Foreign Assistance Act in 1976, which would have lifted the embargo (except on strategic goods) for 90 to 180 days (or more if a substantial accounting of MIAs were obtained during the period), was dropped by Congress when the bill was reenacted following President Ford's multifaceted veto. Some $70-75 million in Vietnamese assets, mostly official bank accounts, and $9 million in Cambodian assets were frozen by U.S. order. Estimates of U.S. investments in Vietnam that fell into communist hands in 1975 run as high as $110 million, with $60 million directly related to oil exploration.[17] Actual private commercial U.S. exports to Vietnam during the last years of the war amounted to a relatively minor $30-50 million.

The trade embargo and the freezing of assets in the United States were not of great commercial consequence to the United States. The chief losers were U.S. oil companies, two of which had obtained leases from the Thieu government in 1973 and 1974 for exploration of offshore tracts. After the fall of Saigon, foreign oil companies, including American, maintained contact with North and South Vietnamese oil directorates, but only in 1976 did the talks reach the stage of fashioning new contracts.[18]

In September 1976 the SRV was happy to assume the membership of the Republic of Vietnam in the International Monetary Fund (IMF), the World Bank, and the Asian Development Bank. The United States perfunctorily opposed SRV membership within the organizations, but it had no support. By January 1977 the IMF announced its first loan of $35.8 million to Vietnam (without U.S. opposition) to cover a more than 10 percent shortfall of exports over previous years. A month-long study mission by a World Bank team was simultaneously getting under way in Hanoi. To benefit from these international efforts, the SRV had to agree to supply the agencies with financial data—which neither the USSR nor China has ever been willing to do.

The actual readiness of each side to discuss normalization of relations was reached in roundabout fashion. Not long after the takeover in Saigon, Secretary of State Kissinger stated that the United States was "willing to look to the future, to gear its policies towards Vietnam to the policies which it pursues toward us, toward its neighbors."[19] This formula remained intact through subsequent speeches by Kissinger and President Ford, with the additional caveat that the United States was "prepared to reciprocate gestures of goodwill—particularly the return of remains of Americans killed or missing in action or information about them."[20] Meanwhile, U.S. intelligence apparently detected no increased involvement by Vietnam in the insurgent movements in Thailand or Malaysia.

As mentioned previously, the visit of the Montgomery Committee to Hanoi in December 1975 elicited a gesture of goodwill— the return of the remains of three American pilots—but it also brought forth the Vietnamese argument that the United States was committed by Article 21 of the Paris Agreement and President Nixon's letter of February 1, 1973, to provide reconstruction aid. The Montgomery Committee maintained the momentum of this exchange by unanimously recommending in March 1976 that the State Department begin direct talks with the Vietnamese. As Congress was considering the embargo-lifting Bingham Amendment, Secretary Kissinger reasserted control over developments by writing the DRV's foreign minister that the United States was "prepared to open discussions with your Government in pursuit of the objective of eventual normalization of relations."[21] The DRV, in reply to this and two more notes, before fixing a meeting of representatives in Paris, reiterated its willingness to discuss outstanding problems with the United States and to normalize relations, but charged that the United States had "shirked its obligation" under Article 21. Each side accused the other of attempting a selective application of past agreements. At the Colombo Conference of Non-Aligned States in August 1976, however, the SRV Prime Minister Pham Van Dong described the reconstruction aid due his country (without reference to the Paris Agreement) as "a question of conscience, responsibility, and honor which [the United States] can by no means elude."[22] After the November 1976 meeting with the United States in Paris, the SRV's communiqué continued this softer formulation, skirting the legal issue of Article 21 and referring to "what had been agreed in the mixed economic commission in Paris in 1973."

The Carter administration did not put together a consistent stance on the question of normalization of relations until the appointment of the Woodcock Commission on February 11, 1976. (There were indications that the new president generally favored normal relations with as many states as possible, including previous pariahs such as Cuba and North Korea.) As already mentioned, UN Ambassador Young and the official Department of State viewpoint differed in the first weeks of the administration with respect to timing. The Woodcock Commission returned from Vietnam in March, however, with assurances of that country's "interest in establishing normal diplomatic relations as quickly as possible." The commission expressed its belief that a resumption of talks in Paris would be most useful in obtaining a fuller accounting for MIAs and recommended a vigorous pursuit of normalization of relations.[23]

On May 3-4, 1977, the talks did resume in the SRV's Paris embassy between delegations headed by U.S. Assistant Secretary of State for Asian and Pacific Affairs Richard Holbrooke and by Vietnamese Deputy Foreign Minister Phan Hien. This first round produced no joint communiqué, but spokesmen for both sides referred to the discussion as "useful" and "frank." The chief Vietnamese delegate recorded his side's view that the United States "had a responsibility to contribute to the healing of the wounds of war and to postwar reconstruction of Vietnam" and stated that the SRV "would increase its efforts" to provide additional information on American MIAs. The U.S. delegation, he revealed, had stated that the United States would not oppose Vietnamese admission to the United Nations and that the U.S. trade embargo (the other "erroneous policy" in Hanoi's perspective) would be lifted as part of the normalization of relations once embassies were established.[24] A second round of discussions was to take place a few weeks later.

The disagreement over how to reach the shared objective of normal relations was narrowed down to tangible elements:

1. the U.S. insistence on a full accounting for MIAs versus the Vietnamese promise that they would try harder

2. the Vietnamese insistence that the United States fulfill an obligation to contribute to the postwar reconstruction of Vietnam versus the U.S. denial of any legal or moral obligation

3. the Vietnamese desire for an immediate removal of the U.S. trade embargo versus the U.S. pledge to lift it once embassies were established

The first issue might be overcome if high U.S. authorities could legitimize the Vietnamese assurances of good faith effort. The second issue would probably require an understanding on procedures for some U.S. contribution to Vietnam's reconstruction at an agreeable amount. The third issue might be solved by Vietnamese acceptance of a few months' delay in the lifting of the U.S. trade embargo—if only the reconstruction aid question could be solved. Reconstruction was thus clearly the sticking point, and it became more intractable the more the U.S. public became aware of it. The second round of talks, held in the U.S. embassy in Paris on June 2–3, 1977, showed no progress, as obstacles were mounted in the U.S. Congress.

Reconstruction Aid to Indochina

In arriving at Article 21 of the Paris Agreement, under which the United States pledged "to contribute to healing the wounds of war and to postwar reconstruction of the DRV and throughout Indochina," the U.S. negotiators avoided the DRV's proposed phrasing, which would have registered "U.S. responsibility for war damage." Nor did the agreement use the term *reparations.* When Japan negotiated an opening of diplomatic relations with the DRV in November 1975, however, a foreign aid contribution of $40 million was included, which both sides implicitly recognized as symbolic reparation for damages inflicted during World War II.

Washington had long used the possibility of postwar reconstruction aid as an inducement to peace—ever since President Johnson's Johns Hopkins speech in 1965. President Nixon, a year before the Paris Agreement, announced a $2.5 billion figure for aid to North Vietnam, contingent upon the end of military operations.[25] The $3.25 billion planning figure in President Nixon's letter to Pham Van Dong five days after the Paris Agreement suggests that considerable secret negotiation had already taken place on this question and that the Christmas bombing of Hanoi had raised the cost of the reconstruction that the United States would consider subsidizing. The Joint Economic Commission, until it suspended meetings on July 23, 1973, worked out a program for grant aid to be provided and commodities to be purchased in the United States during the first year as well as over a five-year period. The program included materials and tools for shelter and building construction, agriculture and food processing, port and transportation infrastructure, energy, and industrial commodities and equipment.[26] But it was never formally agreed to nor submitted to Congress.

As noted previously, in December 1975, six months after the fall of Saigon, the DRV startled the Montgomery Committee by revealing the secret letter from President Nixon to Premier Pham Van Dong dated February 1, 1973. Secretary of State Kissinger, in subsequent meetings with the committee, assured its members that no unconditional commitments had been made to the DRV and that the role of Congress in controlling aid appropriations had been emphasized continually, as well as the precondition of an armistice in Laos and Cambodia.[27]

An armistice had been formalized between the Royal Lao Government and Pathet Lao in Vientiane on February 21, 1973, but the requirements for the withdrawal of all foreign military forces were never enforced with respect to the North Vietnamese presence (estimated at 40,000 in 1974) in the Ho Chi Minh Trail area. The Paris Agreement on ending the war in Vietnam had also attempted to promote peace in Cambodia and Laos by stating in Article 20 that:

b.   Foreign countries shall put an end to all military activities in Cambodia and Laos, totally withdraw from and refrain from reintroducing into these countries troops, military advisers and military personnel, armaments, munitions and war material.

c.   The internal affairs of Cambodia and Laos shall be settled by the people of each of these countries without foreign interference.

These sections included no time limit, and the obligations therefore could be interpreted (as the Department of State did) as "objectives, not present obligations." Rather than removing critical North Vietnamese assistance to the Cambodian revolutionaries, as the U.S. negotiators probably intended, section (c) could be cited by the DRV as justification for not trying to *impose* a cease-fire there, as the Americans were demanding throughout 1973.[28]

A month after the Montgomery Committee visit, the Vietnamese used Senator George McGovern's visit to contend once more that the United States had reneged on the legal obligation of Article 21 and on a written executive agreement (Nixon's letter) to provide reconstruction aid. McGovern's report carefully argued the case for Vietnam's view, namely, that the Paris Agreement remained in effect and that Article 21 (reconstruction aid) was just as binding on the United States as Article 8 (MIA information) was on the Vietnamese. He pointed out that the Paris Agreement was repudiated from the outset by the Thieu government of South Vietnam and that South Vietnamese forces quickly went on the offensive against PRG and North Vietnamese zones of control. The DRV had an initial interest in having the agreement implemented, particularly by the United States, and they therefore acted with surprising restraint. The crucial efforts by the Joint Economic Commission in Paris (March 15 to April 19, and June 19 to July 23, 1973) to agree on the U.S. reconstruction aid broke down when the Nixon administration "seemed to be adding a new condition—a requirement that the Vietnamese somehow arrange a cease-fire in Cambodia."[29]

President Nixon has revealed that in May 1973 (during efforts to resume the JEC talks), he instructed Kissinger to "hit them hard on MIA accounting and on withdrawal from Cambodia as conditions for aid."[30] In April 1973 the news media reported that Kissinger was "angry" with the North Vietnamese for failing to honor a secret "understanding" about obtaining a cease-fire in Cambodia.[31]

In 1976 Hanoi also suggested through Senator McGovern that it was ready to put these legal contentions behind and accept a new format and amount with which the United States would play "some part" in the rebuilding of the country, as "a matter of honor, responsibility and conscience."[32] Laos echoed the Vietnamese line on this issue and doubtless intended to claim a share in reconstruction aid before making any new revelations about missing Americans. Cambodia indicated no interest in the matter.

In May 1976, Senator Edward Kennedy, in a report on refugees, proposed that the United States actively seek reconciliation and normalization with Vietnam and renew its intention to heal the wounds of war, initially through contributions to the international relief and rehabilitation efforts then under way.[33] He pointed out that the UN high commissioner for refugees, the UN

International Children's Emergency Fund, the International Red Cross, the World Health Organization, the Food and Agriculture Organization, the World Food Program, the UN Development Program, and private voluntary agencies were collectively budgeting nearly $100 million for Indochina.[34] Since April 1975, the United States had not made any contribution to UN or international humanitarian programs specifically designated for Indochina, and Congress, in passing the Foreign Assistance Appropriation Act of 1976, had explicitly prohibited the use of U.S. funds in Indochina.

Despite the conciliatory efforts of Senators McGovern and Kennedy and the MIA Committee, the reconstruction aid issue generated only sporadic hostile attention in Washington until the Carter administration resumed talks with Vietnam. In March 1977 the Woodcock Commission had raised interest in a possible breakthrough to full accounting for MIAs, but the May 3-4 talks in Paris led to a provocative and disconcerting commentary reported from Hanoi. The offending Vietnamese statement, to the effect that the United States owed $4.5 billion in reconstruction aid, contrasted with Phan Hien's line in the discussions themselves, where neither the Nixon letter nor a specific aid figure had been raised.[35] A leading Republican conservative congressman, Ashbrook of Ohio, quoting the evening television news account to an unruly late session of the House, proposed an amendment to the State Department authorization bill prohibiting the use of any of the funds "for the purpose of negotiating reparations, aid or any other form of payment to the Socialist Republic of Vietnam." The amendment passed, after only ten minutes' debate, amid a spate of other conservative amendments—which were not successful—in reaction to Carter administration's foreign policy initiatives on the Panama Canal, relations with Cuba, and the United Nations.

Notwithstanding State Department assurances that no "reparations" or "aid" would be negotiated with Vietnam, Congress had seen the U.S. veto on Vietnamese entry to the UN being abandoned, and the legislators were stirred to assert themselves on this suddenly vibrant issue. Amendments to subsequent legislation sought to close every possible avenue by which U.S. funds might reach Indochina.

Perhaps to clear the air and deflect attention to the cloudy record of the Nixon administration in dealing with Congress, the

State Department arranged the release of Nixon's secret letter of February 1, 1973, to Pham Van Dong.[36] The text confirmed the Vietnamese account. President Nixon had written that "the Government of the United States of America will contribute to the postwar reconstruction of North Vietnam without any political conditions," and preliminary studies indicated that the U.S. contribution would "fall in the range of $3.25 billion of grant aid over five years," with other forms of aid to be agreed upon between the two parties. An addendum noted that such other forms of aid "could fall in the range of $1 billion to 1.5 billion depending on food and other commodity needs of the Democratic Republic of Vietnam." Another addendum stated, "It is understood that the recommendations of the Joint Economic Commission mentioned in the President's note to the Prime Minister will be implemented by each member in accordance with its own constitutional provisions." From the context, it appears that this addendum was composed after the original letter, but the State Department gave no indication of the date of its delivery. President Nixon's comment at the time his letter was released stressed that throughout the negotiation of the peace agreement, "the Hanoi Government was under no illusions whatever that any aid program would require approval by the Congress and was conditional on their adherence to the peace agreement." He then asserted that "the North Vietnamese proceeded to break the agreement almost immediately after it was signed" and that by May 1973 he was instructing Kissinger to insist on "MIA accounting and on withdrawal from Cambodia as conditions for aid." During the period of JEC deliberations, the Congress was not apprised of the president's letter and was reassured by Secretary of State Roger's testimony of February 9, 1973, that the administration had "not made any commitment for any reconstruction or rehabilitation effort."[37]

Even though the Vietnamese themselves had broadcast the Nixon letter shortly after the House of Representatives passed, on May 4, 1977, the Ashbrook Amendment barring reparations or aid negotiations, and much as the SRV might insist that the U.S. position on the letter was "trampling upon the most elementary provisions of international law,"[38] the legal argument was not likely to carry much weight in future negotiations. In fact congressional conservatives and isolationists were angry to the point of facilitating the approval of amendments to foreign aid and U.S. contributions to international financial institutions that were designed to "tie the President's hands" and close the door even to indirect assistance to Indochina. In keeping with its new assertiveness in foreign affairs, Congress later insisted (with President Carter's approval) on the observance of human rights by U.S. aid recipients, and the House voted to ban direct or indirect aid to the Indochina states (as well as to Cuba, Angola, and Mozambique).[39] An even more ingenious effort to constrain negotiations with Vietnam was the Dole Amendment, adopted (58 to 32) by the Senate on June 14, 1977, which would require the United States to oppose assistance to Vietnam in international lending institutions and, if the United States were outvoted, to deduct its share of such aid from the next contribution to the institution. An effort to require the United States to vote against any multilateral loans to states that show "a consistent pattern" of violating human rights was narrowly defeated (43 to 50). The emotion aroused by the Vietnam aid issue was shown in the behavior of Democratic Senator John Glenn regarding Dole's amendment. During the brief debate, he voiced the State Department's line in opposition, that "to get tough may be counterproductive" with respect to getting MIA information. A day later, after receiving numerous phone calls "misunderstanding" his position, he himself introduced an amendment barring any commitment by U.S. negotiators "to assist or pay reparations" to the Indochina states. It passed 90 to 2.

The Democratic party leadership in both houses felt hardpressed and insufficiently supported by the White House during these debates. At the same time, it was recognized that President Carter was unlikely to expend much political capital on the foreign aid and lending issues when he faced more crucial contests with Congress over his policies toward the Panama Canal, troop withdrawals from South Korea, Israel, SALT, weapons systems, China, and even Cuba. In September 1977 the administration did push through the final versions of these bills, which excluded provisions that would set new conditions for U.S. participation in international lending institutions. The latter made clear, through a letter from World Bank President Robert S. McNamara, that they would have found such provisions wholly unacceptable.[40]

Since June 1976, any *direct* U.S. contributions to international assistance programs for Indochina have been effectively barred by Section 108 of the Foreign Assistance Appropriation Act of 1976, which stipulated that "none of the funds" made available by the act "shall be used to provide assistance to the Democratic Republic of Vietnam, South Vietnam, Cambodia, or Laos." This act does not restrict, however, the transfer of U.S. contributions to the general purpose funds of international institutions, where they are commingled with the funds contributed by other nations and may end up financing loans or grants to Vietnam. However, as we have seen, many members of Congress were intent on closing this indirect avenue for a U.S. response to the Vietnamese demand for reconstruction aid.

The attempt in Congress in 1977 to place restrictions on U.S. contributions to Indochina states through international agencies had threatened to create a confrontation with the Vietnamese over their insistence on a U.S. obligation to help heal the wounds of war. Even though Congress might hesitate to authorize direct aid to the former enemy—which unlike Germany or Japan in 1945 had *won,* not lost, the war—the Vietnamese might regard the use of U.S. funds by international institutions for relief and rehabilitation as satisfying their demands in principle; yet the U.S. government would not be involved in any transactions regarded as reparations. As the Montgomery Committee pointed out, an estimated $34 million from U.S. contributions to international institutions was expected to be used in 1977 in Vietnam.[41] This included proportionate U.S. contributions to the $35.8 million loan made by the International Monetary Fund in January 1977, the balance of a loan commitment by the Asian Development Bank (made originally to South Vietnam), and commitments from at least three UN humanitarian assistance agencies. A longer-range projection of multilateral aid to Vietnam by the agencies that have been active there (not including the World Bank/International Development Agency) showed a total of $284,383,000 for the period 1976-1980. The relevant organizations were the World Health Organization, the UN High Commission for Refugees, the World Food Program, the UN International Children's Emergency Fund, and the UN Development Program.[42]

Two serious objections to U.S. economic aid to Vietnam might be its impact as a symbol of legitimacy for the new regime, and the demands it might raise for greater U.S. generosity toward long-time friends in the area. It could also be argued that the United States was paying blackmail in return for MIA information and remains. To overcome these objections, the president himself would probably have to speak out on the matter of an international humanitarian concern for "healing the wounds of war." The parallels with Lincoln's magnanimity in 1865 or U.S. aid to postwar Germany or Japan are not exact, but the wellspring of sentiment for reconciliation with old enemies might be tapped. The Vietnamese appear subtle enough and needy enough to accept U.S. reconstruction aid indirectly and without insisting upon a public declaration of repentance or obligation. With Congress insistent on barring the door even to multilateral mingling of U.S. funds in respect to Indochina, however, subtlety appears to count for little.

The four major political issues between the United States and Indochina have rested heavily upon the bitter remembrance of war and the volatility of American public opinion. A resolution of the remaining disagreements will eventually be achieved, but its timing is difficult to anticipate. Party leadership within the Indochina states will play a commanding role in how they orient themselves toward U.S. goals and proposals, and the political and economic development of these states in the coming years will position them decisively for dealing with the United States. To assess the full range of possible relationships between them and the United States, therefore, it is important to examine in some detail their internal development and foreign relations.

2
Vietnam since the Communist Victory

The Socialist Republic of Vietnam (SRV) has emerged as a significant power on the Southeast Asia mainland. Since the unification of the two Vietnams in July 1976, Vietnam has a population of about 50 million (cited by the SRV government as 49,633,000 with a growth rate of approximately 2.9 percent yearly) and a land area stretching more than 1,000 miles from the South China Sea to the Chinese border. With a population ranking sixteenth in the world, almost as large as France, the SRV is the third largest communist nation in the world.

Vietnam also has a major asset, one unusual for a Southeast Asian society, namely, a relatively homogeneous ethnic makeup. Over 87 percent of its population consists of lowland Vietnamese, who live along the Red River delta, the coastal plains of central Vietnam, and the Mekong River delta. They all speak Vietnamese and share a common culture, which has emerged from a largely peasant society engaged in wet-rice cultivation. In addition, the Vietnamese boast a history of centuries of struggle against the Chinese and, more recently, against the French, the Japanese, and the Americans. Thus, with a population that is intelligent and vigorous, among the most dynamic in Southeast Asia, Vietnam has a strong potential for national unity.[1]

The Vietnamese communist revolutionary movement has displayed great strength. Its leadership has remained remarkably stable throughout both the first and second Indochina wars (1946–1954 and 1960–1975). Although the death in 1969 of Ho Chi Minh, the founder of the movement, was a great loss, an indication of the Party's cohesion was the smooth transition to

collective leadership. This leadership developed political institutions and a government that succeeded in organizing a large
segment of the Vietnamese population. The Party has been a successful teacher and guide of the revolutionary movement, and the
various fronts (i.e., Fatherland Front, National Liberation Front)
have been effective in mobilizing the masses. The People's Army
of Vietnam (PAVN) is the most powerful military force in Southeast Asia. It provided the central thrust of the military effort
that outlasted the combined force, at its peak, of some 1 million
South Vietnamese, 500,000 Americans, 40,000 South Koreans,
30,000 Thai, and sundry other forces. This army amassed, in
victory, enormous quantities of U.S.-made equipment and supplies,
including aircraft, tanks, heavy artillery, and armored personnel
carriers—all abandoned by Saigon's military forces.

The new Vietnamese state, on the other hand, is faced with
severe economic problems and the enormous challenge of national
integration following a divisive civil war. The Vietnamese people,
after their protracted struggle, are fatigued, yet more sacrifice is
called for. The country, both North and South, has suffered
enormous destruction, much land has been defoliated, and the
countryside is pockmarked with bomb craters, often filled with
mosquito-infested, brackish water.[2] The new rulers have inherited
a heavy burden of unemployed from the Thieu government, which
was suffering from the economic impact of the withdrawal, beginning in 1970, of 500,000 U.S. troops. In addition, hundreds
of thousands of former military have been demobilized and have
joined the ranks of the unemployed. Former members of the Saigon
bureaucracy, employees of the U.S. mission, and others who
provided services to the foreigners—all are jobless.

A challenging task for the communists will be to integrate into
the new society those of the old society who were hostile to them.
In addition, there remains a deep-seated regionalism, which has
long provided tension between Tonkinese, Annamese, and Cochin-
chinese. More than a million Catholics resided in South Vietnam,
of whom some three-quarters had fled from North Vietnam when
the communists took power there in 1954. The Hoa Hao, a fundamentalist Buddhist sect of more than one and a half million,
have perhaps been even more anticommunist than the Catholics.
The Cao Dai, a syncretic religious sect, have a long record of

resistance to control from the capital. Of the hundreds of thousands of former ARVN paratroopers, rangers, special forces, and others of Saigon's armed forces, many have spent their entire lives in combat against the communists and will not easily join in as enthusiastic members of the new society. Indeed, pockets of active, armed resistance, probably drawn from former military elements and anticommunist religious groups, have created troublesome security problems in the South, even if hopes of defeating the new leadership are vain. In addition, some of the highland ethnic minorities in South Vietnam, disappointed by the policies of the communist leaders, have taken up guerrilla activity, and many intellectuals, professionals, former bureaucrats, and members of the commercial middle class are privately hostile to the new regime.

In confronting a new stage of history, the SRV will be sorely tested. Will the remarkable solidarity of its leadership continue? Other communist regimes, including the Soviet Union and the People's Republic of China (PRC), have experienced bitter factional disputes following the victories of their revolutions. The Third World is filled with examples of heroic revolutionary leaders who proved unsuited to the more prosaic, difficult tasks of national development. Can the SRV leaders, so successful at protracted armed struggle, lead their nation toward successful modernization in peacetime? With victory in 1975, the Party achieved its twin goals of "completing the Socialist Revolution in the North and the liberation of the South." As the leaders now attempt rapid social and economic development, as they "advance the entire nation to socialism, bypassing the stage of capitalism," will they avoid doctrinal rigidity sufficiently to achieve their goals? How has the Party's wartime policy of rapidly expanding its ranks affected its ability to perform its present tasks? Will the Vietnamese population continue to accept the heavy discipline and enormous demands that their wartime leaders imposed upon them?

Finally, what foreign policy options are the victorious SRV leaders likely to choose? In Southeast Asia, what will be their mix of assertiveness and accommodation? In plotting their own independent development, what will be the pattern of delicate choices they must make in the Sino-Soviet dispute? And, after long years of bitter struggle, how will they confront their former enemies in the West, especially the United States?

Although it will be years before the answers to all of these questions emerge, they will of course have an influence upon the development of U.S.-Vietnamese relations.

Leadership

Over the years, there has been frequent speculation about factions within the Vietnamese communist leadership (see Figure 2.1). These postulated factions have been divided into camps such as pro-Soviet versus pro-PRC, pro–building socialism in the North versus pro–prosecuting the war in the South, soft-liners versus hard-liners, pragmatists versus ideologues. It does seem likely that the personality, function, region of origin, and political experience of the leaders have given rise to differences over policy priorities. But it also appears that these differences have been officially submerged into a decision-making consensus. The Vietnamese leaders are dedicated Marxist-Leninists and committed nationalists, shaped by a long revolutionary experience in which a small number of leaders have effectively resolved their differences and developed an essentially common perception of the Vietnamese national interest. Writing in 1969, the U.S. National Security Council's assessment of the Vietnamese leadership was as follows:

> Our knowledge of the existence and significance of any kinds of factions within the Hanoi leadership is imprecise. . . . Different Politbureau members probably ally themselves temporarily with other members on specific issues, and policy decisions are obviously subject to review. The leadership has changed its war and negotiations tactic several times in the last few years, suggesting that members of the Politbureau adjust their view to circumstances. Some members may remain on one or another side of any question, but others apparently shift their ground as they deem necessary.[3]

By all indications, the leadership remains as cohesive and unified after the 1975 victory as it was before. The results of the Fourth Congress called by the Vietnamese Workers' Party (VWP), which met December 14–20, 1976, appear to confirm this assessment.[4] Since the Party had not met in a congress since the start of the second Indochinese war in 1960, its decisions, particularly on leadership, were significant. In the composition of the Polit-buro, the highest decision-making body of the Vietnamese com-

Figure 2.1
SOCIALIST REPUBLIC OF VIETNAM
PARTY STRUCTURE

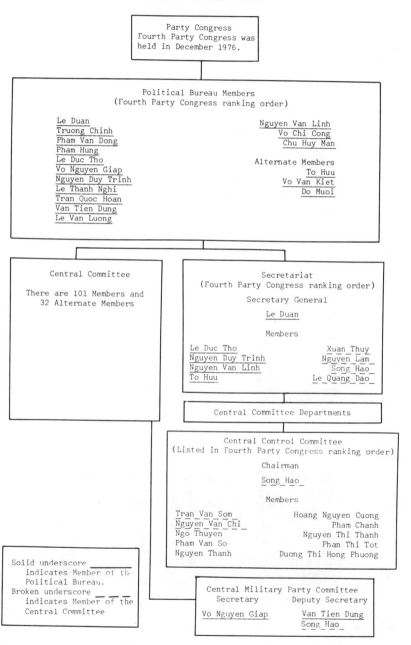

Party Congress
Fourth Party Congress was
held in December 1976.

Political Bureau Members
(Fourth Party Congress ranking order)

Le Duan
Truong Chinh
Pham Van Dong
Pham Hung
Le Duc Tho
Vo Nguyen Giap
Nguyen Duy Trinh
Le Thanh Nghi
Tran Quoc Hoan
Van Tien Dung
Le Van Luong

Nguyen Van Linh
Vo Chi Cong
Chu Huy Man

Alternate Members
To Huu
Vo Van Kiet
Do Muoi

Central Committee

There are 101 Members and
32 Alternate Members

Secretariat
(Fourth Party Congress ranking order)

Secretary General

Le Duan

Members

Le Duc Tho
Nguyen Duy Trinh
Nguyen Van Linh
To Huu

Xuan Thuy
Nguyen Lam
Song Hao
Le Quang Dao

Central Committee Departments

Central Control Committee
(Listed in Fourth Party Congress ranking order)

Chairman

Song Hao

Members

Tran Van Som
Nguyen Van Chi
Ngo Thuyen
Pham Van So
Nguyen Thanh

Hoang Nguyen Cuong
Pham Chanh
Nguyen Thi Thanh
Phan Thi Tot
Duong Thi Hong Phuong

Solid underscore _____
    indicates Member of the
    Political Bureau.
Broken underscore _ _ _
    indicates Member of the
    Central Committee

Central Military Party Committee
Secretary   Deputy Secretary

Vo Nguyen Giap   Van Tien Dung
                      Song Hao

34

Figure 2.2
SOCIALIST REPUBLIC OF VIETNAM
POLITICAL BUREAU MEMBERS
(Fourth Party Congress ranking order)

Le Duan   Truong Chinh   Pham Van Dong

Pham Hung   Le Duc Tho   Vo Nguyen Giap

Nguyen Duy Trinh   Le Thanh Nghi   Tran Quoc Hoan

35

Figure 2.2 (continued)

Van Tien Dung   Le Van Luong   Nguyen Van Linh

Vo Chi Cong   Chu Huy Man

ALTERNATE MEMBERS

To Huu   Vo Van Kiet   Do Muoi

munist movement, the Congress ratified continuity. The Politburo was enlarged to seventeen members (fourteen full members, plus three alternates) from its previous size of thirteen (eleven full and two alternates) (see Figure 2.2). All but one of the Politburo members (the seventy-one-year-old Hoang Van Hoan) were reappointed, and all of the new members were elevated from previous positions on the Party Central Committee. Only two members (Ho Chi Minh and Nguyen Chi Thanh) had died since the Third Party Congress in 1960. Le Duan moved from his role as primus inter pares following the death of Ho into a more distinct Party leadership role as general secretary. (The post of chairman of the Party was left vacant, in deference to the memory of Ho.) The apparent order of importance within the Politburo was changed only slightly, with Le Duc Tho moving into fifth place (from sixth place) and Vo Nguyen Giap moving to sixth (from fifth). The average age of the members of the Politburo dropped only one year, from sixty-six to sixty-five.[5]

The second most important decision-making body of the Party, the Central Committee, was expanded even more significantly than the Politburo. Before the Fourth Party Congress, there were 53 full members and 24 alternate members, a total of 77. The Fourth Party Congress expanded the full members to 101, plus 32 alternates, reaching a total of 133. New members account for half of its full members and all of its alternate members, or 65 percent of its total membership. Thus, although the first generation of revolutionary leaders still holds the key positions, new participants are being drawn into decision-making roles. Of the 30 full or alternate members dropped from the Central Committee in December, most were old or had withdrawn from active public life in the previous few years. Of the first 47 Central Committee members—all of whom had served in the previous Central Committee—the average age is about sixty. Most of them had joined the Party during the 1930s, or at least before the August Revolution of 1945. The 86 new members appear to be several years younger than those reappointed, although information on the ages of all is not available.

The departure of four generals at their politically prime age raised speculation about the current influence of the military.

There was an increase in the overall military representation on the Central Committee (six of the top eleven PAVN generals are on the Central Committee),[6] but its proportional share of the Central Committee membership declined (in 1960 30 percent of the Central Committee members were military officers; in 1976, 23 percent.) In spite of the army's importance for so long, it appears that the Party still firmly commands the gun.[7]

It comes as no surprise that the leading public personalities of the Provisional Revolutionary Government (PRG) and the National Liberation Front (NLF) do not appear among the Party's high decision-making institutions. The PRG president, Huynh Tan Phat, was awarded the post of vice-premier in the Council of Ministers and the former NLF chairman, Nguyen Huu Tho, was named to the largely honorific post of vice-president of the SRV, but neither appears in the Central Committee. The absence of prominent PRG and NLF personalities within the Party Central Committee should not obscure the fact that the VWP's policy organ has long had a healthy representation of high-level Party cadres born south of the seventeenth parallel. It is evident from postwar behavior and Party accounts that the VWP leadership based in Hanoi directed the revolution in South Vietnam throughout its duration.[8] Namely, the revolution in South Vietnam was directed by the VWP Central Committee's directorate for South Vietnam (generally labeled Central Office for South Vietnam, or COSVN), headed since 1967 by Pham Hung, now thought to be the fourth-ranking member of the Politburo. Presenting the NLF and, subsequently, the PRG as leader of the southern struggle was a VWP political tactic, designed to help mobilize southern popular support, to reduce danger of retaliation against North Vietnam before 1965, and to attract international support for the "spontaneous" southern struggle against the oppression of the U.S.-supported regimes of Ngo Dinh Diem and his military successors.

The Party

A directive of the Fourth Congress, setting forth the Party's doctrine and tasks, neatly summarized the Party's critical role in building socialism:

> The Party creatively applies Marxism-Leninism to the conditions existing in our country. It defines the basic principles of proletarian dictatorship as they apply to Vietnam. These include Party leadership, State control and collective mastership by the people. The Party fixes the State's internal and external policy lines. It establishes the key policies and programs required for the political, military, economic, ideological and cultural advance of the society. The Party—through its members in State and mass organizations, leads the people in implementing these Party lines and State programs and policies. Party members must be exemplary in assuming this leadership. Party leadership over the State is absolute [and] comprehensive. As Lenin has said, no state organ must ever resolve an important political or organizational problem without a directive from the Party's Central Committee.[9]

During the thirty-year revolutionary struggle, the Party has proven an effective instrument for mobilizing popular participation. It has maintained discipline among its cadres, adapting the communist techniques of democratic centralism to local conditions. Although the Party is not immune to ideological rigidity, its pervasive practice of criticism (*Kiem Thao*) has pressed it toward constant examination of its faults and self-correction. Although the leaders lavished praise and self-congratulation upon the Party at the Fourth Party Congress, they also focused upon certain of its shortcomings and prescribed certain remedies.

Perhaps the official change of the Party's name at the Fourth Congress—from Vietnam Workers' Party to Vietnam Communist Party (VCP)—was made in part to emphasize the Party's new goal of social revolution and to promote solidarity with other communist countries.[10] The Party newspaper noted that the name was changed to "reassume" the name first chosen by Ho Chi Minh on February 3, 1930 (when he formed the Party in Hong Kong from three separate organizations and then obeyed the Comintern's order to rename it the Indochinese Communist Party).[11] According to an official Democratic Republic of Vietnam (DRV) Party history, "Following the Communist International's instructions, the session decided to change the Party's name to Indochinese Communist Party because the Vietnamese, Cambodian and Laotian proletariat have politically and economically to be closely related in spite of their differences in language, customs and race."[12] Evidence of how the Party leaders in 1976 linked their communist ideology with nationalism can be seen in General Secretary Le Duan's statement: "Nation and Socialism are one. For us Vietnamese, love of country now means love of Socialism."[13]

As was evident in the pronouncements at the Fourth Party Congress, Party leaders felt that quality had been sacrificed to quantity during the wartime years of recruitment and that an intense effort must be made to reinvigorate the Party. Referring to the Party expansion, Le Duc Tho noted that there had been excessive concentration "only on quantity" and a belief "that zealous people were [automatically] qualified for Party membership." Consequently, the VWP had recruited people with "low political awareness, thus in reality lowering the standards of Party members and adversely affecting the class and vanguard nature of the Party."[14] In the final decade of the war, the Party expanded from 760,000 in 1966 to 1,553,500 members at the time of the Fourth Party Congress.[15] In the future it intended to weed out unworthy Party members. The errors of some Party cadres, as the Party's theoretical journal *Hoc Tap* noted, included "parochialism, regionalism, localism, lack of concern for the general good, and lack of socialist cooperative spirit."[16] General Secretary Le Duan, in delivering the Central Committee report, deplored "scrambling for positions, enmity and envy, over-exaltation of past achievements and self-complacency, claiming merits for oneself while blaming others' shortcomings, etc. It is precisely these evils—and not any serious differences of viewpoints and directives—that are the main causes for disunity here and there in the Party."[17] The Party will be reinvigorated not only by the reeducating or expelling of delinquent cadres but also by applying more rigorous standards in selecting new members. A greater effort will apparently be made to strengthen the working-class component of the party; reliance upon the middle peasants and the urban petite bourgeoisie, which characterized the now completed "national democratic revolution," must end.[18]

The Party in South Vietnam has special problems. Politburo member Le Duc Tho, discussing Party building, reported that "grass roots Party level organizations suffered heavy losses," and that "hundreds of thousands of cadres and Party members sacrificed their lives or were sent to prison."[19] In view of the enormous destruction of the Party in the South, province Party organizations there have smaller memberships than those in the North. For example, Dong That Province (formerly Kien Tuong in the Plain of Reeds) has only 4,000 members, but Hai Hung and Nghe Tinh provinces in the North have 80,000 and 160,000, respectively. Ho Chi Minh City (Saigon), with twice Hanoi's population, has a Party organization only half as large.[20] This paucity of Party cadres is an important reason for the heavy assignment of Party cadres from the North to duties in the South.[21] The Party-building program raises special problems in the South. There, the poor peasants and farm laborers, who have had no experience with collectivization, are still dominated by "small producer mentality," and the more educated elements are largely bourgeois and thus undesirable for Party membership.[22] Thus, building the southern segment of the Party may have to await the creation of new classes through socialist transformation and education, and since southerners are recruited only gradually, Party cadres from the North will continue to be assigned to the South in large numbers.[23]

Doctrine on National Reunification

The communist victory in the spring of 1975 was apparently as unexpected in Hanoi as it was in Saigon and Washington. Hanoi's political strategy for South Vietnam had anticipated a more gradual accession to complete power and, during the transition, a period of shared power with the third force, perhaps even with reactionary elements of the old order. Thus, the VWP envisioned the continuation of two separate governments in North and South Vietnam.

With the rapid, unanticipated disintegration of the Thieu government in April 1975, the VWP was faced with the responsibility of governing all of South Vietnam. A Military Management Commission (MMC), under the leadership of Senior Lieutenant General Tran Van Tra and composed largely of military elements, was given this responsibility. As the MMC, with PAVN units as well as regional and local militia units, asserted the new communist authority and reestablished order throughout the South,

"People's Revolutionary Committees" were set up at all levels to carry out local administration. The PRG continued its formal existence, and in July 1975—indicating that the VWP was still contemplating two separate governments—both the DRV and PRG submitted applications for entry into the United Nations.

Shortly thereafter, the VWP obviously revised its plans for two separate administrations in the country and moved rapidly toward its cherished goal, the reunification of Vietnam. Its justification for doing so without awaiting the further transformation of South Vietnamese society (as required in the earlier doctrinal assumptions) was that international conditions were favorable to rapid consolidation. The revolutionary forces had been successful in Laos and Cambodia, thus enlarging the area of security for a united Vietnam, and socialism had now become a world system with a "combined force much bigger than imperialism."[24]

At the reunification conference in November 1975, its chairman, Truong Chinh, enunciated the Party's plans for unification. The immediate task, he stated, is to advance the entire nation to socialism, thus "bypassing the stage of capitalist development." The "socialist revolution includes socialist transformation and socialist reconstruction." The North is currently building socialism, and the South must simultaneously "complete the remaining tasks of the People's national and democratic revolution" and begin the "step-by-step" socialist transformation of the national economy. Completion of the national democratic revolution requires the construction of a "people's revolutionary administration," the repression of reactionaries, the reeducation of former, "puppet" military and civil servants, and the abolition of the feudal system of land ownership, which is to be done through "the land to the tiller program."[25]

In expounding the Party's assumptions that would guide the integration of the South and North, Truong Chinh noted similarities and differences in the two zones. Both zones, of course, have always been led by a single, genuine Marxist-Leninist party. Both have had a national unity front led by the worker-peasant alliance. But the North is farther along the road to socialism than the South, and the South must be helped to catch up.

Economically, the North has but two main sectors: the state-owned economy and the collective economy. The remaining individual economy is negligible. The South has five economic sectors: the state-owned economy, the collective economy, the joint state-private economy, the private capitalist economy, and the individual economy. Socialist ownership of the means of production, socialist production relations, and a planned economy have only just begun in the South, but they are advanced in the North. The South must gradually transform the private capitalist industry and commerce, agriculture, handicraft, and small trade along socialist lines, establishing state and collective management or (in a transitional phase) state-private management.

As for social classes, the North's exploiting class (capitalist and landlord) has been "reformed," and only the working class, the collective peasant class, and a stratum of socialist intellectuals remain. In the South, there are the working class and peasantry, the petite bourgeoisie, and the national bourgeoisie (all deemed to be acceptable). But the comprador capitalist class, remnants of the feudal landlord class, and some private peasants and petite bourgeoisie whom South Vietnamese society has deformed—must be reformed.

In the North, Marxism-Leninism has played the leading cultural and ideological role in society. It is the core of a socialist culture responsible for developing a new socialist man—imbued with patriotism and proletarian internationalism and whose "socialist virtues" include love for productive work, protection of public property, class love, and the spirit of socialist cooperation. By contrast, the South still suffers from the "evil influences of U.S. neo-colonialism and negative influences of feudalist ideas." These must be erased and replaced by a "scientific, popular and socialist culture as well as socialist-minded men and women."

Truong Chinh summarized the full process of reunification as follows:

> The completion of reunification of the homeland is carried out not only by blotting out the provisional military demarcation line which, in fact, was already blotted out at the end of 1972, not only by the free movement of the people in both zones, (this will be achieved step by step) nor only on the State plane. To complete national reunification is to complete the unity of the political and social systems in the two zones, more concretely speaking, of the economic

structure, relations of production, social composition, state organization, constitution and legal system, culture and ideology.[26]

In summary, the South was to be amalgamated into the North, and all its sociopolitical institutions were to be merged into northern institutions—those of the central leadership of the Vietnamese Workers' Party. This merger would take place under the Party's careful leadership and would embrace the government and administration, the mass organizations, the legal and educational systems—indeed, all institutions.

Government: Reunification and Structure

At the Reunification Conference, Truong Chinh noted that "in the whole process of completing national reunification, reunification on the State plane is the main link." Thus, elections for a single national assembly—the highest organ of the state— were set for April 26, 1976, exactly one year following the "liberation" of the South. On that date, voters throughout Vietnam elected 492 members to a national assembly, the first all-Vietnam election since early 1946, when the DRV, led by Ho Chi Minh, was attempting to prevent the French from regaining control in Vietnam following the Japanese occupation.[27]

In the North 249 deputies (of 324 candidates) and in the South 243 deputies (of 281 candidates) were elected. The Party had clearly selected the National Assembly candidates to include representatives from top echelons of the Party and government (33 percent), high army officers (16 percent), intellectuals (16 percent), religious groups (5 percent, including several Catholic priests), workers (9 percent) and peasants (21 percent). Twenty-four percent of the deputies were women, 23 percent were under the age of forty, and 12 percent were non-Vietnamese minorities. Candidates were formally nominated by the Fatherland Front in the North and by the National Liberation Front in the South. As the total number of candidates indicates, most voters had no choice, although they could cast a blank ballot. It is not surprising, then, that according to the official report, 50 percent of the deputies were elected with more than 90 percent of the votes and that all received at least 60 percent of the votes.[28] A vigorous campaign was mounted to bring out all eligible voters, and 98.77 percent were reported to have gone to the polls. Those ineligible to vote were former Republic of Vietnam military officers, government officials, civil servants, and members of the former bourgeois political parties. (However, an announcement later in 1976 declared that 95 percent of the former soldiers and officials of the Thieu regime had attended reeducation courses and would be permitted to vote in future elections.)

The campaign was characterized by official exhortation to fulfill the remaining revolutionary tasks. Posters with photographs of the candidates and a list of their revolutionary achievements were distributed, but candidates were not permitted to make speeches. The Party interpreted the election results as indicating that the people "love socialism and they are united behind the VWP leadership." Less partisan observers, if not sharing this enthusiastic conclusion, would concede Nguyen Huu Tho's claim that the "front organizations, mass organizations, electoral organizations and cadres, and information and propaganda organs [have striven to] overcome difficulties to fulfill tasks, displayed organizational and working abilities, satisfactorily carried out the task of motivating and educating the people and strictly implemented Party policies and State law."[29]

The assembly election and its first session (the Sixth National Assembly, called the "Unification Assembly"), which met from June 24 to July 2, 1976, brought no surprises in the personalities who emerged as prominent. At the top of the list in North Vietnam was the venerable Ton Duc Thang, the incumbent president who was reelected president of the SRV. The new general secretary of the Vietnamese Communist Party, Le Duan, was elected to the assembly; the number two man of the Party, Truong Chinh, was renamed chairman of the Standing Committee of the National Assembly, its most important post; and Pham Van Dong was again chosen as prime minister. Reappointed as vice-premiers were General Vo Nguyen Giap, Nguyen Duy Trinh, and Le Thanh Nghi, all prominent Politburo members. Three new vice-premiers identified with the Party organization in the South were appointed. Most important was Pham Hung, now the fourth-ranking Politburo member, who had secretly led the Party organization in the South (COSVN). Vo Chi Cong, a newly appointed Politburo member associated with the southern Party organization, was another, and Huynh Tan Phat, former president of the PRG (who was not appointed to a prominent position in the Party), was a third.

Among its decisions, the Sixth National Assembly adopted a new name for the nation—the Socialist Republic of Vietnam (SRV)—and appointed a thirty-six-person drafting committee, under the leadership of Truong Chinh, to draft a new constitution. In addition, it adopted a new national flag and a national anthem (both from the DRV), renamed Saigon Ho Chi Minh City, and designated Hanoi the national capital.

According to the DRV Constitution of 1959, which is still the fundamental law for the SRV until the promulgation of the new constitution, the National Assembly is the highest organ of the state, with legislative, administrative, and judicial powers (see Figure 2.3). The assembly elects the president and two vice-presidents of the Republic, appoints the Council of Ministers and National Defense Council, elects the president of the Supreme People's Court and the chief people's public prosecutor, and adopts the State Plan. In fact, the Party leadership, in particular the Politburo, makes the substantive decisions, which are pro forma carried out by the National Assembly. The genuine power holders are the top Party members, particularly the Central Committee members, who are interspersed throughout the key governmental institutions.

The National Assembly is supposed to meet twice yearly to provide a sounding board for the pronouncements of high Party officials, which are applauded by National Assembly members. The actively working element of the National Assembly is its Standing Committee, which serves as a permanent executive body. It is composed of a chairman, seven vice-chairmen, a general secretary, and thirteen permanent and two alternate members. At its July 1976 meeting, the National Assembly established six commissions: bank, inspection, nationalities, planning, price, and science and technology.

The executive authority of the new SRV, as in the DRV, is the Council of Ministers, consisting of the prime minister, seven vice-premiers, twenty-nine ministers, and six heads of state organizations of ministerial level. As in the other governmental bodies, policy is guided by the strategic placement of top Party leaders in

Figure 2.3
SOCIALIST REPUBLIC OF VIETNAM
GOVERNMENT STRUCTURE

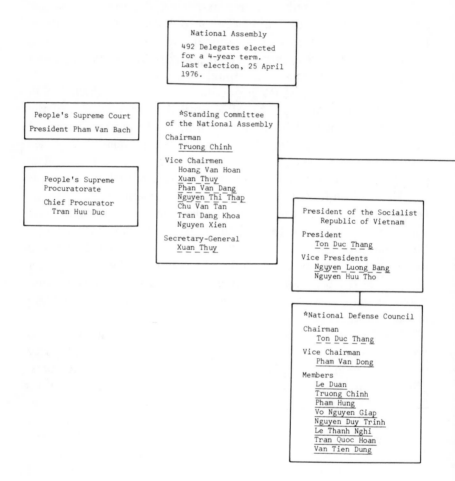

Figure 2.3 (continued)

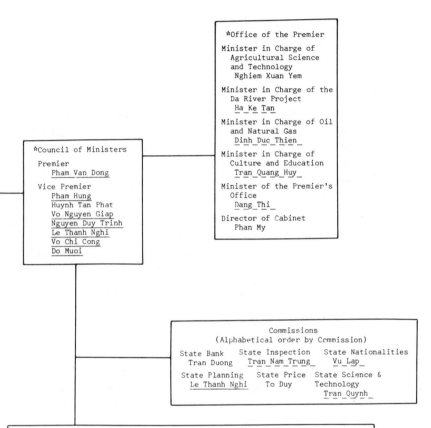

the executive posts. It should be noted that unlike the largely honorific seats in the National Assembly, ministerial posts do have genuine executive functions in the government, even for those who are not Central Committee members.

The new administrative system, promulgated for the entire country in December 1975, now has four levels: the center (with the capital at Hanoi), thirty-five provinces (a reduction from sixty-one) and three cities (Hanoi, Haiphong, and Ho Chi Minh City), the district, and the commune. At each level there is "a people's council," which serves as the organ of state power, conducting its administration. The judicial system is a People's Supreme Court, elected by the National Assembly for five years; and at the local level, local People's Court judges are elected by the corresponding People's Council. For law enforcement, there is the office of the people's supreme public prosecutor, whose head is also formally elected by the National Assembly for five years, and a system of local-level prosecutors' offices.

Steps were taken to amalgamate most of the separate southern mass organizations into their northern senior counterparts. An initial conference in mid-June 1976 in Ho Chi Minh City, followed by a second conference in Hanoi in July, took steps to integrate the National Liberation Front of the South and the Fatherland Front of the North. The South Vietnam Liberation Trade Union was absorbed into the Vietnam Federation of Trade Unions.[30] The Youth Liberation Association and the Student Liberation Association, both of South Vietnam, were integrated into the Hanoi-based Vietnam Youth Federation. The Women's Liberation Association and other southern women's associations were absorbed into the northern-based Women's Union. The Liberation Press Agency merged with the Vietnam News Agency, and the South Vietnam Patriotic and Democratic Journalists Association became part of the Vietnam Journalists Association.[31]

Economic Problems and Prospects

The reunification of North and South Vietnam in 1975 joined two potentially complementary economies, which will require a considerable period of adjustment before meshing into the rapidly developing, economically powerful state that the leadership envisages. Although the SRV is the third most populous communist country in the world, its per capita gross national product was estimated to be under $200 in 1976. This puts it slightly ahead of India but behind the Philippines and China.[32] Nonetheless, Vietnam is favored with natural resources. Only 16 percent of its total land area is cultivated, and 51 percent is covered by forest, with fertile soil enriched by an abundant flow of water. The North has rich coal deposits, which have been used to produce much of its electrical power and could be further developed for export. There are also important deposits of zinc, tin, iron ore, and uranium and small quantities of tungsten, lead and antimony, manganese, gold, cobalt, aluminum, and platinum. In 1971, industry and handicrafts accounted for 43.9 percent of the GNP in North Vietnam, and agriculture contributed 30.5 percent.[33]

The economy of the South, on the other hand, is largely based on agriculture, forestry, and fishing, with about three-fourths of the population engaged in agriculture at the end of the war. Before 1965 the region had been a net exporter of rice, but during the war, it is estimated, more than a million hectares of land were abandoned.[34] Mineral deposits in the South are not extensive, and the industrial sector is relatively new, with the exception of textiles and food processing. U.S. economic aid contributed greatly to the development of some light industry in the South, which produced a variety of consumer goods, such as shoes, bulbs, and electrical appliances. Foreign petroleum companies had been active in exploring offshore oil deposits, and up to their withdrawal in March 1975, they had reportedly invested some $100 million in sixteen tracts now claimed exclusively by Vietnam. In contrast with the North, the economy of South Vietnam in 1972 acquired only 7 percent of its GNP from manufacturing, mining, and quarrying.[35]

The economic organization of the North and South is also fundamentally different. In the South, land redistribution was effectively carried out under the Thieu government during the war on the basis of private ownership, but in the North agriculture was collectivized. In addition, substantial foreign participation in industries and banks existed in the South only. The difference in currency systems between the two economies has been allowed to continue into 1977, with the relative values set at a level that depreciated the southern money. Rice cultivation in the South previously existed side by side with cash crops such as tea, rubber, jute, and aromatic plants, which played a significant part in the economy. During the war the cities became swollen and overpopulated—Saigon grew from 2 million to 4 million—to the point of being unable to meet the most elementary needs in health, transportation, and water supply by the end of the war.[36]

The trade patterns of North and South were also quite different. The North ran a growing trade deficit throughout the war, a deficit that was directed overwhelmingly toward the socialist countries (92 percent in 1970), with foreign aid or long-term loans covering the imbalance. Since that time, trade with nonsocialist countries has grown to 28 percent of the total and will probably continue in this direction. Japan accounted for 39 percent of this nonsocialist bloc trade in 1975, but the Soviet Union was easily North Vietnam's largest trading partner in 1975. The latter was also the largest donor to the North Vietnamese during the entire period after the Geneva Agreement, contributing approximately $2.2 billion in economic aid (nearly all in grants) between 1955–1975. During the same period, the People's Republic of China contributed $1.8 billion in grants. For the current five-year plan of unified Vietnam, the Soviet Union is expected to provide somewhat more ($2.4 billion) than the previous twenty-year total, mostly in soft loans, and China will provide somewhat less ($1.5 billion) in soft loans. The East European socialist states may add another $700 million in grants and loans. During the twenty-five years in which the United States extended economic and military assistance to South Vietnam, it gave $7.8 billion in economic aid, and by 1973 the RVN's trade deficit of $5.64 billion was being balanced largely by U.S. government expenditures on goods and services. An estimated $110 million had been invested privately by Americans in South Vietnam, primarily by U.S. oil companies.[37] U.S. government assistance in the South contributed to the creation of "one of the best transport networks in the Far East," including Cam Ranh Bay port, which is one of the best natural harbors in Asia, and an airport system that far exceeds present civilian requirements.[38]

The war's economic impact on Vietnam's infrastructure, however, was adverse and severe in the area subjected to U.S. bombing and artillery barrages. In March 1976 a special report to the secretary general of the United Nations outlined the damage:

> *In the North,* the situation is as follows: Railway systems: all damaged, many completely destroyed. . . . Large and medium size road and rail bridges: damaged and often completely destroyed. . . . Waterways for inland and maritime shipping, and harbors and docks: damaged or destroyed. Rolling-stock: locomotives, wagons, trucks, boats: largely destroyed. Industries: Rolling stock-repair shops: completely destroyed; electric generating stations, fertilizer factories, tobacco factories, mechanical engineering and iron and steel plants: destroyed or seriously damaged. . . .
>
> *In the South,* the situation looks less than favorable. . . .
>
> There are quite a large number of "blank zones," where all vegetation was, so to speak, ruined by the use of defoliants and other chemicals and these should be brought back into full cultivation as a matter of urgency.
>
> To this tremendous damage in the North and South must be added the losses in equipment . . . , the displacement of population from areas of military operations, and the countless losses of human life caused by the war, among both military personnel and civilians.[39]

The UN Mission was visibly struck by the social consequences of the war as well as the physical damage, and for this reason it advocated a relief and rehabilitation program. Urgent attention was needed by the 3 million unemployed and the 5 million others who were either dependent upon them or displaced peasants, refugees, former soldiers, or office workers and laborers whose jobs had been temporarily suspended. In addition, sufficient food for the population had to be provided, and reestablishment of the communication routes for resettling people had to receive top priority. With this in mind, the mission strongly advocated the development of the agricultural sector and endorsed the government's policy of establishing New Economic Zones.[40] Ironically, although the population displacement and unemployment were much more severe in the South, the level of consumption there was so much higher at the war's end that a "leveling of the South" began as northern troops and cadres entered the southern cities and towns. Much of the South's best rice was shipped north in exchange for inferior grades. Private property was confiscated, usually in the guise of collecting taxes, and mounting inflation obliged the middle class (including the Chinese in Cholon) to sell their personal belongings and household goods before joining the ranks of the poor, to whom special food assistance was available. Northerners were the most ready purchasers of such consumer goods during the "vast garage sale" in Ho Chi Minh City.[41] The more privileged members of the Party or civil service were reportedly flying South on shopping tours for the "four treasures": refrigerator, television set, electric fan, bicycle.

Within a week of the fall of Saigon, the Economic and Social Council of the United Nations issued an appeal to all states to come to the assistance of the peoples of Indochina. The secretary general of the UN sent his personal representative to survey the needs and generate support among possible contributing governments. Largely as a result of these efforts, the United Nations coordinator for rehabilitation assistance to Vietnam was able to report in November 1976 that "as far as immediate humanitarian relief needs are concerned, they have been largely met," and he announced his intention to continue serving donor countries and UN agencies with information on the reconstruction requirements and progress of Vietnam.

In August 1976 it was announced that South Vietnam was self-sufficient in food, though this condition proved to be short-lived. At the year's end the Hanoi–Ho Chi Minh City rail link was reopened with fanfare, for the first time in thirty years. With provisional bridges and shortages of equipment, the trip took four to five days. In 1976 UN agencies and programs (not including international banks or the IMF) disbursed $33.4 million in aid to Vietnam and projected a disbursement of $86.7 million in 1977. The IMF provided $35.8 million, and the Asian Development Bank was projecting an expenditure of $13 million in 1977.[42] Direct bilateral aid from noncommunist states projected for the first year after formal unification was estimated at $162.1 million, and France agreed to increase its aid availability in May 1977. In November 1977, French aid credits were contracted for a $207 million steel complex, which over ten years will double Vietnamese output to 500,000 tons.[43]

Economic Strategy

The unexpected inheritance of full control of the southern economy in 1975 required a period of improvisation, rehabilitation, and transition before an economic plan for the entire nation could be prepared. At the Fourth Party Congress in December 1976, the revised five-year plan (1976–1980) was finally announced. The Party leadership boldly set high goals for yet another period of struggle to carry out the socialist revolution and achieve "large-scale socialist production within about twenty years."[44] Even though the economy was beset with duly acknowledged difficulties and even though there were "still notable discrepancies between the two zones," the Party exhorted the nation to plunge ahead into what was sometimes characterized as its "Third Resistance."

As Le Duan pointed out, the North had shifted "from a colonial and semi-feudal regime with an extremely backward agricultural economy to a socialist regime." In the South, however, he saw the socialist transformation just beginning:

> the exploiting classes remain; the poisons of the enslaving culture and the social evils caused by U.S. neo-colonialism as well as the influence of bourgeois ideology in society remain heavy; the reactionaries are still operating against the revolution; the negative aspects of capitalism and the spontaneous character of small production are still to be overcome.[45]

Further difficulties, on a national scale, were acknowledged by the leadership, in particular the small scale of production; low labor productivity; the deficiencies in food, raw materials, equipment, and fuel; and an imbalance of imports over exports. Nonetheless, the two fundamental tasks set by the Party were "to insure the needs of the people's life while carrying out accumulation in order to build the material and technical basis of Socialism."[46]

The official unveiling of the five-year plan stimulated speculation about factional disagreement within the leadership over the basic economic line. A pragmatic rather than purely ideological strategy seemed to have been agreed upon, but not without considerable disputation beforehand. Western observers were not wholly in agreement as to whether the Vietnamese were basically following a Soviet or Chinese model of economic development. Perhaps the best answer is that they are working out an essentially Vietnamese model, cognizant of the experiences of both fraternal states.

The most striking feature of the five-year plan was its emphasis on achieving "a leaping development of agriculture." Although Le Duan had given clear priority to heavy industry in his address to the National Assembly in June 1976, his presentation of the five-year plan stressed that this priority was to be based on the development of agriculture and light industry, which "have not been given due importance."[47] Agriculture and fishery and forestry industries were to receive 30 percent of the investment under the plan, and 35 percent would go into industry. In the latter sector, engineering industry would be emphasized in order to serve the food producing, forestry, and light industry sectors. Communications and transport would be rapidly expanded, and preparations made for future large-scale construction.

Another major goal of the plan was to organize the labor force so as markedly to increase productivity. The chief element in this plan was to be the development of districts into agro-industrial units of production and economic management. Some 488 such districts were projected for the nation as a whole. A massive redistribution of population is also planned. In addition to the approximately 700,000 persons already resettled by 1977, 4 million more persons are to be moved by 1980 from large urban centers, primarily in the South, to the underpopulated areas. Such population shifts are to continue into the 1980s as well. The human costs of such a program were acknowledged, in the press at least, with the comment that "the fact is that those who have sought refuge in the towns for so many years have lost the habit of farming, and the erstwhile soldier, officer, or merchant does not welcome becoming a peasant again."[48]

The other major economic goals of the plan are to "achieve socialist transformation in the South" and to "perfect the socialist production relations in the North." Furthermore, and particularly relevant for foreign policy, the Party is determined to "rapidly increase the sources of export, first of all agriculture and light industry products [and] broaden economic relations with foreign countries," which would include nonsocialist states.[49] The major emphasis in international trade must be to acquire advanced technology and thus to achieve a better division of labor and higher productivity in order to contribute to the accumulation of capital and a broadening of imports. Despite the insistence on short-term objectives, the Party leadership insists that the improvement of the people's "material and spiritual life is the cardinal task" of the Party and state "and the highest objective of economic development programs." In the next five years, the Party will strive to ensure enough staple food, decent and warm clothes, and common household goods for everyone. In addition it "must step by step meet the demands of the people for electric fans, clocks and wristwatches, radios, television sets, sewing machines."[50]

A final and critical economic objective found in the plan is to "vigorously improve trade, prices, finance and banking operations," while at the same time setting up "a new system of economic management on a national scale." Thus, a better use of prices to regulate supply and demand, of budgets (both national and local) to improve the implementation of economic development programs, and of tax policy to help regulate the sources of income as well as a banking system to supply credit capital for production—all are mentioned as desirable and necessary.

The particular production targets set for 1980 are noteworthy as goals, but at this point they are less significant than the predicted investment totals incorporated in the five-year plan. The government foresees a total investment of $7.5 billion during the five-year period. Outside economists have estimated that about 40 percent of this amount ($890 million per year) will have to be financed from foreign aid (mostly grants and soft-term credits).[51] To facilitate the bridging of the financial investment gap in these ambitious plans, the SRV in early May 1977 issued translations of its new foreign investment regulations. These were not only pragmatic, but the Citibank in Hong Kong called them "the most unconventional foreign investment regulations to be published by any Socialist government." It also pointed out that the regulations were merely general principles and that as article 26 specifies, "if need be the SRVN government may approve more advantageous terms in favor of the foreign party."[52] This phrase would doubtless be invoked by investors seeking to obtain a guarantee against nationalization longer than the ten to fifteen years offered in the code, as well as even more favorable tax provisions.

Assessment

The ambitiousness of Vietnamese economic and social planning, as demonstrated in this five-year plan, is not inconsistent with its endurance and determination during the two Indochina wars. In deciding to subject the South both to a "socialist transformation" and a program of "socialist construction" simultaneously, the Party is attempting to take a shortcut toward the fulfillment of its revolutionary goal. At the same time the leadership has quietly given the word that a period of at least twenty years will pass before the achievement of the ideal modernized society. Nonetheless, the general features of the economic plan are rational in Western economic terms, since they concentrate upon the development of agriculture, fisheries, and forestry in the short term, rather than move dogmatically toward heavy industrialization. They also face up soberly to the fact that foreign assistance in the future will move away from nonrefundable grants, which sustained the DRV in wartime. In presenting the plan, the leadership also acknowledged the country's major problems in reaching self-sufficiency in food (including natural adversities, which continue to occur) and in acquiring needed foreign exchange while overcoming an enormous trade deficit.

It would be remarkable, indeed, if Vietnam were to achieve its target of a 15 percent annual rate of economic growth, but it may very well show the strong growth in exports the plan stresses.[53] In mid-1977 the World Bank appeared favorable toward the development of coal for export as well as toward irrigation projects in the Mekong delta.[54] The Asian Development Bank was also reviewing a number of projects originally discussed with the Republic of South Vietnam, projects that could soon be reactivated using the previous loan commitments. Bilateral assistance has also come to Vietnam from European countries' token contributions to postwar relief and reconstruction, with more substantial amounts from France and Sweden.[55] The keystone of financial progress, however, would be the United States, whose potential assistance the Vietnamese doubtless foresee as substantially greater than any other nonsocialist state, and furthermore as something to which they are legally and morally entitled.

Vietnam's attractiveness as a place for foreign economic assistance, investment, or trade will depend considerably on its ability to overcome serious deficiencies in managerial personnel and performance. The Vietnamese themselves admit that they are plagued with bureaucratic red tape and abuse of power, which they exhort themselves to eliminate. As Le Duc Tho put it in his address to the Fourth Party Congress, "The organizational apparatus of many sectors and localities is cumbersome, authority and responsibilities are not clearly defined, work methods are bureaucratic, remote from the masses, and divorced from reality, and decentralization, particularism, localism and departmentalism are still rather widespread."[56] Foreign investors may not be as patient as even the Party leadership in dealing with the administrative deficiencies of an economy so lacking in experience in peacetime management and exposure to international standards of flexibility and decision making. Thus a critical test of the SRV's ultimate practicality may be its readiness to send substantial numbers of personnel abroad for training in advanced management technique.

A further key to Vietnamese economic development will be the rate of collectivization of agriculture imposed upon the South. It is not clear how rapidly the achievement of "collective mastery" in agriculture is to be pushed, although the goal has been enunciated. The imprecise Party pronouncements on this subject into early 1977 suggest that no firm decision has yet been taken. The fact is that rice farming in the collectivized system of the North has been less productive than the basically private farming of the South, where land reform, some mechanization, and high-yield seed varieties and fertilizer increased production by 25 percent in the last decade of the war. The Party's goal for southern agriculture is the giant agro-industrial production unit based upon the district, which is to average somewhat more than forty square miles of cultivated land.[57]

The Party is quite aware of the "grave errors" it committed in its first collectivization campaign in the North in 1954. After the initial excess of zeal, which included executions of landlords, the process moved successfully step by step from labor exchange teams to cooperatives, to large-scale cooperatives and double or triple cropping. In the new South the first step—the formation of labor exchanges—seems to be well under way, and some fifty State farms have also been opened since mid-1975. The New Economic Zones, which are being developed out of virgin or abandoned land for transplanted urban populations, lend themselves easily to this form of organization. Thus various agricultural production units have been tried and stabilized by the new leadership in Vietnam. Southern agriculture was already improving its productivity under U.S. assistance during the war, however, and whether communist organization on a larger-scale, centrally planned basis can continue this improvement without incurring major political resistance and economic slippage will be a major test of the new order. In June 1977, Politburo alternate member Vo Van Kiet announced that in the South all industry and agriculture would be state-controlled by the end of 1979.[58]

There is good reason to believe that the Vietnamese would like to become economically less dependent upon the Soviet Union and the People's Republic of China. Western visitors have been given to believe that the Vietnamese have had enough of what they see as Russian inefficiency and insufficiency of assistance. Large-scale dependence on China, with whom the Vietnamese have territorial disputes over the Paracel Islands, also has manifest disadvantages. The Vietnamese have a strong desire for national independence. Their readiness to encourage foreign investors with rather flexible investment regulations and their rapidly growing trade with Japan, Hong Kong, and Singapore indicate a readiness to edge away from the economic dependency necessitated by the war. In their attempts to lure back the oil companies that had explored the offshore tracts for the South Vietnamese government, the new regime may be holding major areas for renewal of operations by U.S. companies, since they frankly wish to have the best technology available. Again an intriguing dilemma arises: despite the vision, zeal, and practicality of the Vietnamese communists, they still must overcome political bitterness left from the past and ideological differences of the present and future in their relations with Americans. Yet a mutually profitable accommodation is conceivable.

With all the deficiencies of its economy—in management, resources, financial capital, and productivity—Vietnam has such obvious potential that its neighbors cannot help wondering how long it will remain behind in level of development. In terms of natural resources, its development prospects are "as good as any in the Third World,"[59] and its labor force of 22 million will be supplemented for some time to come by its 600,000-man army. The success of its zealous drive to modernize the economy will depend on the skill and sensitivity of its political leaders and on their ability to develop adequate management. The SRV will certainly not be another Burma economically, but it probably cannot expect to equal in the short run the present rate of development of neighbors such as Singapore or Malaysia.

Foreign Policy

Some Foundations of SRV Foreign Policy

The Vietnamese communists were euphoric about their victory. For them it represented not only the achievement of their cherished goals (of liberating the South, unifying the nation, and establishing socialism in the North), but more fundamentally they believe they have helped alter the world strategic balance. In the VCP perspective, there are three revolutionary currents abroad in the world today that are determining the "development of human society." These three currents, which are "impelling the transition of the world from capitalism to socialism," are: the establishment of a socialist system by the USSR, the PRC, and other countries; the growth of the national liberation movements in Asia, Africa, and Latin America; and the growing struggle of the working class in the capitalist countries. The Vietnamese war of national liberation was at the vanguard of this worldwide struggle against U.S.-led imperialism—their victory, therefore, was a turning point in the world's history.

This belief that they played a critical role in a larger struggle against imperialism, reinforced by lavish worldwide praise for their remarkable accomplishment, naturally stimulates the Vietnamese to encourage other national liberation movements. Their Southeast Asian neighbors fear that the Vietnamese pride of accomplishment might be translated not only into rhetorical encouragement of the insurgencies in their countries, but also into the supply of arms, logistic support, and training. On the other hand, the SRV leadership, in defining the new challenges they confront, has given overwhelming importance to modernization. The struggle against economic underdevelopment, they frequently note, is their third new war of resistance. In repairing the damage of the war and launching into a program of rapid economic growth, they are pushed to concentrate their attention upon internal problems. Their pragmatic inclinations encourage amicable relations with their Southeast Asian neighbors, a stable external environment, and increased commerce.[60] An interest in attracting capital and, more important, the most advanced technology, inclines the SRV leaders to seek active interchange with the West, even the United States.

The SRV's foreign policy principles enunciated at the Fourth Party Congress provide a framework out of which specific policies will be developed. The first principle calls for "militant solidarity with fraternal socialist countries," avoiding any hint of favoritism in the Sino-Soviet dispute. SRV neutrality in this dispute has had an activist tendency, as evidenced by the frequent quotes from Ho Chi Minh's testament that the Vietnamese must do their best to "restore and consolidate" solidarity between their major allies.

A second principle recognized a "special relationship" between the Vietnamese and the fraternal peoples of Laos and Cambodia, with no suggestion of the tensions between the SRV and Cambodian leaders. As for Vietnam's other neighbors in Southeast Asia, the Party resolution, using language that caused consternation when first pronounced following the 1975 communist victory, states that they "fully support the just struggle of the peoples in Southeast Asia for national independence, democracy and genuine neutrality . . . without military bases and troops of the imperialists." This was coupled with a commitment to the Third World to support "the struggle of the peoples of Asia, Africa and Latin America against imperialism and old and new colonialism . . . to actively contribute to the struggle of non-aligned countries against imperialism's policy of aggression and domination."[61] There was anxiety that this language might presage a Vietnamese communist effort to support "national liberation movements" in Southeast Asia,[62] although subsequent evidence that the Vietnamese were not pressing their involvement has been reassuring, at least temporarily. This resolution gives no clear indication of Vietnamese intentions, since it adds that the SRV is prepared to "establish and develop relations of friendship and cooperation with other countries in this area on the basis of respect for the other's independence, sovereignty and territorial integrity, non-aggression and non-interference in the other's internal affairs, equality, mutual benefit and peaceful coexistence."

In summary, the VWP often describes the dual tendencies in its fundamental policy as a combination of "patriotism closely intertwined with proletarian internationalism." The patriotism includes the element of nationalism, jealousy of its independence, and the pursuit of national self-interest; and the proletarian internationalism is expressed in Hanoi's ideological commitment to Marxism-Leninism, its alliance with the communist powers, and its identification with the national liberation struggles of the Third World.

SRV Perception of the United States

Official Vietnamese communist documents and public rhetoric are pervaded with the belief in a threat from "U.S.-led imperialism." The Fourth Party resolution notes that

> U.S.-led imperialism is feverishly preparing for a new world war, pursuing neo-colonialism and hitting back at the revolutionary movement. It schemes to retake lost positions, crush the national liberation movements and hamper the development of socialism. It plots to keep the newly emerging countries in the orbit of capitalism, to retake outlets, sources of raw materials, energy and investment areas. This is the basic policy of U.S. imperialism aimed at carrying out its scheme of world hegemony. The U.S. imperialists wanted to roll back the Vietnamese revolution and to reverse the general situation in the world, but after twenty years of involvement in Vietnam, with almost ten years of direct aggression against Vietnam by hundreds of thousands of troops by the U.S. and satellites, they were defeated and compelled to withdraw their soldiers. The total defeat of the U.S. in its aggressive war in Vietnam was a turning point, marking the period of decline of U.S. imperialism. Its military, political and economic weakening has plunged the capitalist world into an all-around and irremediable general crisis.

In keeping with their fundamental assumptions, the Party called for "a united anti-imperialist front" directed against U.S. imperialism.

Although the SRV assumptions suggest that Hanoi's leaders will remain suspicious of the United States in the foreseeable future, their pragmatic tendencies attenuate their ideology. The Vietnamese are eager to acquire U.S. technology, particularly for the exploitation of offshore oil, and they have frequently made public their interest in having U.S. oil companies resume their efforts to drill for oil in their South China Sea deposits. They strongly desire U.S. aid, and they believe that the Americans owe it to them. As for strategic considerations, though the Vietnamese align themselves with the socialist countries, their strong sense of nationalism leads them to hedge against too heavy a reliance on the USSR or the PRC.

SRV Relations with the Indochina States

Laos. Current SRV relations with Laos reflect the Vietnamese communists' intimate involvement in the development of the Lao revolutionary movement. The Vietnamese communists played a decisive role in the creation of the Lao communist movement (the Pathet Lao, PL) after World War II and have since provided critical advice, assistance, and military force, which helped to bring it to full power.[63]

Though clearly the junior partner in their long struggle, the Lao communists have shared goals with their Vietnamese allies. Both groups fought first against French colonial rule and then continued their resistance against what they perceived as U.S. neocolonialism. Since their adversaries drew much powerful support from the Americans, the relatively weak Lao communists leaned heavily upon the Vietnamese communists and embraced a similar ideology. During the formative years of the Lao communist movement, the Vietnamese gave counsel and support for the development of institutions strongly resembling their own.

The ruling communist party of Laos today, the Lao People's Revolutionary Party (LPRP), grew out of a Committee on Laos, established in 1936 by the Indochinese Communist Party (ICP) under the leadership of Ho Chi Minh. The ICP, with almost exclusive Vietnamese membership, directed the formative years of the Lao communist movement in the first Indochina war (1946–1954). The ICP authorized a separate Lao party in 1951, but it was not until March 1955 that the Lao People's Party (LPP, renamed the LPRP in February 1972) was actually founded with 300 Lao members.[64] The LPP followed the model of Vietnam's Lao Dong Party and continued to receive guidance and assistance from Vietnamese advisers.

The Vietnamese, in providing support to the Lao communists during the second Indochina war (1960–1975), were interested in three primary goals: the protection of their borders, access to South Vietnam, and the establishment of a politically congenial regime in Laos. In their concern for security, the Vietnamese communists sought to assure themselves that neither the adjacent territory in Laos nor the ethnic minorities living there would be used by their enemies for attacks against North Vietnam. The corridor through Laos to South Vietnam, commonly referred to as the Ho Chi Minh Trail, became especially important to the DRV after 1959, when it stepped up the infiltration of men and supplies for the insurgency in South Vietnam.

After the communist victories in Indochina, relations between Vietnam and Laos continue to be close. Vietnam provided a variety of assistance to Laos, including emergency shipments of food and access to the sea, following Thailand's blockade of the frontier in November 1975. In July 1977, the Vietnamese and Lao signed a series of sweeping military and economic agreements, including a twenty-five-year friendship treaty, which provided for Vietnamese financial aid and loans to Laos, and a detailed border pact with military provisions and agreement on common approaches to foreign policy and domestic issues.[65] The joint communiqué affirmed the "special relationship" between Vietnam and Laos. The Vietnamese agreed to permit the use of Da Nang as a duty-free unloading area for Laos and, according to intelligence reports, have been improving the road network linking Laos to Vietnam. Western diplomats in Bangkok believed that the agreements ratified the presence in Laos of 20,000 to 30,000 Vietnamese troops, who are engaged in road building, logistic activities, and support of the Lao government's efforts to suppress resistance activities. The official announcements noted that the four-day visit to Laos led by VCP General Secretary Le Duan and Prime Minister Pham Van Dong was the highest ranking delegation ever to leave Vietnam and that 100,000 Laotians turned out to welcome them. As the Lao communist links with Vietnam expand, landlocked Laos will continue to shift from Thailand to Vietnam for access to the outside world.

Laos clearly follows Hanoi's foreign policy line and pursues domestic development based on the SRV model. Nevertheless, the exact extent of Hanoi's control or influence is not evident. Although the Lao communist leaders were greatly dependent upon Vietnam in the earlier phases of their revolutionary movement, they are now in effective control of their country and have political and administrative institutions that can stand on their own. Having achieved power in such close cooperation with the Vietnamese, and sharing their ideological framework, it is not surprising that they see things as their Vietnamese allies do and that they emulate the policies of their senior partners. Most of the Lao leaders speak Vietnamese, some have Vietnamese wives (Nouhak, Souphanouvong) or had Vietnamese parents (Kaysone's father was Vietnamese), and all have spent years during the first and second Indochinese wars in collaboration with Vietnamese counterparts. Moreover, directing a backward country of 3 million people next to a relatively powerful nation of 50 million, the Lao leaders recognize their weakness and have an interest in friendly cooperation with the Vietnamese. On the other hand, with the growth of nationalism in Laos, it would be natural for the Lao communist leadership to be sensitive about their sovereignty and to resent any Vietnamese attempt to dominate. It is not impossible that there are hidden tensions, but there have been no public signs of discontent among the Lao leaders over excessive Vietnamese dominance. For their part, the Vietnamese have demonstrated that even during the great wartime PL dependence, they were discreet and indulgent concerning Lao nationalist sensitivities.

Thus, no matter how much control or influence Hanoi has within the inner councils of Laos, it seems likely that in the foreseeable future, Lao and Vietnamese foreign policy will operate in tandem, with the Vietnamese steering the course. Lao leaders might attempt to counterbalance Vietnamese influence through relations with the USSR and the PRC, but the Lao will probably not take any action in which the Vietnamese might have a serious interest without first clearing it with them.

Cambodia. Although much less has been revealed about the Communist Party of Kampuchea, which rules Cambodia, the important role of the communists in its founding and early development is evident, notwithstanding the Cambodian leaders' rewriting of Party history to exclude the period of Vietnamese dominance. Like its counterpart in Laos, the Cambodian Party grew out of the Indochina Communist Party (ICP), founded by Ho Chi Minh in 1930. In 1951, when the ICP decided to establish separate parties, the Pracheachon, or People's Party, was founded (along with the VWP in Vietnam in 1951 and the LPP in Laos in 1955, as already noted).[66] The Pracheachon's statutes were modeled on those of the VWP, and the secretary general, Sieu Heng, had worked closely with the Viet Minh. But in contrast to the situation in Laos, the Vietnamese did not nurture a Cambodian communist party that came to power dependent upon Vietnamese efforts. The Vietnamese communists did provide critical assistance to the Cambodian communist movement from the outbreak of war in Cambodia in 1970 until 1972, when Vietnamese assistance diminished and the Khmer communists, with Chinese supplies, operated independently, with relatively little Vietnamese advice and support.[67] By the time the Cambodian communists, or Khmer Rouge as they were popularly called, seized Phnom Penh in April 1975 (two weeks before the fall of Saigon), they were clearly an independent revolutionary force whose relations with Vietnam were, at best, formally correct.

Vietnamese residents of Cambodia, under pressure from the new leadership, soon moved to South Vietnam, and there were reports of armed conflict between Vietnam and Cambodia over disputed territory. According to these reports, Vietnamese forces, in June 1975, seized the Wai Islands, which Cambodia also claimed (and these were subsequently returned to Cambodia), and there were armed clashes, including Vietnamese bombing at other frontier areas. A "high-ranking" Cambodian delegation, said to be the first to represent the new government abroad, traveled to Hanoi in June 1975, apparently to discuss border problems between the two countries.[68] In late July, the SRV's highest-ranking leader,

Le Duan, led a Vietnamese delegation to Phnom Penh, which produced a formal communiqué. Two months later, there were conversations between Le Duan and Cambodia's Vice-Premier for Foreign Affairs Ieng Sary in Peking, with the Chinese apparently assuming an active role as mediator. Subsequently, formal diplomatic relations were resumed between Vietnam and Cambodia, and a Vietnamese ambassador moved to Phnom Penh in September 1975.[69]

Diplomatic relations were maintained until December 31, 1977, when the Cambodian authorities severed diplomatic ties, charging the SRV with "aggression against the territory of Democratic Cambodia."[70] A statement by Cambodia's president, Khieu Samphan, charged that "since September 1977, the SRV Armed Forces, consisting of several infantry divisions from Hanoi and several hundred tanks and artillery pieces supported by airplanes, have launched a continuous large-scale aggressive offensive" against Cambodia.[71] Subsequent statements by both sides confirmed that there had been intermittent military clashes since May 1975, which had been hitherto concealed from the press. Numerous attempts at a negotiated solution of the border dispute had been undertaken, principally at Vietnamese initiative, it appears, but, according to Premier Pham Van Dong, the Cambodians severed all contact with the Vietnamese in April 1977 and "stepped up encroachment on our territorial sovereignty on an increasing scale."[72]

The Vietnamese launched a major attack against Cambodia in September 1977, and the fighting continued, with the Vietnamese reportedly occupying as much as 400 square miles of Cambodian territory at the end of the year.[73] Refusing to accept the Vietnamese call for negotiation that accompanied its attack, the Cambodian leaders ruptured diplomatic relations and proclaimed that they would not agree to negotiations until the Vietnamese halted their "aggression" and all Vietnamese troops had been withdrawn from Cambodian soil. As the fighting continued into January and February 1978, there was an escalation of rhetoric on both sides. The Cambodians charged, in a broadcast on January 26, that the Vietnamese

> continuously interfere in our national affairs, cause disturbances in our country and nibble at our border territory. Particularly since the

middle of 1975, because Vietnam's goal is to swallow Cambodia's territory and force Cambodia into an Indochinese federation under its control, and because Vietnam is no longer fighting the U.S. imperialists and their lackeys and thus needs no more help from Cambodia in the form of economic assistance, food, sanctuary and transportation routes as it did during the war, the annexationist, expansionist Vietnamese have openly, continuously and wantonly encroached on Cambodia's national independence, sovereignty and honor.[74]

The Cambodians asserted further that the Vietnamese intention to make Cambodia their "satellite and servant" derived from Vietnam's own doctrine; "no imperialist power is behind it."[75]

The Vietnamese denied that they had annexationist or expansionist intentions, rejected the charge that they wished to force Cambodia into an Indochinese federation, and insisted that they had never interfered in the internal affairs of Cambodia.[76] They charged that the Cambodians had penetrated Vietnamese territory, shelled civilian towns and villages, and had committed a wide range of atrocities, including the murder of Vietnamese and Cambodian residents. The Vietnamese authorities brought domestic and selected foreign journalists to observe the sites of the Cambodian incursions into Vietnam. In contrast to the Cambodian pronouncements, the Vietnamese statements frequently emphasized an undying friendship between the Vietnamese and Cambodian *peoples* and continued to propose a negotiated solution. In early February 1978, a Vietnamese proposal called for the establishment of a demilitarized zone on both sides of the border along with international supervision. The Vietnamese suggested three possible forms of supervision: a United Nations role, a body to be formed from nonaligned nations, or a supervisory organization like those formed under the Geneva Agreement of 1954 and the Paris accord of 1973.[77] At the time of this writing, the Cambodians had not accepted these Vietnamese appeals for negotiation, and the clashes and denunciatory rhetoric continued.

As of February 1978, the strategy of the Vietnamese in their conflict with Cambodia remained unclear. The major Vietnamese attack of September 1977 appeared designed to demonstrate Vietnam's superior strength and clear determination to assert its position and to persuade the Cambodian leaders to negotiate a settlement of their border differences. The defiant reaction of the Cambodians revealed the intensity of their anger, the depth of the Cambodian historic national suspicion of the Vietnamese, and the fiercely independent attitudes of the Cambodian leaders. The Vietnamese undoubtedly have the military capability to seize any objective in Cambodia, including Phnom Penh, with little difficulty, and could install a government sensitive to Vietnamese wishes. But the costs of such a policy would be high. Cambodia enjoys the public support of China, and even with the Soviet Union's endorsement, the Vietnamese have to face the prospect of Chinese pressure and possible retaliation. Furthermore, an expansionist Vietnam might lose some of the international support it had won during its war against the United States, and endanger some of its economic assistance. Moreover, an adventure in Cambodia would divert Vietnam's energies away from its massive internal problems of reconstruction and socialist transformation. It is not possible, at this juncture, to ascertain whether there was any truth in the Cambodian charges that the Vietnamese had been trying to overthrow Phnom Penh's leadership and install a client government.[78] The Vietnamese did hint, in early 1978, that they might be at the limit of their patience and that if the Cambodian authorities "continue to violate Vietnamese territory, to commit new crimes against the Vietnamese people and to refuse to negotiate, they will be duly punished. They must be held responsible for all consequences."[79]

The tensions between Cambodia and Vietnam have deep roots. Vietnam expanded to its present boundaries at the expense of the Khmer Empire, which once included the bulk of Cochin China (South Vietnam). Consequently, Cambodians have historically regarded the Vietnamese as imperialists who have seized Khmer territory. Furthermore, the French employed Vietnamese as colonial administrators in Cambodia (and Laos) at the echelon below the French, relegating the Cambodians to inferior positions. Vietnamese also came to Cambodia during the colonial period as merchants, sharing commercial activities with the Chinese in Phnom Penh and in the provincial towns, inspiring further resentment from an overwhelmingly agricultural people, who, in characteristic fashion, are suspicious of foreign merchants. The ferocity of the anti-Vietnamese pogroms by the Khmer populace in 1970, under the Lon Nol regime, is an indication of the hostility that many Cambodians harbor for the Vietnamese. The border issues mentioned above, both in regard to the mainland, where the French-drawn frontiers of the nineteenth century are in dispute, and to a number of offshore islands in the Gulf of Siam, have provided a source of contention out of which the frontier war erupted.

Although Hanoi and its Lao junior partner have been careful to straddle the Sino-Soviet dispute by maintaining correct relations with both powers while tilting in the Soviet direction, Phnom Penh has clearly aligned its policy (its pronouncements on nonalignment notwithstanding) with the PRC. These differing orientations in the Sino-Soviet dispute have provided another source of tension between Cambodia and Vietnam. For Cambodia, close relations with China represent a counterbalance to possible pressure from Hanoi. In addition, there is a striking difference between the Vietnamese and the Cambodian manner of consolidating power and doctrine on the next stage of the revolution. For example, the Vietnamese reportedly expressed astonishment and displeasure at the Cambodian forced evacuation of the cities in April 1975. Thus, the revolutionary allies, which had so often expressed their "militant solidarity" during their struggle against foreign "imperialists," were themselves engaged in serious conflict in early 1978.

Vietnam and the future of Indochina. Do the Vietnamese wish, as the Cambodians charge and as many analysts believe, to form an Indochina federation they will dominate? Various reasons have been given for this belief. The Vietnamese dominated the Indochina Communist Party, whose goal was to expel the French from Indochina. (However, although communism was to replace colonialism in Indochina, it was never explicitly stated that Vietnamese communists would rule Laos and Cambodia.) Some Western historians contend that France took over and achieved the dream of the rulers of precolonial Vietnam to rule Laos and Cambodia.[80] It would not be uncommon for a former colony to wish to succeed the colonial power in ruling its total domain (e.g., Indians defined India as the territory ruled by the British; Indonesians defined Indonesia as the territory ruled by the Dutch).

According to a resolution of the VWP's Seventh Plenum in October 1940, one of the party's goals was the establishment of an Indochinese democratic federal republic.[81] During the second Indochina war, VWP cadres used the *Indochinese People's Revolutionary Movement* or similar terms to refer to the coordination of the movements in Laos, Cambodia, and Vietnam. These Vietnamese phrases may have evoked images of institutionalized coordination, which the Cambodians, and even the Lao, did not share.[82] At junctures in both the first and second "resistance wars," the Vietnamese set up "united front" organizations: in 1951, the Viet Minh established the "United Front of Vietnam, Laos and Cambodia"; in 1970, in China, the DRV and the National United Fronts of Laos, Cambodia, and South Vietnam held a Summit Conference of the Indochinese Peoples. These former alliances could provide, it is asserted, the structure for bringing together the three Indochina nations in a union that Hanoi would dominate.

At a minimum, some contend, the Vietnamese will absorb the highland regions of Laos, where tribal minorities from Vietnam spread across the frontier. The Vietnamese communists have long been sensitive about the questionable loyalty of the minorities who have straddled their frontiers with Laos.[83] In 1954–1956, some Tai tribes, presumably remnants of the French-trained Tai Federation troops, went into rebellion. According to DRV sources, they were centered in Lao Cai and Ha Giang provinces, tying down "hundreds" of PAVN and regional force units in "bandit suppression."[84] Up to December 1955, the government reported, 5,200 such "bandits" and over 4,000 firearms had been seized. Certainly the fact that the highlands of Laos contain ethnic minorities who are even more numerous in Vietnam gives the Vietnamese an acute interest in Lao internal affairs. One historian of Vietnam contends that "Nothing, indeed, will more easily shape the future of Laos than the belief possessed by almost every ruler of Vietnam, Communist or non-Communist, that Vietnamese governments have a permanent interest in Laos, because the political boundaries of the 'nation' of Laos do not coincide with the actual geographic distribution of ethnic groups in Indochina."[85] The highland minorities of Laos have not demonstrated great affection for the lowland Lao and have shown little loyalty to governments ruling them from the plain in Vientiane. It is possible, as some contend, that the Vietnamese will one day rectify the unwise borders imposed by the French colonial power, although provisions in the twenty-five-year friendship treaty the two countries signed in July 1977 may have reassured the Lao that the Vietnamese have accepted these borders.

With a population of 50 million, as contrasted with approximately 7.5 million Cambodians and 3 million Lao, the Vietnamese are clearly the most powerful of the Indochinese nations. They are a vigorous people and have a history of expanding into their neighbors' territory. Of course, the Vietnamese may somewhere have a blueprint for dominating Indochina. It is conceivable, too, that even if they do not, the inherent historic trends of the region will again produce Vietnamese expansion.

On the other hand, it is possible that the Vietnamese do *not* aspire to dominate their neighbors in Indochina. They might well be satisfied to have friendly states on their frontiers, states that would be sensitive to their interests and would consult them on matters of primary concern. Important factors reinforce such independent development on the part of the Indochina states. Nationalism has grown to significant proportions in Laos and even more so in Cambodia, and there would be resistance to Vietnamese domination, especially in Cambodia, where, as noted above, there is such active suspicion of the Vietnamese. Although the Lao resent the Vietnamese less intensely than the Cambodians do, they look back with anxiety on the historic record of Vietnamese expansion into Laos. The lowland Lao are drawn closer to the Thai than to the Vietnamese by similarities of language, religion, and culture. Furthermore, Indochina's neighbor to the north would tend to counterbalance possible Vietnamese ambitions. Although it supported Vietnam in its war against the "American imperialists," the PRC is not likely to look with favor upon a Vietnamese move to dominate Indochina. Khmer and Lao nationalists, recognizing the counterbalance that the PRC can provide, would look to China for assistance. The PRC is now the dominant external power in Phnom Penh, and it maintains influence in Laos, including an estimated 15,000 troops engaged in the construction of a road network that leads from China to the Thai border. Thus, the factors countervailing a Vietnamese tendency toward long-term expansion

in Indochina may predominate, although Vietnam's border conflict with Cambodia raises new uncertainties about the future of
Indochina.

Relations with ASEAN States

ASEAN reaction to communist victory. Although communist
victory in Indochina was ultimately expected, the rapid collapse
of the Saigon government in the spring of 1975 came as a shock to
the ASEAN states (Association of Southeast Asian Nations, composed of Thailand, Malaysia, Singapore, Indonesia, and the Philippines). Furthermore, the final victory crystalized anxieties among
the Southeast Asian leaders about what posture the new Indochinese communist regimes, especially the Vietnamese, would take
toward them. They saw communist Vietnam as the foremost military power on the Southeast Asian mainland, made even more
powerful by the formidable windfall of weapons, vehicles, and
supplies so munificently provided by the United States to the
Thieu government. Their fears of Vietnamese military power were
reinforced by Hanoi's later pronounced intentions to maintain,
even strengthen, its military forces. Would Hanoi be inclined to
use this power directly to expand its area of control or influence?
Some ASEAN leaders believed that even if the Vietnamese leaders
waited some years to consolidate their dominance of Indochina,
they already exercised effective domination over Lao policymaking. Some ASEAN leaders also feared that the Vietnamese would,
in time, turn aggressively to the northeastern regions of Thailand,
populated by peoples who speak Lao or Thai.[86]

The most serious concern of the ASEAN leaders was the impact of the communist victory in Indochina upon insurgencies in
Southeast Asia. Many feared that communist Vietnam, flushed
with victory and a self-proclaimed leader of national liberation
movements, could not ignore calls for assistance from local communist groups. Thailand is plagued with a communist-led insurgency not only in the northeast Lao-Thai area, but also in the
north among the hill tribes (especially the Meo) and in the Muslim
regions of the south bordering Malaysia. Since the 1960s, the
Vietnamese communists had been training, in North Vietnam and
Laos, a relatively small number of Thai revolutionaries operating
largely in the northeast. Now that the communists in Laos con-

trolled the 1,000-mile frontier with Thailand along the Mekong, the Thais feared that the Lao and Vietnamese would collude in augmenting rebel attacks against them and that training of rebels to infiltrate Thailand would mount.

In Malaysia, the communist insurgency, which recruited principally from ethnic Chinese, was again troublesome on the mainland (West Malaysia), particularly in the areas bordering Thailand, and also on the island of Sarawak. In the Philippines, there was a tenuous truce with Muslim rebels in Mindanao, and the communist-led New People's Army was seen by the government there as a potential threat, if not a current challenge. Although Indonesia was not facing a communist insurgency, Indonesian leaders continued to entertain morbid fears of an internal communist resurgence, despite the massacre in Indonesia of tens of thousands of communists and the decimation of the party organizations following the abortive coup in 1965. Similarly, in Singapore, although Lee Kuan Yew's tightly run ethnic Chinese city-state was not confronting an active insurgency, there was concern that a communist political movement, over which Lee achieved ascendance in a tense political struggle in the 1950s, could grow once again.

Although most Southeast Asian leaders had long derided the simplistic projections of Southeast Asian dominoes toppling in rapid succession following a communist success in Indochina, the communist takeovers in 1975 rekindled the fear of the ripple effect that communist Indochinese provocations could have in the area. Anxiety mounted that heavy pressure on northeast Thailand, internal Thai political problems, and the declining U.S. presence and willingness to act in the region might lead to communist domination of Thailand. This would, in turn, affect Burma, itself already suffering from communist insurgency, ethnic conflict, and serious political mismanagement. These and similar visions gained increased currency in Southeast Asia after the spring of 1975.

Most Southeast Asian leaders expected that, at a minimum, the Vietnamese would be troublesome, with public exhortation favoring revolution in their countries. They were particularly concerned about Hanoi's proclamations that "the Vietnamese peoples fully support the struggle of the peoples of the Southeast Asian nations for independence, democracy, peace and social progress" and

about its urgings to Southeast Asians to "foil all neo-colonialist
schemes and tricks of American imperialists and reactionaries,
restore true national independence and sovereignty and restore
the ownership of the Southeast Asia region to the Southeast
Asians."[87]

Another concern of ASEAN leaders—probably of greater importance than the communist victory in Indochina—was the conclusion that the debacle in Indochina had affected the United
States so profoundly that it might fully withdraw its influence
from the region. An expression of this assessment—one of many
pronounced by Southeast Asian leaders—came from President
Marcos of the Philippines, who told a reporter, "the U.S. has, after
Vietnam, of course, wanted to forget all about southeast Asia, a
bad dream."[88] Concern about this possibility actually began in
the late 1960s, as the United States began to reduce its forces in
Indochina and negotiate a withdrawal. As these calculations
regarding U.S. intentions were evolving among Southeast Asian
leaders, they were shocked to learn in the summer of 1971 that
Secretary of State Kissinger had been secretly negotiating a U.S.
opening to China. This raised anxiety that China would also
expand its influence in the region, along with the Vietnamese
communists, as the United States abandoned Southeast Asia to
its own resources. Though there had been ambivalence over U.S.
influence, there surely was no enthusiasm to see it replaced by
either a PRC or Vietnamese influence.

SRV position toward ASEAN states. Despite their early fears
about aggressive Vietnamese intentions following the victory,
ASEAN leaders were reassured, at least temporarily, by the
moderate SRV posture. The Vietnamese emphasized their interest
in developing normal diplomatic relations and commerce with
their neighbors. Their earlier pledges to assist the "just struggles"
of the peoples of Southeast Asia for national liberation were
muted in favor of emphasis on state-to-state relations based upon
the Bandung principles of "respect for each other's independence,
sovereignty and territorial integrity, non-aggression, non-interference in each other's internal affairs, equality, mutual benefit
and peaceful coexistence." Propelled by their pragmatic interest
in increasing trade, attracting foreign capital, and importing
technology, the Vietnamese concluded that normalized relations
with their Southeast Asian neighbors, as well as with the indus-

trialized West, would best serve their interest in rapid modernization and would reduce their heavy reliance upon their socialist
allies. Moreover, as the SRV was the most powerful nation on the
Southeast Asian mainland, it was interested in making its influence
felt in regional affairs.

One early signal of the Vietnamese interest in accommodation
came in the spring of 1976, when the new communist governor
of the National Bank of (South) Vietnam attended a meeting of
the Asian Development Bank, called for economic cooperation in
the region, and invited foreign assistance to Vietnam.[89] Even more
encouraging was the new, friendly tone toward relations with
Southeast Asian nations enunciated by SRV Foreign Minister
Nguyen Duy Trinh after the official reunification of Vietnam in
July 1976. He called for the establishment of "relations of friendship and cooperation" with the countries of the region and a
"lasting peace."[90] Then followed a goodwill tour of Malaysia,
Philippines, Indonesia, Singapore, and Burma by Deputy Foreign
Minister Phan Hien, during which Vietnamese friendly intentions
were expressed. The ASEAN leaders responded in kind, and
almost all Southeast Asian states began negotiations for establishing or improving relations with Hanoi.

Hanoi made it abundantly clear that its interest was in improving bilateral relations with Southeast Asian nations, not in
cooperating with the ASEAN organization, for which it expressed
grave mistrust. The ASEAN members have intermittently made
advances toward Hanoi regarding membership. Following the
Paris Agreement of January 1973, an ASEAN foreign ministers'
meeting in February issued a cautious press release stating that the
ministers had concluded that "it was desirable to expand the
membership of ASEAN at the opportune time to cover all the
countries in Southeast Asia." Meeting no favorable response, in
1974 ASEAN leaders launched a proposal for an " 'Asian Forum'
to discuss problems of vital interest to the region [and] to remove
misunderstanding and dispel suspicion, when and where they
exist."[91] But again they were rebuffed. After the communist victories in Indochina, the ASEAN states emphasized that they had
never envisaged ASEAN as a military organization. Although most
of ASEAN's members recognize the futility of attempts to attract
Hanoi into any form of cooperation with the ASEAN organization,
some have held out the hope that the "Asian Forum" proposal

might be revived as a mini-Helsinki meeting to confirm the borders and establish a modus vivendi among Southeast Asian states.[92]

But the Vietnamese hostility toward ASEAN has been consistent. In the summer of 1976, a Vietnamese Foreign Ministry spokesman announced that "we decidedly do not tolerate any scheme to revive ASEAN's none-too-bright past and to sell this organization's outmoded and bankrupt policy." Premier Kaysone Phomvihan of Laos was even blunter in refusing his country's cooperation with ASEAN as an organization.[93] Both Vietnam and Laos still see the hand of U.S. imperialism in ASEAN. In their joint declaration announcing their twenty-five-year treaty of friendship in July 1977, the two states condemned the United States for maintaining troops and bases in the region and for "plotting to take advantage of ASEAN to oppose the trend toward genuine independence, peace and neutrality."[94]

Although the Vietnamese and Lao have made frequent exhortations in favor of neutrality, they find unpalatable the ASEAN resolution for a "zone of peace, freedom and neutrality," first propounded in 1971 by Malaysia and formally accepted by the other states (although with an evident lack of enthusiasm for any concrete implementation in the near future). When the Malaysian delegate introduced this ASEAN resolution to the Colombo summit conference of nonaligned nations in August 1976, Lao President Souphanouvong denounced it vigorously. The Vietnamese delegation added that it agreed with the Lao position, although it emphasized that the SRV policy of improving bilateral relations in Southeast Asia had not changed.

SRV bilateral relations with its Southeast Asian neighbors—with the important exception of Thailand—have been steadily improving, although temporary setbacks have occurred. All the Southeast Asian states have felt relieved that Hanoi has not sold or significantly increased its free donations of U.S. weapons, which it captured in such huge amounts in South Vietnam.[95] Southeast Asia was reassured, at least temporarily, that Hanoi had neither expanded its efforts in the Thai insurgency, to which it has long given low-level support, nor become involved in the Philippine or Malaysian insurgencies.[96] Hanoi could take heart from the formal demise in June 1977 of the moribund Southeast Asia Treaty Organization (SEATO) (whose underlying treaty the

United States had cited in pursuing the Vietnam war)[97] as well as from the almost complete departure of U.S. military personnel from bases in Thailand in 1976.

SRV relations with Malaysia, which had been cooled somewhat by the Lao and Vietnamese performance at the Colombo conference, were improved by the Malaysian foreign minister's visit to Hanoi in June 1977. Agreement was announced on sending Malaysian technical experts to help the Vietnamese rubber and palm oil industries. Vietnamese-Philippine diplomatic relations were launched following Phan Hien's goodwill tour in 1976, and some commercial exchanges have been initiated. Continuing points of contention between the SRV and the Philippines are the presence of U.S. naval and air bases at Subic Bay and Clark Field as well as conflicting claims to the Spratly Islands. The Singapore leaders are more skeptical than most Southeast Asians about the peaceful intentions of the Vietnamese, but they have responded affirmatively to Vietnam's shopping list of needed supplies in early 1977. The military leaders of Indonesia, perhaps even more than the Singapore leaders, feel an anxiety about Vietnamese long-term strategy in the region and are concerned lest Vietnam be excessively assisted in rapid industrialization. Nonetheless, correct state-to-state relations are under way between the two countries. A specific bone of contention was Hanoi's highly vocal support for the Revolutionary Front for an Independent East Timor (FRETILIN) and its denunciation of Indonesia's annexation of East Timor.

Several factors account for the serious tensions between Vietnam and Thailand. At the root of these tensions is the centuries-long competition between the two nations.[98] Most recently, Thailand sent more than 20,000 troops to the U.S.-South Vietnamese war effort in Vietnam, something that Hanoi cannot easily forgive. In addition, Thailand secretly provided more than 15,000 military "volunteers" in Laos against the revolutionary side. Thailand was also the headquarters of SEATO, and, at peak periods, Thai soil held more than 40,000 U.S. troops and five U.S. air bases, from which U.S. bombing raids were conducted against Vietnam and Laos. At the collapse of the Thieu government, part of the Saigon government's air force and navy fled to Thailand with their vessels. The PRG claimed this property, but the Thais rebuffed it. Bitter recriminations followed. Thailand has been a haven for refugees from all three Indochina states, with most coming from Laos across the 1,000-mile border along the Mekong River. Vietnam and Laos accuse Thailand of supporting these "reactionary elements" as well as hostile guerrilla raids within Laos.

The Thais, too, have many grievances against the Vietnamese. They have been seriously concerned by long-term Vietnamese support of insurgency, particularly in the northeast. Although somewhat relieved that the Vietnamese have not increased their support to the insurgents since April 1975, they still feel vulnerable to hostile Vietnamese activities. The Thais have suspected (justifiably or not) that the Vietnamese residents of northeast Thailand, who had fled from Vietnam and Laos during the first Indochina war in the early 1950s, are helping the insurgents in Thailand. Some 40,000–50,000 of these early Vietnamese refugees remain in Thailand, under pressure from the Thai government and in danger of harassment by local anti-Vietnamese groups. The SRV has protested the Thai treatment of this Vietnamese minority, and the Thai government has made efforts to repatriate them to Vietnam, but it has received no cooperation from the SRV.

Despite these sources of tension, SRV-Thai relations improved during 1976, and diplomatic relations were agreed upon, although ambassadors were not exchanged. However, these moves toward accommodation were set back by the military coup d'etat in Thailand in October 1976, which overthrew the moderate government of Seni Pramoj and replaced it with a more firmly anticommunist regime. Both Hanoi and Vientiane denounced the coup as the work of U.S. imperialists and Thai reactionaries, and their radio broadcasts strongly denigrated the new leadership. The Thai leaders, in turn, were sharply critical of the Indochinese communist regimes. Thai-Vietnamese relations again improved following the overthrow of the short-lived Thanin regime in October 1977 and its replacement by a government led by General Kriangsak Chamanan, who pursued a more accommodating policy toward his Indochinese neighbors. Furthermore, the outbreak of the border war with Cambodia in late 1977 led Vietnam to pursue friendly relations with Thailand as well as with the other ASEAN members. Vietnam was concerned, it appears, that the PRC's support for Cambodia, its role as a mediator of Thai-Cambodian tensions, and its benevolent attitude toward ASEAN might isolate Vietnam in the Southeast Asian region.

Vietnam and the Third World

Although identified with the socialist nations, Vietnam has carefully cultivated an active role in the Third World. In August 1975, it joined the nonaligned group at their foreign ministers' conference in Paris and in the following year took an active role, as already noted, at the conference in Colombo. The Vietnamese have formed close ties with Algeria, with whom they share common bonds of struggle against French colonialism, and with Yugoslavia, a socialist state that asserted its independence from its powerful Soviet mentor. In the Middle East, the SRV has had its closest political ties with the Arab militant states (Libya, Iraq, Algeria, the People's Democratic Republic of Yemen), but it has also actively pursued commercial ties with the conservative, oil-producing countries of Iran, Kuwait, and United Arab Emirates, seeking supplies of petroleum, technology for exploration of its own oil, economic assistance, and trade. In Latin America, the SRV has developed especially strong ties with Cuba. As early as 1969, after the formation of the PRG, Cuba sent an ambassador to the "liberated" areas in South Vietnam. Since the 1975 victory, there have been several exchanges of high-level delegations as well as agreements for the exchange of professionals and cultural cooperation.[99]

SRV Relations with the Socialist States

The Sino-Soviet conflict. Since the emergence of the Sino-Soviet dispute in the early 1960s, Hanoi has engaged in a delicate balancing act to maintain good relations with both its major supporters—China and the Soviet Union—even as most of the smaller communist states found it necessary to choose sides. Although it has created difficulties for the Vietnamese, the Sino-Soviet conflict has also provided certain opportunities. During the war, when the revolutionary effort against "American imperialism" attracted such widespread support, both the USSR and the PRC gave substantial military and economic assistance. Each claimed the leadership of a revolutionary bloc, and neither wanted its competitor to seem more devoted to the Vietnamese war of national liberation. With peace, this Sino-Soviet competition has diminished, although both Moscow and Peking are still eager to prevent the growth of the other's influence in Vietnam. The Soviet policy of containment is oriented toward preventing China from expanding in Indochina, and the Chinese see the Soviet presence in Indochina as a threat of Soviet "encirclement" of China.

Thus, though the Soviets and Chinese give greater importance to their conflict with each other and to their relations with the United States than to their relations with Vietnam, the SRV has benefited by continuing to extract assistance from both sides without committing itself irrevocably to either. After the Vietnamese communist victory in 1975 (as well as during the war), the Soviets provided substantially more assistance than the Chinese, and the Vietnamese have tilted toward Moscow. But the SRV has not publicly taken a side in the dispute. It has not, for example, joined the Soviets in walking out on Chinese officials, nor has it joined the Chinese in boycotting conferences in Moscow. From Hanoi's perspective, the Sino-Soviet dispute not only tends to increase the material assistance it receives from both, but also provides Vietnam with the opportunity to counterbalance the political influence of one with the other, thus helping to protect its own sovereignty.

Despite these advantages, the Vietnamese have long been uneasy about the Sino-Soviet differences. When these differences degenerated into a virulent conflict, the Vietnamese, as committed Marxist-Leninists, saw the danger to world socialism as well as to their own dependence upon these two powers. Thus, the SRV continues to press for reconciliation of its two allies, in keeping with the counsel given by Ho Chi Minh, in 1969, in his last will and testament.

Soviet Union. Relations with the Soviet Union have been especially fruitful for the SRV in recent years. Massive Soviet military aid to the DRV came at the critical time of the DRV's conventional military offensive in the spring of 1975. Although their military assistance has sharply declined since the end of the war, the Soviets are still the largest single donor of economic assistance although they are shifting a larger portion to a reimbursable basis. An exchange of visits by high-level delegations from the SRV and the Soviet Union was the occasion for signing a series of agreements on economic, scientific, cultural, and political cooperation. The SRV has taken measures to coordinate its economic relations with the Soviet-guided Council for Mutual Economic Assistance (CMEA) (technically as an observer member), and it participates in the CMEA-related International Investment Bank and International Bank for Economic Cooperation.[100]

The SRV foreign policy has tended toward the Soviet line on several issues. In Africa, Hanoi has praised the leadership groups in Angola and Zaire, groups that Moscow supported and Peking denounced. In the Middle East, the SRV has supported the Soviet position. In Southeast Asia, where the SRV policy positions are determined more by its own intrinsic interests in specific issues than by its weighing of Chinese and Soviet positions, Hanoi has been closer to the USSR—in its condemnation of U.S. military bases in the Philippines (and earlier in Thailand)—than to the PRC, which has been silent on the question. Both Hanoi and Moscow have been critical of ASEAN as an organization (although their criticism was muted in early 1978), but Peking has been tolerant of ASEAN, seeing some advantage in its moves to strengthen regional ties and to promote neutralization, which, the Chinese believe, would inhibit Soviet expansion. SRV spokesmen, to Peking's displeasure, have noted that "détente is irreversible," even though Hanoi appeared unenthusiastic about the marked improvement of U.S.-Soviet relations shortly after the Vietnamese victory. But the SRV has been careful not to side with Soviet direct criticism of the PRC, and it has given the PRC no ground for suspecting military collusion with the Soviet Union. Rumors in Southeast Asian capitals have intermittently raised the specter of a Soviet naval base at Cam Ranh Bay in Vietnam, but it seems highly unlikely that the SRV would offer naval facilities to the Soviets on Vietnamese shores, which the PRC would undoubtedly regard as a serious provocation.

From Hanoi's point of view, the Soviet Union has certain advantages over the PRC as a political ally. Distant from Vietnamese territory, the Soviet Union does not inspire the same anxieties. There is not the long-standing historic conflict that divides Vietnam from China. The Soviets are richer than the Chinese and can offer some modern technology (although the Vietnamese, as they have sometimes told Western visitors, greatly admire the more advanced Western technology). The Soviets are not so wary of an expanded Vietnamese influence in Indochina and might even welcome the spread of Vietnamese hegemony in Laos and Cambodia, as a counterbalance to Chinese influence.

Despite certain natural preferences for closer ties with the Soviet Union than with the PRC, the SRV is understandably cautious in relations with the Soviets. The current Vietnamese leadership can soberly recall how the Soviets, in pursuit of their larger interest in Europe, bargained away Vietnamese goals at Geneva in 1954 (in pressing Vietnam to accept a partition at the seventeenth parallel) and again subordinated Vietnam to its own interests in improving relations with the United States in the early 1970s. For the Soviets, whose proposal for an Asian collective security agreement has been politely rejected by the countries of Southeast Asia, Vietnam and Laos offer an opening for Soviet expansion in Asia and containment of China.[101] But the Vietnamese, though looking to the Soviet Union for assistance in their development efforts, are likely to continue steering a middle course in the Sino-Soviet conflict, although veering at times toward the Soviet side.

The People's Republic of China. Hanoi's relations with Peking have been publicly cordial, although tensions between the SRV and PRC are evident. Characteristic of SRV pronouncements was the message of General Vo Nguyen Giap, SRV minister of defense, to his counterpart in the PRC: the Vietnamese people's "historic victory and the great success of socialist reconstruction in North Vietnam are inseparable from the support and assistance of the fraternal socialist countries including the great, effective support and assistance of China."[102] Although Peking did not accord visiting Vietnamese delegations as much fanfare as Moscow did, important agreements were signed in September 1976 providing for a Chinese interest-free loan to the SRV, commodity exchanges (including important food shipments from China), and arrangements for scientific and technical cooperation. Like Soviet help, Chinese assistance must now be paid for, on favorable terms, by the SRV.

One source of Vietnamese-Chinese tensions has been their dispute over the Paracel and Spratly islands in the South China Sea and, possibly, differences over their land frontier.[103] In

January 1974, Chinese forces cleared out the forces of the Thieu government from the Paracels and occupied them. Although silent at the time of the Chinese move, the Vietnamese communists are known to claim these islands. In April 1975, the DRV ousted the Saigon government's garrison on six of the Spratly Islands and occupied them. (The various Spratly Islands are claimed by the Philippines and Taiwan as well as by the SRV and the PRC.) Complicating the rival claims is the presumed presence of oil on or near the islands. When a Swedish-Filipino joint venture to explore for oil in the Spratlys was announced, the PRC, in June 1976, proclaimed that "any foreign country's . . . exploration and exploitation of oil and other resources in the Nansha [Spratly] Islands area constitute encroachments on China's territorial integrity," a statement obviously aimed at the Vietnamese as well.[104] The Vietnamese communists were already on record as committed to "defend their sovereignty." As long as these claims remain unresolved, they can create friction—although probably not serious armed clashes—between the SRV and the PRC.

Another source of Sino-Vietnamese tension arises from a clash of political goals in the region.[105] China, proud of its own revolutionary origins, is likely to resent Vietnamese competition for the symbolic leadership of the region's communist revolutionary movement. Furthermore, the SRV is now a rival with China for state-to-state influence in Southeast Asia. In Cambodia, the PRC is the only significant outside power with influence, thus counterbalancing possible Vietnamese (and Soviet) leverage. The Chinese support for the Cambodian position in the border war, although publicly cautious, has brought increased strains in Sino-Vietnamese relations. Probably the most serious Vietnamese deficiency, in the Chinese view, is that the SRV does not understand that the Soviet Union rather than the United States is the main threat to the security of Southeast Asia. The Chinese are disturbed that the SRV continues to embrace the Soviet Union, accepting its aid and finding no fault in Soviet assistance to Laos, while denouncing U.S. bases in the Philippines and the U.S. presence in Thailand. The PRC apparently fears that a further U.S. withdrawal from the region would benefit not itself, but more likely the Soviet Union and, perhaps, Japan, who would fill the "vacuum." The Vietnamese, who lived for centuries under Chinese hegemony, are ambivalent about China, admiring much in China but remaining suspicious of Chinese power. As a great Asian power that customarily received tribute from the lesser powers to the south, China expects respect or, perhaps, deference. The proudly nationalist Vietnamese, who still celebrate their historic struggle against Chinese control, are extremely sensitive about their independence. Thus, important differences in the Vietnamese and Chinese perspectives make it likely that Sino-Vietnamese relations will remain cool.

The Industrialized Nations and International Organizations

Although ideologically aligned with the socialist camp, the SRV has actively pursued diplomatic and commercial relations with the industrialized countries of the West and has actively sought membership in a variety of international organizations. The SRV's primary motivation appears to be the search for economic assistance and political safeguards for its independence.

The Western country with which the Vietnamese feel the most familiar, although not always the most friendly, is, of course, France. The Vietnamese leaders studied in French colonial schools (a few studied in France), speak French, and are familiar with the French approach to problems. Although they fought bitterly against the French colonial rule, they still respect French culture. Moreover, as the Americans replaced the French as the "imperialist power," past French injustices have faded somewhat in the Vietnamese memory. DeGaulle's opposition to U.S. policy in Indochina was welcome and served to maintain relations between the French and Vietnamese communists. The Vietnamese, therefore, found Paris suitable as a meeting site for U.S.-Vietnamese talks.

Immediately after the communist victory, Franco-Vietnamese relations underwent a period of turbulence. The French ambassador to the former Thieu government and other important French personnel were expelled from South Vietnam. With the seizure of power, there were differences between the French and the new rulers of Vietnam over compensation for French financial losses in South Vietnam and over exit rights from the country for French residents and dependents, many of whom were ethnic Vietnamese. These differences were resolved in lengthy talks in Hanoi with a French delegation in late 1975, during which there was also agreement on French economic and cultural cooperation, including provision for the return of the French cultural mission to Saigon. French oil companies have been contacted for assistance in oil exploration in Vietnam, and a sizable purchase of French fertilizer and other products has been consummated. In April 1977, Pham Van Dong made a state visit to France, during which French investment, technical assistance, trade, and aid were discussed.

Relations with the Scandinavian countries have been perhaps the most cordial of any relations between the communist government in Vietnam and the West. During the war, the Scandinavians, particularly the Swedes, provided humanitarian assistance and political support to the DRV. In 1975, Sweden gave Vietnam $10 million to build a hospital and entered into an economic agreement for 1975-1976 quite favorable to the SRV. In mid-1976 Norway, whose offshore oil technology is among the most advanced in Western Europe, offered Vietnam $50 million in assistance for offshore oil exploration.

The Vietnamese are ambivalent toward Japan, but they are well launched into fruitful economic relations. There is a great Vietnamese admiration for and curiosity about Japan, an Asian nation that has achieved remarkable economic development. At the same time, there is a lingering fear of a fascist and imperialist Japan.[106] Vietnam and Japan normalized diplomatic relations in October 1975, and a Japanese ambassador took his post in Hanoi in early 1976. Japan has been generous in economic assistance to Hanoi (which the Vietnamese initially regarded as reparations for Japanese damage to Vietnam during World War II). This aid amounted to 5 billion yen in 1975, and grants in June and October 1976 were for 6 billion yen and 8½ billion yen.[107] Japan is now the most important nonsocialist trading partner of the SRV. For the Japanese, Vietnam provides a market and source of raw materials and helps limit Chinese and Soviet influence and keep the sea-lanes open. For the Vietnamese, Japan provides primarily valuable trade, aid, and advanced technology.

The SRV has been prompt in taking up the former South Vietnamese membership in international organizations that can serve its needs in economic development. The Asian Development Bank (ADB), the World Bank, and the International Monetary Fund (IMF) have accepted this succession to membership. Both the World Bank and the IMF sent economic study missions to Vietnam in 1976 and 1977. The ADB was preparing in 1977 to reactivate projects planned in South Vietnam before the communist victory. The United Nations Development Program (UNDP), whose exploratory missions were welcomed in Vietnam, has allocated some $44 million in assistance for 1977–1981. Other agencies providing assistance include the World Health Organization (WHO), the UN High Commission for Refugees (UNHCR), UNICEF, the World Food Program, and the International Red Cross. At the regional level, the SRV has participated in the Economic and Social Commission for Asia and the Pacific (ESCAP) and has agreed with Laos and Thailand (but without Cambodia) to reactivate the Mekong River Development Project, which could provide development of hydroelectric, irrigation, and drainage schemes. As mentioned earlier, the SRV has adamantly refused all probes for cooperation with ASEAN, which it regards as a front for U.S. imperialism. As noted earlier, the SRV's application for UN membership was approved by the Security Council in July 1977, following withdrawal of the U.S. veto. On September 20, 1977, the General Assembly approved the admission of Vietnam to the United Nations, with a record number of 105 countries cosponsoring its application.

3
Laos since the Communist Victory

Communist Accession to Power

In Laos twenty-five years of national division and conflict came to an end in May and June 1975, when rightist political and military leaders and their U.S. support system were expelled from the country. A bloodless seizure of administrative power by "people's committees" then spread through the districts and towns of Laos, followed by local elections in November and the sudden establishment of the Lao People's Democratic Republic (LPDR) on December 2, 1975. The previously semisecret Communist Party of Laos subsequently moved its full strength into the new government in Vientiane and announced that its goal was an independent, prosperous, socialist state.

The Paris cease-fire agreement and the U.S. withdrawal from Vietnam had set the stage for this remarkable political transformation. On February 21, 1973, three weeks after the Paris agreement, the communist-led Lao Patriotic Front (LPF) and the Royal Lao Government (RLG) reached a corollary agreement in Vientiane.[1] Fourteen months later, a warily negotiated protocol to the agreement was implemented by the formation of an equally balanced Provisional Government of National Union (PGNU) in Vientiane. The royal capital and administrative capital cities were "neutralized" by the formation of joint police forces and matching

---

For this chapter, the authors have drawn upon their published articles: "New Stages of Revolution in Laos," *Current History*, December 1976; "Laos 1976: Faltering First Steps Toward Socialism," *Asian Survey* 17, no. 2 (February 1977); and "Laos 1977: The Realities of Independence," *Asian Survey* 18, no. 2 (February 1978).

army detachments of royal and "patriotic" forces. The rest of the country, however, remained fixed in the cease-fire pattern: the Lao Patriotic Front exclusively controlled almost four-fifths of the territory while participating simultaneously in the coalition PGNU, which controlled the remaining, more populous villages and towns along the Mekong River. North Vietnamese troops remained in Laos in the eastern regions even after the deadline for withdrawal.

Understandably, the anticommunist leaders, who had lost so much territory during their U.S.-assisted military campaigns for fifteen years against the Pathet Lao forces and their North Vietnamese advisers and fighting units, resented the unfavorable bargain negotiated by the neutralist prime minister, Prince Souvanna Phouma. The requirement of unanimous agreement before any action by the provisional government, the access of communist ministers to authority and information in Vientiane without granting reciprocal privileges in their own "liberated zone," the indefinite recess imposed upon the National Assembly while an appointed National Political Consultative Council (NPCC) under the adroit chairmanship of the "Red Prince" Souphanouvong issued policy pronouncements and promoted their popular acceptance—all struck them as illegitimate and ominous.[2] In retrospect, some Lao leaders who have now found refuge in the United States and France characterize the Vientiane Agreement as their "death warrant," and Pathet Lao (PL) historians treat it as a "great victory," which helped to shift the balance of forces in their favor. Its strict implementation became a major party slogan and remained so until the abolition of the monarchy in favor of a socialist republic, months after the agreement had lost its original force and intent.

The communist victory during the PGNU period was shaped not only by revolutionary doctrine but also by external events. The fundamental factor was the fall of Saigon and Phnom Penh to communist forces and the removal of U.S. support and presence in Vietnam and Cambodia. This created an "historic opportunity" for the leadership of the Lao People's Revolutionary Party (LPRP), and they were ready to mobilize "the masses throughout the country to rise up to seize power in the areas controlled by the Vientiane reactionaries in the shortest possible time."[3] "Three strategic blows" were struck: by the forces of the population, by supporting armed forces, and by defectors from the "puppet troops" of the Royal Armed Forces. Students occupied U.S. AID offices and living compounds in May 1975, which brought about the termination of the program and the reduction of the U.S. mission in Laos to fewer than thirty persons.[4] After a virtually bloodless takeover during the summer of 1975, the Party prepared the ground for the "voluntary" resignation of King Savang Vatthana and Prime Minister Souvanna Phouma in December 1975 and the establishment of the Lao People's Democratic Republic.

The Party

Leadership

During the struggle for power, the ruling communist party, now called the Lao People's Revolutionary Party (LPRP), kept secret its role in directing the revolution and did not make public the identity of its members. With victory, the Party emerged from the penumbra and has now identified a political bureau, whose seven members are the most powerful of the country's leaders. The most important is Kaysone Phomvihan, general secretary of the Party and prime minister of the LPDR. Having spent most of the last thirty years in clandestine revolutionary activity, including a decade of directing the revolution from a cave complex in Sam Neua Province, from which he descended to Vientiane only in 1975, Kaysone still seldom appears in public in Vientiane and rarely receives foreign noncommunist visitors. Born in Savannakhet, in southern Laos, in 1920, Kaysone is the son of a Vietnamese father, who served as a secretary to the French resident officer, and a Lao mother. Kaysone studied at the faculty of law of the University of Hanoi and according to an official biography, participated in 1942 "in the student struggle against the colonialist French and Japanese fascists."[5] He was one of the first Lao members of the Indochinese Communist Party.

Nouhak Phoumsavan, one of four deputy prime ministers and also minister of finance, is probably second in the Politburo. Born in Savannakhet in 1914, the son of a peasant family, Nouhak had only an elementary school education. While in the trucking business, hauling merchandise between Laos and Vietnam, Nouhak became involved with the Indochinese Communist Party in the early 1940s and was a founding member of the LPRP. Phoumi

Vongvichit, a deputy prime minister and minister of education, sports, and religious affairs, is the son of a former governor of Vientiane Province. Though only a secondary school graduate (Collège Pavie), Phoumi is regarded as one of the intellectual leaders as well as a founder of the Party. Phoun Sipaseut, a deputy prime minister and foreign minister, was born in Savannakhet, where he attended grammar school before entering the French colonial public works administration. He was an early member of the Lao Issara (Free Lao) Movement in 1945, opted for the group that continued cooperation with the Vietnamese following the Lao Issara's dissolution in 1949, and became a charter member of the LPRP. Fifth and sixth are Khamtai Siphandon, a deputy prime minister and minister of defense, and Sisomphon Lovansai, vice-president of the Supreme People's Council.

Probably seventh in the Politburo is Souphanouvong, president of the LPDR and president of the Supreme People's Council. The acknowledgment of Souphanouvong as a member of the Politburo resolves a long-standing debate regarding his real political power. Some observers accepted as fact Souphanouvong's past public posture as the primary leader of the revolutionary movement, but others contended that he was a mere figurehead, whose princely origins, traditional prominence, and theatrical personal qualities were being exploited by the "real" Lao communists for their political advantage. Souphanouvong is a dedicated Marxist-Leninist who fills certain honorific posts but also serves, about seventh in rank, as a Party decision maker.

The most remarkable qualities of the Lao communist leaders are their longevity and cohesion. These qualities appear to be surpassed only by their Vietnamese mentors in the communist world—and perhaps not at all in the noncommunist world. Most of the Party's Central Committee members have served together since they joined the resistance against the French following World War II. They retained their impressive cohesiveness both during armed struggle against their adversaries and during the periods of cease-fire and coalition governments in 1957, 1962-1963, and 1973-1975. In 1977, Souphanouvong, at age sixty-eight, was the oldest of the Politburo members, and Khamtai Siphandon, at age fifty-one, was the youngest. Although the top leaders are mature, they are not as old as the eleven men in the North Vietnamese Politburo, whose average age in 1975 was sixty-five.[6]

Perhaps the most arduous period for the Lao communist leadership was the decade of war following the breakdown of the coalition government in 1963 until the cease-fire of 1973. During this devastating wartime decade, the LPRP operated from a cave complex in Sam Neua, near the northern border with Vietnam, under heavy U.S. aerial bombardment. The dangers were great, food was scarce, the caves were damp, and life was difficult. But as is frequently the case, danger and sacrifice seemed to weld the group together. Their adversaries of the Royal Lao Government, who enjoyed relative luxury sustained by U.S. assistance, were, on the other hand, divided into cliques and factions. Throughout its long tenure, there has been no evidence of a purge within the Central Committee of the LPRP.[7]

Most communist leadership groups have, at some time in their history, suffered from factionalism. One might expect to find in Laos, as in Vietnam, differences among leaders based upon personality, function, region, social class, education, and even linkages to foreign allies. Over the past decade, analysts have speculated that the Lao leaders were divided into factions variously labeled as: Indochina communist vs. Lao nationalist, Sam Neua group vs. Vientiane group, hard-liners vs. soft-liners, modest social origins vs. upper-class origins, and ideologues vs. pragmatists. But there is no evidence that such factions have ever been a serious source of division among the leaders. Among the explanations for this unusual cohesion is long and effective tutelage by the Vietnamese communists, whose own remarkable record suggests they have great talent for achieving unity within the leadership. Furthermore, a common ideology, an effective organizational framework, and, as noted earlier, long service under great danger and adversity have created strong bonds among the leaders.

The LPRP leaders do show marks of a "cave mentality"— toughness, implacable opposition to the bourgeois life, deep suspicion of those outside the revolutionary movement, reliance on clandestine operations, humorlessness, ideological rigidity, and zealous commitment to the revolutionary cause. They are self-professed Marxist-Leninists, and although such avowal comes as no surprise, the LPRP leaders had so successfully camouflaged their ideology that there was widespread speculation within Laos as to whether the revolutionary leadership was "communist" or "nationalist." Actually, the LPRP leaders are both communist and nationalist.

Lao communism has a heavy imprint of Vietnamese influence. Lao communists frequently use concepts and slogans identical to those of the Vietnamese and adopt similar policies. This, too, is not surprising, since the ICP, dominated by Vietnamese communists, directed the Lao communist movement until at least 1955, when the Lao People's Party (later the LPRP) was founded, and afterward continued to give important guidance and support. Most LPRP leaders speak Vietnamese, and all have traveled frequently in Vietnam. Although Vietnamese advisers operate clandestinely and their exact role is not clear, we know that the Vietnamese still provide important guidance to their Lao allies.

Ethnic Representation

In a nation whose population is only half lowland Lao (Lao Loum) and half a variety of highland minorities, it is noteworthy that the LPRP leadership is overwhelmingly lowland Lao. Of the twenty-three members of the Party's Central Committee, there appears to be but a single minority group member, Nhiavu Lobaliayao, a prominent Hmong (Meo; Lao Sung), even though the geographical base of the Lao communist movement was for more than a quarter of a century in the upland regions of Laos. The most prominent ethnic minority leader, a Lao Theung tribal chief from southern Laos, Sithon Kommadam, was a member of the less important Central Committee of the Lao Patriotic Front and a vice-president of the Supreme People's Council. (Sithon's death on May 1, 1977, brought forth a declaration of national mourning for five days and celebration of his role as "a great patriot of the Lao nation and representative of the people of Lao Theung nationality.")[8]

In view of the LPRP's profession of ethnic egalitarianism, the lack of minority group representation in the Party decision-making bodies is a serious shortcoming. The simplest explanation may be that the Lao communist leaders, like their noncommunist Lao counterparts, are condescending toward the upland minority groups, considering them uncivilized (the word *Kha,* which the

Lao use to designate the Lao Theung minorities, means "slave") and unintelligent. The lowland Lao have for centuries dominated the less developed upland peoples, and Lao history is peppered with revolts by tribal minorities against them.

National liberation movements have generally been led by the more "evolved," secular-educated, urban-oriented segments of society. The Lao Theung and the Lao Sung have few members with secular education or urban roots and have been least touched by "Lao nationalism." There have been reports that the LPRP has been active, particularly during the past decade, in recruiting younger minority group members for advanced education abroad as well as for responsible middle-level positions within their bureaucracy.[9] The actual extent of that recruitment and the access of these minority cadres to decision-making positions within the Party will be an important element in the political future of Laos. It seems likely that Laos, like plural societies elsewhere in the world, will feel the growing demands for access to power from the numerous ethnic groups within the society. As the LPRP leaders intensify their efforts at political mobilization and economic modernization, there will undoubtedly be a concomitant increase in communal demands.[10]

Party Organization

The National Congress of the LPRP is designated as the commanding authority of the Party, but, as is usually the case in other communist party systems, this is a mere formalism. Since its founding in March 1955, the Lao People's Party (as distinct from the ICP) has held only one Party congress (Figure 3.1). The First Congress founded the Party in 1955.[11] The Second Party Congress did not meet until February 1972, when it was convened at Vieng Say in Sam Neua Province. At that congress, the Party's name was changed from the Lao People's Party to the Lao People's Revolutionary Party in order, in the words of an official history, "to conform itself to the class character and requirements of the leadership."[12] No record of either the First or the Second Party congresses has been made public.

Party policy is made by a Central Committee composed of nineteen full and four alternate members, which is, in turn, dominated by a seven-member political bureau (see Figure 3.2).[13]

Figure 3.1
LAO PEOPLE'S DEMOCRATIC REPUBLIC
PARTY STRUCTURE

```
┌─────────────────────────────────────────┐
│            Party Congress                 │
│      (Second Party Congress was           │
│        held February 1972)                │
└─────────────────────────────────────────┘
```

```
┌───────────────────────────────────────────────────────┐
│                  Political Bureau                       │
│                                                          │
│   Kaysone Phomvihan          Phoun Sipaseut             │
│   General Secretary                                      │
│                              Khamtai Siphandon          │
│   Nouhak Phoumsavan                                      │
│                              Sisomphon Lovansai         │
│   Phoumi Vongvichit                                      │
│                              Souphanouvong              │
└───────────────────────────────────────────────────────┘
```

```
┌───────────────────────────────────────────────────────┐
│                  Central Committee                      │
│                                                          │
│   Full Members                                           │
│                                                          │
│   Chanmi Douangboutdi          Sanan Soutthichak        │
│   Kaysone Phomvihan            Sisavat Keobounphan      │
│   Khamsouk Saignaseng          Sisomphon Lovansai       │
│   Khamtai Siphandon            Somseun Khamphithoun     │
│   Ma Khaikhamphithoun          Souk Vongsak             │
│   Maichantan Sengmani          Souphanouvong            │
│   Maisouk Saisompheng                                    │
│   Meun Somvichit               Alternate Members         │
│   Nouhak Phoumsavan                                      │
│   Phoumi Vongvichit            Khambou Soumisai         │
│   Phoun Sipaseut               Khampheng Boupha, Mrs.   │
│   Sali Vongkhamsao             Nhiavu Lobaliayao        │
│   Saman Vilaket                Sisana Sisan             │
└───────────────────────────────────────────────────────┘
```

```
┌─────────────────────────────────┐
│  Solid Underscore ____ indicates │
│  Member of the Political          │
│  Bureau.                          │
└─────────────────────────────────┘
```

Figure 3.2
LAO PEOPLE'S DEMOCRATIC REPUBLIC
POLITICAL BUREAU MEMBERS

Kaysone Phomvihan   Nouhak Phoumsavan   Phoumi Vongvichit
General Secretary

Phoun Sipaseut   Khamtai Siphandon

Sisomphon Lovansai   Souphanouvong

The LPRP directs and develops the policy of the Lao communist movement, unifies and disciplines Party members, who are the leading force ("vanguard") of Lao society, and maintains liaison with "fraternal" parties abroad. Like ruling communist parties elsewhere, it maintains control by placing its Party leaders and cadres throughout the key institutions of the government, administration, and army.

We do not have reliable estimates of the current LPRP strength. Party membership in 1968 was estimated at 14,000.[14] At that time the Lao communist movement controlled a population of approximately 1,000,000, making the ratio of Party members to population under its control at 1.4 percent (compared to 3.13 percent of the DRV population in December 1970 and to 5.77 percent of the Soviet population who were full members of the Communist Party in 1969). The LPRP now dominates all of Laos, approximately 3,000,000 people. Even though Party strength must have grown, we have seen no indication of a sizable recruitment campaign, so that the ratio of Party members to population under its control has probably declined. Thus, Party numbers are well below those of the well-developed communist parties elsewhere and undoubtedly below the level the Lao Party leadership desires. It has seemed probable that the LPRP leadership would undertake a strong recruitment campaign to increase the ranks of the Party, but in view of the continued secrecy of the Party operations, we have no evidence of such an undertaking.

The Party continues to give importance to mobilizing participation by all segments of the society into a variety of mass organizations under the umbrella of the Lao Patriotic Front (LPF). At the village level, the peasantry are drawn into three organizations—of men, women, and youth. These are linked together in zonewide associations, which hold intermittent training meetings at rallies at the canton, district, and province level. A variety of functional organizations, such as the Lao Federation of Labor and the Lao Journalists Association, brings together special interest groups. A cluster of organizations serves the foreign policy interests of the regime. Such groups as the Lao-USSR Friendship Association, the Afro-Asian Solidarity Committee, the Committee for the Support of the Reunification of Korea, and the Lao-Vietnam Committee for Economic, Cultural, and Scientific Cooperation are used to issue various proclamations of support and to host receptions for fraternal foreign delegations.

Party Secrecy

As already noted, despite the public declaration of the Party's leading role in the revolution, many of the Party activities and Party membership lists remain secret. Although Politburo and Central Committee members who participate in public ceremonies have been identified, the full membership has not. Deliberations of the Party's ruling organs are kept secret, except for the announcements of resolutions to guide public policy. Party cadres within the bureaucracy, the army, and other key institutions do not reveal themselves, and as the authors learned from Lao refugees in Thailand in 1977, their non-Party coworkers often can identify only the most important members.

This style of clandestine operation has followed a consistent pattern since the creation of the Party. The Indochina Communist Party, founder of the Lao communist movement, operated secretly within Vietnam during the colonial period, since its members were in danger of arrest by French authorities. The ICP's Committee on Laos, established in 1936, worked underground for these same security reasons. As Lao nationalism began to incubate, there were political reasons for the maintenance of clandestine operations. It would have been unwise to reveal to the Lao public that a communist party run by Vietnamese was striving to lead the Lao nationalist movement. Secrecy continued to surround the Lao People's Party after its formation in 1955. As Party spokesmen have noted, because the Party leaders assumed that the Lao masses were not sufficiently developed to be told that a communist party was leading the revolution, "front" tactics were used from 1955 to 1975.

Until 1970, there was no public reference within Laos to the existence of a party.[15] In a published article in October 1970, Secretary General Kaysone did refer to a "genuine revolutionary party"—although he did not then label it as the PPL—and distinguished it from the LPF as the leader of the revolutionary movement.[16] As late as the summer of 1974, Prince Souphanouvong, as president of the National Political Consultative Council of the post-cease-fire coalition government, recoiled in annoyance

at a question the authors posed about the Party.[17] He insisted
that this was an internal affair that did not concern outsiders
and maintained, in keeping with his party's practice, that the LPF,
of which he was president, was in command. In late 1975, however, when the Lao communists were in unchallenged control of
the country, spokesmen revealed that the Party had directed the
revolution from the outset.

One advantage of the Party's clandestine method of operation
during its periods of legal political struggle was that it could
deceive its political adversaries. The RLG elite were remarkably
naive about the decision-making processes of their communist
adversary. Their own political model followed a traditional Southeast Asian pattern, heavily suffused with patron-client relationships, and they poorly understood modern organizational politics.
Indeed, interviews with former Vientiane-side cabinet ministers
in 1977 in France have revealed vast ignorance about the most
basic facts of the Party. Some actually did not know that a communist party directed "Pathet Lao" decisions. Those who had
some suspicion of a communist party were vague about its organizational procedures. Even relatively sophisticated Vientiane-side
ministers could seldom name more than a few members of the
LPRP Politburo. As one former minister told us, "We didn't know
their organization, or their internal processes. We only had a
general belief that their line was dictated from Sam Neua which
was, in turn, dictated from North Vietnam."

Secrecy provided tactical flexibility to the LPRP. It was easier
to negotiate a political accommodation with right-wing RLG
leaders through the LPF than it would have been through an open
communist party. The RLG elite would have seen a communist
party as a frightful threat, but many saw the LPF as simply "left-
wing nationalists." Thus, those Party personalities who could
best deal with RLG counterparts were assigned to operate under
the LPF umbrella. The Party has applauded its own political
astuteness:

> The Party finally grasped the strategy and correctly applied tactical
> policies to the realities in Laos, particularly in struggling to join

knew how to consolidate and expand the revolutionary forces, to lead the struggle with appropriate methods, to encircle the enemy, to rally the revolutionary forces so that they would grow stronger.[18]

Although secrecy is no longer necessary, the long practice of clandestine operation has created certain habits that are not easily abandoned, so that Party leaders continue to find a rationale for retaining a certain secrecy about the identity of the Party cadres. They harbor an active suspicion that there is widespread internal sabotage supported by malevolent outside forces. In the words of Kaysone, "Many of us do not yet clearly understand . . . that every enemy of the revolution is taking all possible means to restrict, obstruct, and sabotage the independence of our nation in an arrogant, stubborn manner. Obviously, some of us, satisfied with our victories, have lacked vigilance."[19] Keeping the identity of Party cadres secret may be a means of maintaining surveillance over the suspected saboteurs within the bureaucracy, the army, and other agencies. Obviously, former Vientiane-side officials are suspected of lacking enthusiasm for—or of active hostility to—the new regime. Further, masking the identity of Party cadres may be a means of camouflaging organizational weakness. The Party ranks are probably thin in many of the government agencies, but since nonmembers do not know who is watching them, they must be more vigilant.

Government and Administration

On December 1–2, 1975, a "National Congress of People's Representatives" was convened to preside over the formal demise of the Provisional Government of National Union and to proclaim the new Lao People's Democratic Republic (LPDR) (see Figure 3.3). It met secretly—not until December 4, two days after it ended, did the public learn of the congress through radio pronouncements. The announcements proclaimed that the congress had ratified King Savang Vatthana's abdication and "voluntary" renunciation of his royal wealth and that it had accepted the resignation of Prince Souvanna Phouma as prime minister of the PGNU. Thus, the congress was used to give legitimacy to the wide-ranging changes the LPRP engineered.

100

Figure 3.3
LAO PEOPLE'S DEMOCRATIC REPUBLIC
GOVERNMENT STRUCTURE

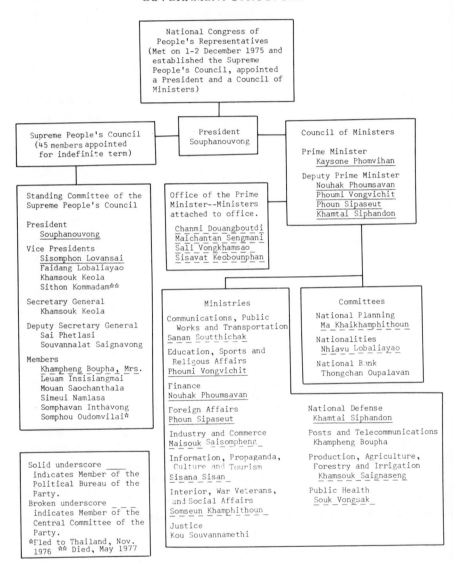

Formally convened by the LPF and consisting of 264 members, the congress consisted of delegations representing diverse groups. There were 27 members (the largest group) of the LPF Central Committee, 4 members from the Patriotic Neutralist Front (PNF) Alliance Committee, 6 Buddhist bonzes, youth and intellectuals, as well as delegations from each province and the Vientiane municipality.

The congress announced that Souphanouvong was named president of the LPDR, the ceremonial post of chief of state. It further proclaimed the formation of a forty-five-member Supreme People's Council (SPC) to fulfill "the need to have a legislative organ to draft the constitution and promulgate the laws of the LPDR." Souphanouvong was also named as president of the SPC. Like the LPF, the SPC has representation from diverse elements within the society, including prominent ethnic minority chiefs, a few former neutralists, and leaders from various occupational groups. Thus, the SPC provides recognition to prominent personalities whose constituency the LPRP wishes to mobilize, and these representatives in turn help to legitimize the LPRP policies they are convened to applaud.[20] (It appears that the LPF has declined as an instrument of mobilization, although personalities are still identified as members of its Central Committee. There has been no report of a LPF Central Committee meeting, and no public indication that the Central Committee, last appointed in 1964, has been changed.)

Of four vice-presidents of the SPC, one is "patriotic neutralist" Khamsouk Keola; another is Faidang Lobaliayao, a prominent Meo chief; and a third was Sithon Kommadam, a well-known Lao Theung (Alak/Loven) tribal leader from southern Laos (who died in May 1977). The fourth vice-president, Sisomphan Lovansai, is, along with Souphanouvong, a member of the Politburo. (He and Souphanouvong are the only members of the Party Central Committee serving on the SPC.) Two former Vientiane-side officials of the PGNU were named to the Thirteen Member Standing Committee, and two members of the royal household—Prince Khamchan Phetsalat and Crown Prince Bong Savang—were made members of the SPC.

At the same time the king's "voluntary" abdication was announced, an LPDR spokesman stated that the former king was appointed as "supreme adviser" to the president of the LPDR. Both the former king and the crown prince withheld their presence from the SPC, however, to the displeasure of Party leaders, and this may have helped precipitate their arrest in March 1977. A more immediate factor was the increase in anticommunist guerrilla activity in the vicinity of Luang Prabang. The LPRP authorities may have been concerned that the guerrillas might involve the king and crown prince in their dissidence—perhaps by "liberating them" or making them a popular rallying point. The Lao Foreign Office has denied rumors of the king's execution and has announced that the king and crown prince are being held by LPDR authorities "to insure their safety" (probably somewhere in Sam Neua or Phong Saly provinces).

Problems of Administration

According to the Party's doctrine, the "national democratic" revolution has been achieved. The next stage will be the "gradual advance toward socialism, by-passing the development of capitalism." The Party's new action strategy, laid out in the Third Resolution of the Party's Central Committee, was announced in May 1976. The resolution calls for the simultaneous implementation of three revolutions: a production relations revolution, a technical revolution, and a cultural and ideological revolution. (The same three revolutions were called for at the inaugural session of Vietnam's new National Assembly.)[21] Economic development is seen as most important, since changes in other sectors flow from it. An effort will be made to expunge the "vestiges of the enslaving, reactionary and depraved culture of the old, rotten regime." During the transformation of the economy, the influence of the "comprador" bourgeoisie (judged to be tools of the imperialists) and "feudalists" is to be eliminated and their property confiscated by the state. The "national" bourgeoisie (entrepreneurs who are deemed patriotic) may undertake joint enterprises with the state, which will provide guidelines and controls.[22]

A serious problem facing the new regime is the paucity of competent administrative cadres. In the wake of the LPRP victory in 1975, more than 100,000 persons fled across the Mekong, including large numbers of Vientiane-side civil servants, many of them well-trained technicians. Throughout 1976 and 1977, the flow of refugees to Thailand continued, averaging an estimated 1,000 per month in early 1977 and increasing to 1,500 per month for the year as a whole, as economic conditions worsened and the government cracked down on Meo insurgents. In interviews conducted by the authors in Thailand in the spring of 1977, former Lao civil servants who had recently arrived cited a number of reasons for their flight. Fear of being sent off to a "reeducation" center was a powerful incentive to flee. One interviewee, who had been weighing the pros and cons of departure, decided to traverse the Mekong at night in a pirogue with his family immediately after learning that he was to be sent to a reeducation center the following morning. (At least 20,000 Vientiane-side officials who remained in Laos after the communist takeover were incarcerated in such reeducation camps.)[23] Discontent with frequent "seminars," boring training sessions, onerous demands for "voluntary" labor duty in gardens and fields, and heavy-handed bureaucratic methods were also cited as reasons for departure by former Vientiane-side civil servants.

Other reports from Laos, particularly of overzealous bureaucratism, echoed these grievances. During the initial months of the new order, a peasant needed a laissez-passer to leave his province, his district, or even his village. He often needed a paper authorizing him to sell his products at the local market, causing the food supplies in town to dry up and prices to soar. In Savannakhet, bureaucratic excesses had produced such popular discontent during the spring of 1976 that both Kaysone and Nouhak, during ostensible visits to their mothers, who were still residing in their native towns, took public steps to relax some of the most stringent measures.[24]

Although the new leaders decided to utilize the skills of some of the former Vientiane-side bureaucrats, they mistrusted them and kept them under surveillance. During several periods in their first two years of power, groups of former Vientiane-side civil servants were rounded up and shipped off for reeducation.

Among the problems recognized by Party leaders are arrogance of Party cadres toward the masses, lassitude following the end of the war, poor organization and faulty coordination, and inadequate training of cadres. There was constant tension, too, between the leaders' concern for political loyalty and technical competence, the classic communist choice between "Red" or "Expert." As Kaysone has stated:

> We must be concerned with promoting old cadres. However we must be specifically concerned with building, promoting and leading new cadres in all movements. At the same time we must re-educate and re-train officials of the old administration and transform them into cadres of the revolutionary administration who wholeheartedly serve the public and the new system.[25]

Former Vientiane-side bureaucrats feel that they are serving in a bureaucratic minefield. There is always the danger that they will be blamed for sabotage when there are shortcomings in administration. The new agricultural tax, introduced in November 1976, created widespread discontent among the peasantry. For many peasants, especially those who had been living in noncommunist territory, this was the first tax on their product they had ever paid. The tax was complex, which made it even more difficult to collect. The minister of agriculture, Khamsouk Saignaseng, in a frank interview with a reporter, acknowledged the difficulty in collecting the tax and laid the blame on a combination of sabotage by "enemy agents" who had infiltrated the administration and erroneous interpretation of the tax law by ill-equipped cadres, which had led to some excesses and peasant discontent.[26] Apparently, then, civil servants, especially those employed by the former government, are extremely careful not to take the initiative, an attitude labeled administrative "attentism" during the days of colonial Indochina.

There has been intermittent guerrilla activity since the communist accession to power, with ambushes on government installations and vehicles and the interdiction of roads and bridges. In the late summer of 1977, insurgents temporarily occupied several towns in the northwest, and in early fall they blew up storage tanks near Savannakhet and blasted some barges in the Mekong River near Nong Khai. Among the areas under most serious harassment were the northern sector, where Meo tribesmen, former members of General Vang Pao's CIA-supported army, operated, and in the southern panhandle, where bands of former government soldiers and right-wing political elements made sporadic attacks. There were reports that some dissidents unassociated with the old regime had joined the resistance activity.[27] An added difficulty for the government has been the guerrillas' advantage of sanctuary across the long Mekong River boundary with Thailand, where they could find support and recruits from Lao refugees in the camps. The Lao authorities charged that the Thai regime, with the encouragement of the United States, was supporting the insurgency. Although some local Thai military commanders probably gave Lao insurgents low-level support with a few rifles and supplies in return for tactical intelligence, there were no solid indicators that either the Thai central government or the U.S. government was actively supporting the insurgency. The Lao military forces had help in dealing with the insurgents, it appears, from Vietnamese military units in Laos, whose strength in 1977 was estimated at 20,000 to 30,000. The insurgents succeeded in diverting government resources to the maintenance of security and in preoccupying the attention of Party leaders, but the resistance did not appear to threaten seriously the stability of the regime.

There were other indications, in addition to resistance activity and refugee exodus, that important sectors of the population were discontented with life under the new regime. By early 1978, the communist authorities had released only a handful of the more than 20,000 former government civilian and military officials whom they had incarcerated in "reeducation" centers in 1975. A few of the prisoners' families were informed in 1977 that they could move into the thinly settled northeastern provinces near the camps, raising apprehension that even when released from the camps, "reeducatees" would not be permitted to return to the cities along the Mekong. As already noted, the agricultural tax imposed in 1976 raised serious discontent among the peasants, many of whom had never before paid taxes on their production.

There were signs that the zealous communist work ethic was not congenial to the easygoing life-style of the Theravadda Buddhist Lao peasant. There was reported discontent with the regime's heavy demands for corvée labor on public projects, such as the digging of irrigation canals, and with the requirement to work during Buddhist holidays. The humorless, heavy-handed bureaucratism and frequent nighttime political indoctrination meetings were not endearing to the peasants, and there was resentment at the introduction of limited forms of cooperative farming. One reporter noted that superstitious farmers have blamed the new regime for last year's poor harvest, because the regime had banned the traditional fireworks festivals that the farmers believe fertilize the clouds.[28]

Economic Prospects

The economic history of Laos, in the words of its new prime minister, has been one of "abject poverty and backwardness." Even though Kaysone sees his country as rich in natural resources and possessing great potential in agriculture, forestry, and water resources, the "colonialists and feudalists" kept it economically stagnant for centuries. The new leadership, however, expected Laos to advance directly to socialism, bypassing the stage of capitalist development.[29]

There is no disputing the economic backwardness of Laos, a landlocked country of dense jungle and rugged mountains. In 1976 its per capita GNP was estimated at $70. Its arable land, estimated at 8 percent, has been poorly cultivated, generally on a one-crop-per-year basis and, in many areas, by the slash-and-burn techniques of migratory mountain tribes. Its rich timber resources (60 percent of the country is forested) have been haphazardly exploited for export. Its mineral resources have been inadequately surveyed and seriously exploited only in the case of French-owned tin mines. The French treated Laos as a colonial backwater in which imported Vietnamese filled their minimal needs for administrative personnel and semiskilled labor. The small native commercial class was also dominated by Vietnamese, as well as by Chinese and other foreigners. In the early 1950s, only about a dozen Lao students per year graduated from secondary schools. Two decades later, the literacy rate was estimated at only 12 percent. The population of about 3 million people is small for the vast area of the country (91,428 square miles), but its rate of growth has been held down by a death rate of 2.4 percent, versus a birthrate of 4.2 percent. In September 1976 the government announced a ban on contraceptives, in an effort to build up the nation's population.[30]

In such a setting, industry has played only a tiny part in the Laotian economy. In 1970, about 2 percent of the labor force was engaged in light manufacturing, and over 80 percent was employed in agriculture, fishing, and forestry.[31] Ranked by number of establishments, the most important manufacturing enterprises were sawmills, mechanized rice mills, printing presses, brick factories, ice cream plants, and distilleries. Largely with U.S. assistance, plants had been developed for cigarettes, rubber sandals, soft drinks, plastic household products, barbed wire, and other domestically consumed products. In the Pathet Lao zone, during the war, very primitive but ingenious production facilities were developed, often in caves, to produce farm implements, pharmaceutical products, and woven material. The transportation system for the limited internal trade of Laos relied upon a minimal road network left by the French, which was unevenly improved during the war in the U.S.-assisted areas and laid waste in the U.S.-bombed areas. For two decades, Chinese engineering teams have been building roads in the northern provinces, but they seem to be in no hurry to finish this program. For foreign trade, the easiest outlet has traditionally been across the Mekong into Thailand, but a French colonial roadway leads across the mountains to Vietnamese ports, and the SRV is apparently ready to restore it to full use.

The war in Laos gave the country the dubious distinction of being the most heavily bombed, per capita, in the history of warfare. By 1972 the United States had dropped twice as much tonnage on Laos as on North Vietnam, but the economic impact of the bombing was primarily to displace people rather than to destroy productive resources.[32] The war also distorted the economy of the gradually shrinking area administered by the Royal Lao Government; up to 90 percent of the RLG's annual budget of about $40 million was derived from foreign assistance.[33]

Besides project assistance—which was more than $30 million in fiscal year 1973—a Foreign Exchange Operations Fund (FEOF) was maintained for eleven years by the United States, France, Japan, the United Kingdom, and Australia to help stabilize the Royal Lao economy, which enjoyed an artificial prosperity far beyond its means. In 1974–1975, the U.S. contribution to this fund was $19.6 million, out of a total foreign contribution of $28.1 million. Although a U.S. AID pamphlet blandly asserted that "the fund has enabled the government to provide essential services for the people . . . and has permitted sufficient economic growth to avoid economic stagnation and serious unemployment," a brief walk through Vientiane during the later years of the war quickly revealed the inordinate number of imported luxury items that the hard currencies had actually financed: Mercedes Benz automobiles, hi-fi equipment, television sets, whiskey, and motorcycles for teenage sons of rich Chinese and Lao officials became the perfect symbols, cited in Pathet Lao propaganda, of the corruption and inequity of the "feudalist-colonialist" regime.

The most expensive U.S. economic operation in Laos was refugee assistance: an estimated $27.5 million in fiscal year 1973. The number of refugees receiving both food and rehabilitation assistance amounted to over 350,000 at the end of the war, and close to 700,000 persons—one-quarter of the population—were displaced during the course of the war. "Relief and resettlement" covered everything from emergency evacuation "in anticipation of military action" to transportation to relocation sites where all the basic facilities were supposed to put refugees on the same economic and social level as that of the nonrefugees in the area.[34] Many other vital projects in "humanitarian assistance"—such as malaria control and public health development—were supported in the Royal Lao Government area by U.S. and some European and international organization assistance.[35]

Under the administration of the World Bank, the Nam Ngum Dam, a major hydroelectric and irrigation project, was completed in 1971, with the United States contributing over half the $29.1 million cost for the first phase. The projected U.S. contribution to the second phase was cancelled after the expulsion of U.S. AID in 1975, but West Germany stepped in to fill the gap. Since 1972 Laos has been supplying electrical energy to Thailand from the Nam Ngum powerhouse. This not only creates one of the largest sources of foreign exchange for Laos but also has maintained a functional linkage between the two sometimes hostile neighbors. Further hydroelectric and irrigation projects on the Mekong River were studied during the war, to the point that in

May 1977 Thailand considered it expedient to continue regional cooperation with Laos and Vietnam (Cambodia has dropped out of the organization) in the Mekong River Development Committee.[36]

The expulsion of U.S. AID by means of "spontaneous popular demonstrations" against their offices and personnel in May 1975 deprived the Lao government of the financial and technical core of its economy. The FEOF disappeared, the road maintenance and airways system terminated abruptly, the DDT spraying stopped, and PL 480 food shipments and refugee relief and maintenance ended. In November 1975, a shooting incident on the Mekong River prompted Thailand to impose a blockade on Laos, which created a severe food shortage and immediate inflation of prices in Vientiane. This crisis may have helped accelerate the decision of the Party leaders to complete the seizure of power in the old Royal Government areas by overthrowing the monarchy and establishing the Lao People's Democratic Republic on December 1, 1975. The so-called coalition government had neither attacked private property after May 1975 (except for expropriating a few "traitors") nor undertaken socialist reorganization. Yet the popularity that attended the initial expulsion of corrupt "feudalist" families and "colonialist" U.S. aid structures had been squandered through mismanagement, maladroitness, and sheer ignorance on the part of Party cadres and followers. The Lao National Congress of People's Representatives, which met on December 1–2, 1975, provided the occasion for outlining a new economic strategy for the country.

The fundamental objective was to use agriculture and forestry "as the basis for industrial expansion." Through research, promotion, and supervision, productivity in these two fields was to be rapidly developed in order to attain self-sufficiency in food. (During the last years of the war, the RLG area had imported from 50,000 to 70,000 tons of rice per year and well over half the animal proteins consumed.)[37] In the industrial sector, the initial emphasis was to be upon restoration of operations and upon supervision and assistance for private-sector light manufacturing plants. The state would expand its network of trade agents and cooperatives so as to ensure the proper distribution of essential goods among the people, and it would also control all exporting and importing. Private traders would continue their operations under state-controlled prices. The state would control land and water transportation, but a private sector would continue to exist. Laos expected "to cooperate with Vietnam to construct a road to the sea." New tax policies, state-owned banks, and better budgeting were also in prospect. Economic assistance would be sought from both socialist and other countries, "on the basis of equality and mutual interests and without any strings attached." And even though all these plans were to develop the basis for the "march forward to socialism" (bypassing the stage of capitalism), considerable scope was left at this point for joint economic ventures between the state and the private sector and for noncollectivized agricultural production.

In land-abundant Laos, the customary system of land ownership was that whoever cleared and cultivated the land was considered the legitimate proprietor. There was very little absentee ownership and landlordism, and little need for land reform in any section of the country. The overriding agricultural problem has been minimal cultivation and inadequate redistribution of surplus products from some regions to areas of insufficiency. Thailand served both as an importer of rice from southern Laos and as a supplier of rice to the central and northern provinces. In its first year, the LPDR encountered adverse weather, but the prime minister proudly asserted that "no cases of starvation were reported" in the country and that "the towns are now basically self-sufficient in food supply." In 1976, however, it was necessary to import rice—an estimated 120,000 tons—and a severe drought in 1977 made the deficit for that year much higher, perhaps more than 200,000 tons before the 1978 harvest.[38] An emergency appeal for food assistance for Laos was made by the World Food Program in the fall of 1977. Numerous messages to the Party cadres and the people exhorted special efforts to increase productivity by dry season rice growing, clearing new farmland and reclaiming abandoned rice fields, and constructing irrigation facilities. Most importantly, "new productive relations" were sought through the formation of labor exchange teams. As noted earlier in regard to Vietnam, this is doctrinally the first step in the direction of "collective mastery" in agriculture, yet it has been undertaken very gingerly in Laos. As the prime minister pointed out in his report to a joint SPC-cabinet meeting in February 1977, labor exchange units would be the basic step in agriculture during the "next few years"—employing such devices as collective loans, sharing of animal labor, collective purchase and selling methods, and work teams for expanding irrigation facilities. This step would set the stage for "converting to the socialist cooperative system." The Party had decided that "currently, it is inappropriate to consolidate agricultural cooperatives into a single unit because various conditions for the operations, management and guidance have not yet been fully guaranteed."[39] As an editorial in the *Siang Pasason* put it:

> At a time when our country has just entered a new revolutionary era, we must be careful to mobilize the farmers step by step to walk along the Socialist path of collectivism, in order to conform to the degree of their understanding as well as to the present material and technical foundations of agriculture. In the immediate future we must organize unity and labor exchange units which correspond to the degree of awareness in the level of organization and production management which will be accepted by the farmers. . . . The leading organs at all levels must pay attention to managing and promoting the farmers' enthusiasm to a higher degree . . . the most important thing is that we must be careful, not hasty, so that after setting up these units, the farmers can understand the effectiveness of collective organization and become energetic in their work.[40]

An additional measure to attain self-sufficiency in food was the encouragement of vegetable farming by families and work groups of all sorts, including government ministries. The tending of lettuce and other vegetable plots during and after normal workdays, despite the efforts to stimulate emulation campaigns, was ridiculed by many refugees after leaving the new republic. Special "voluntary" work teams for helping in the harvest or digging irrigation canals, even when joined by the prime minister himself in a rare public appearance, were not likely to sustain the "joyous atmosphere" mentioned in the official accounts.[41] It was easier to instruct the Lao People's Liberation Army that one of its "three major tasks" was the "boosting of production" than it was to enforce effective implementation. Encouraging the migratory mountain people (Lao Theung and Lao Sung) to shift from migratory to sedentary farming was also difficult. Admonishing people to practice thrift became almost redundant in an economy of scarcity; and a new tax on agricultural production, starting in November 1976, became a major controversy. Although the minister of agriculture, as mentioned above, attributed difficulties in collecting the tax partly to "enemy agents," the government also exerted itself through editorials and official speeches to achieve legitimacy for its unprecedented measure to raise income.[42] In December 1976 Phoumi Vongvichit even promised that "we will pay this tax only for a certain period of time. After we have found other sources of income the agricultural tax may be reduced or abolished."[43] Yet the tax continued in early 1978, at even steeper rates, and was likely to remain the principal source of public revenue.

Heavy industry in Laos cannot seriously compete—as it does in Vietnam—with agriculture for resources. The large enterprises in this economy have been cement plants, breweries, or furniture factories. The new government has made it quite clear that industry is to serve the needs of agricultural and forestry production, primarily by providing tools, repair facilities, and processing plants. Thus the pattern of basically light industry, which in 1972 manufactured thirty-four different products and employed an average of only twenty workers in the Royal Lao Government area, will not change under the new regime. Nor can the Lao consumer look forward to obtaining household appliances or items of comfort or pleasure from his domestic manufacturing sector. For the moment he has been instructed by his leaders to regard the feeling of "collective-mastery and self-reliance" as his revolutionary reward. As Kaysone put it in a report to the SPC in June 1976:

> all Lao patriots . . . have encountered difficulties because their life style has been changed. Nevertheless they are all ready to face these difficulties for the sake of the independence and freedom of the country, and prefer to live a miserable life as the masters of their own country and destinies in order to build and develop the country instead of a happy life enslaved by foreigners.[44]

A strategy of building up the Lao economy through greater exports will offer only slight relief in the near term. In the past, half of the legally recorded exports of Laos were in tin and 40 percent in timber, with coffee, cotton, hides, benzoin, and sticklac making up most of the rest. During the war, in the RLG area, imports exceeded these approximately $3 million worth of exports by as much as 13 to 1.[45] The largest part of this import trade came from Thailand, which also benefited from much smuggling across the river. The second-largest part came from Japan, and the United States and France accounted for about a quarter of the regular imports. The leadership can propose little in this area except that mineral resources be energetically surveyed and exploited and that the sources of capital in the country be further exploited through more efficient organization of labor and through thrift in the use of materials.

Despite the Party's economic pronouncements at the People's Congress that established the new republic, detailed economic planning was not forthcoming during the next year and a half. As Phoumi Vongvichit put it, at the end of the first year,

> Regarding economic construction, our country is truly backward agriculturally. There are many projects that must be carried out. Some projects will be carried out this year and others will be done next year. At present we cannot adopt four-year or five-year plans as in other countries. In the next few years we will map out our plans year by year. We will map out long-term plans after the necessary foundations are laid down and after the people have reached unanimity in their way of thinking. For the time being we will work things out gradually.[46]

The state budget during the first year of the LPDR was not publicly revealed, but in April 1977, when the finance minister presented a draft budget for 1977, he referred to an earlier budget while continuing to hold back on details of either plan.[47] With the flight of trained civil servants continuing and with many others in reeducation camps, the capacity of the new government to plan and direct even so backward an economy remains limited. Not only are skills in short supply, but also attitudes are inappropriate. As Kaysone acknowledged in his report of June 1976:

> Public organizations remain disorganized and decentralized . . . the method of working and leading is haphazard and not organized . . .

the attitudes and understanding of our cadres, combatants, and people have not been promptly changed to conform to the situation. Many of them hold that when the administrative power has been seized throughout the country, every task of the revolution has been accomplished and everything will be easy. As a result, they fall back on an attitude of peace, relaxing and paying no attention to taking care of their responsibility toward work.[48]

Despite these personnel deficiencies, Laos looks forward, as does Vietnam, to the use of districts (not provinces or enterprises) as the basic economic-administrative unit in the country.

A three-year plan was set up in 1977, and individual development projects were to be prepared with the help of consultants from Japan, financed by the UN Development Program, and executed by the Asian Development Bank. The preparation of an $8.2 million loan project for the approval of the International Development Association (IDA), covering irrigation projects, pig multiplication units, and rice cultivation research, indicated the readiness of the beleaguered government to adapt itself to international standards of planning and accountability. A token of this pragmatic adjustment to World Bank standards, as well as of the ability to learn from mistakes, was the cutting of the budget deficit and the rate of monetary expansion by about two-thirds in 1977. Consumer prices, which were rising at a rate of 400 percent in the free market in 1976, rose less than 50 percent in late 1977. Government-controlled shops provided government employees in the cities with their basic necessities at fixed prices, and the free market began toward the end of 1977 to show more goods available—through the easing of restrictions on transactions and imports, the reopening of more local production enterprises, and the arrival of commodity aid.

Even though imports have been cut drastically since 1975, exports cover only one-fifth the cost. (Foreign aid, which used to cover most of the royal government's public expenditures, still provides for about half of the LPDR's budgetary expenditures. The high price of coffee was one bright spot in the 1977 export picture, but foreign exchange earnings will remain woefully insufficient, notwithstanding potential expansion in hydroelectricity (from the Nam Ngum Dam), timber, and mineral exports. More effective management of timber exploitation and expansion of mineral extraction could substantially increase earnings, but both projects will require considerable capital investment and time to achieve. The prospect for 1978 is a current account deficit even higher than the roughly $60 million in 1977, because of greater food imports. Trade deficits of about $70 million may continue for another decade and will roughly equal the foreign assistance requirements.[49]

From the start, the LPDR has insisted upon its readiness to receive assistance from "fraternal countries, friendly countries and other international organizations." This plank has also been punctuated with recurring demands that the United States fulfill its obligation to "heal the wounds of war." The aid received, however, has been so weighted in the direction of the Soviet Union and other "fraternal countries" that Kaysone found it necessary to refute the "slanderous charges against us that the request of our government for assistance from fraternal countries is not much different from the puppet administration which lived on U.S. aid." The difference, he asserted, is that the socialist countries were enabling Laos "to become self-reliant and self-sufficient."[50]

The details of economic aid agreements with the Soviet Union, China, and Vietnam have not been revealed, but it is thought that Soviet aid, running between $30 and $40 million, will in 1978 amount to three times the Chinese package. Even though all the East European bloc countries have made contributions to Laos, particularly during the hardship period of the blockade by Thailand in late 1975, East Germany, the largest bloc contributor, has not provided as much aid as West Germany has.[51] For 1977, Sweden, West Germany, and the Netherlands planned to give $15 million in aid to Laos.[52] An increased effort was promised by India, following a visit by President Souphanouvong in January 1977, and Iraq was also sought out for a contribution. The OPEC Special Fund, France, and Japan have made significant aid commitments. The second phase of the Nam Ngum Dam construction project should eventually contribute to economic development. Laos has also indicated its readiness to continue working with the Mekong River Development Committee toward further development of its waterpower.

The idea of foreign commercial investment in Laos is not altogether unthinkable, especially if Thailand's new government continues to allow transshipment of all non-security-related goods. The LPDR is apparently ready to negotiate with "friendly" foreign contractors for the exploitation of timber and possibly tin, with Laos simply receiving a percentage of the earnings without a share in the management. Given the inexperience and dearth of managerial cadres in the government, this appears to be a practical choice. Meanwhile, the state has worked at tasks in which its administrators have demonstrated some capability, such as the resettlement of several hundred thousand wartime refugees (with the assistance of the UN high commissioner for refugees) and the raising of literacy in the nation.

Given the extreme backwardness, lack of resources, and landlocked situation of Laos, it is small wonder that Vietnam is able to exert a special political influence over the country. The twenty-five-year Treaty of Friendship and Cooperation, formalized between the two countries on July 18, 1977, was accompanied by a three-year economic assistance agreement, which may be aimed at road building. For the first time, loans, rather than simply grant aid, reportedly were included. It seems likely that the previous precarious reliance upon Thailand for access to the sea will now be exchanged for greater economic and political dependency upon Vietnam. Thailand, after imposing a de facto blockade on the transshipment of goods to Laos from July 1977 until after General Kriangsak Chamanand's government was established in November 1977, appeared ready to cooperate more with Laos in 1978. It remains a question whether Thailand will still be a haven for Lao insurgents and whether these activities will seriously handicap the economic progress so desperately sought by Laos. If the Thai government does not augment these insurgent efforts, severe economic disruption seems unlikely, even though the threat may promote a continuing military presence by Vietnamese forces in Laos. With or without insurgents, however, the prospect for Laos is grim: shortages of material and food, inept administration, and dependency upon foreign economic assistance may extend many years into the future.

Foreign Policy

In its external relations, the young republic has been chiefly concerned with obtaining economic assistance for its immediate needs and with developing its relations with its major supporters in the socialist camp, while dealing warily with states that could be "neocolonialist." As noted earlier, the expulsion of the U.S. AID mission from Laos in June 1975 and the termination of the Foreign Exchange Operations Fund put the new republic's principle of self-reliance and independence severely to the test. Laos has subsisted with emergency food and materials from the Soviet Union, China, Vietnam, and even Cambodia, as well as with donations from virtually all the other socialist states, from nine major international organizations, Australia, India, Burma, Sweden, the Netherlands, and France. By 1978 the LPDR took price in maintaining diplomatic relations with more than fifty states, and it broke relations with Israel, demonstrating Third World solidarity.

Relations between Laos and Vietnam have been, in the words of both, like "lips and teeth," with Vietnam retaining its role as the dominant external power within Laos. As noted earlier, their close relationship was cemented in a twenty-five-year friendship treaty signed in July 1977. Lao relations with Cambodia have been outwardly friendly, despite the military clashes during 1977 between Vietnam and Cambodia. Cambodia provided small amounts of aid to Laos in 1977 in the form of rice, salt, and dried fish. President Souphanouvong made an official visit to Cambodia in December 1977, but if one of his missions was to mediate the conflict between Vietnam and Cambodia, as the press speculated, it obviously failed in view of Cambodia's rupture of diplomatic relations with Vietnam on December 31, 1977, and the eruption of fighting between them.

During the public speeches, neither Lao nor Cambodian spokesmen mentioned the wartime slogans of "Indochinese solidarity." Rather, the Cambodians used Souphanouvong's visit to stress their friendship with the Lao, in contrast with their animosity toward the Vietnamese. In a radio broadcast welcoming the Lao delegation, there was little doubt that the Vietnamese were targeted along with other enemies: "The Cambodian and Lao peoples are brothers who have shared weal and woe, share their characteristic politeness and honesty and have similar traditions, customs and cultures. . . . Our two countries have continually enjoyed good relations to the dissatisfaction of the enemies—the colonialists, imperialists, aggressors, expansionists and annexationists."[53] At a banquet honoring the Lao delegation, Cambodian President Khieu Samphan proclaimed that his country "would resolutely prevent any foreign country from stationing forces on its soil" and added an only slightly veiled warning that Lao soil must not be used as a base for Vietnamese forces to launch attacks against Cambodia.[54] A few days after the Souphanouvong delegation returned to Vientiane, the Vietnamese foreign minister, Nguyen Duy Trinh, paying a friendship visit to Laos, emphasized the "special relationship" between Vietnam and Laos, and warned that "no vicious maneuver can weaken this relationship."[55]

Although Laos has generally followed the foreign policy line of Vietnam, which has been more closely linked to the Soviet Union than to China, the LPDR has made an effort to maintain good relations with both the Soviets and the Chinese, cautiously straddling the Sino-Soviet dispute. The Soviets have been the largest suppliers of economic and technical assistance to Laos, including a variety of aircraft as well as pilots and maintenance personnel. A curious Soviet donation in 1977, which seems to enhance neither the LPDR's military nor economic capability, was a gift of about a dozen MIG-21 fighter planes. There are few Lao pilots and technicians for such aircraft, and aviation fuel, which Thailand has not been willing to transship, even after lifting its de facto blockade in November 1977, is unavailable. Total Soviet personnel in Laos was estimated, in early 1978, to be between 500 and 600 (about half the U.S. strength three years earlier). The Party leadership has readily acknowledged Soviet aid in glowing terms: "At all stages of our revolutionary struggle the CPSU and the government and people of the Soviet Union have constantly rendered us tremendous support and effective aid."[56] Relations with the PRC have also been friendly and respectful. Laos seems to recognize that it cannot afford to cast its lot definitively with the Soviets or Vietnam on issues affecting China. The Chinese have continued road construction in the northern areas and reportedly keep 15,000 laborers on hand for such work. Among other aid, the Chinese gave Laos 8,000 bicycles, which were particularly valuable because of the stringent gasoline shortage.

Thailand is of vital importance for Laos, because of Laos's traditional dependence upon trade in rice and other products across the Mekong River border and upon Thai ports and roads for overseas commerce. Strained relations had been improving until the military coup d'etat in October 1976 brought to power the rigid and anticommunist government of Thanin Kravichien and deepened the mutual suspicion between the two countries. Lao statements then stressed even more heavily the "fraternal friendship between the peoples" of the two countries, which the acts of the "warlord clique" could not shake. The Lao commentaries pledged "wholehearted support" for the "fraternal Thai people in their struggle for freedom and true national independence."[57] The capacity for reciprocal harassment was clear. Kaysone warned in his National Day address in 1976 that if those who hold power in Thailand "continue to follow evil imperialist schemes by further fostering and supporting exiled Lao reactionaries and counter-revolutionary elements opposing the Lao people . . . they must bear full responsibility for all consequences arising from their actions."[58] In similar fashion, the Thais charged the Lao communists with supporting the communist insurgency in the north and northeast of Thailand. Following another military coup in Thailand in October 1977, which ousted Thanin, the new government of General Kriangsak Chamanand initiated a marked improvement in Thai-Lao relations. As discussed earlier, the new Thai government was more accommodating than its predecessors toward the communist Indochina states. Although it barred certain "strategic" military supplies, it restored most of the transit trade to Laos, which was still stalled by the de facto blockade, and lifted the prohibition on private commerce with Laos. In December 1977, Laos and Thailand announced the resumption of commercial air services between their two capitals.

The improvement in Lao-Thai relations at the end of 1977 was part of what appeared to be an amelioration of relations between the ASEAN countries and Laos, following an earlier period of strain. As mentioned earlier, the Lao delegation, at the fifth nonaligned summit conference in Colombo in August 1976, had jarred the ASEAN states by criticizing the well-known ASEAN resolution on making a zone of peace in the area. Lao amendments in support of "the legitimate struggle of the people" against neocolonialism, to enable them to become "truly independent, pacific and neutral," had angered Malaysia in particular and eventually precluded any conference resolution on the subject.

Earlier statements in July by Kaysone had indicated that the Lao government saw ASEAN as an imperialist organization set up following the dismantling of SEATO,[59] even though Laos was ready, as was Vietnam, to maintain normal relations with member states. It is not clear to what degree the Lao were acting at Colombo as proxies for the Vietnamese. The Colombo episode expressed the latent contradiction in the twin policies pursued by Laos and Vietnam—that is, of normalizing interstate relations while championing people's struggles against neocolonialism. By mid-1977, as Vietnamese-Cambodian clashes were increasing, Vietnam and Laos seemed concerned about the PRC's endorsement of ASEAN, its close relations with Phnom Penh, and its role as mediator of Thai-Cambodian tensions, and they may have tried to improve relations with ASEAN to insure they would not be isolated in the Southeast Asian region. In June 1977 the Malaysian foreign minister, apparently acting as a special emissary for the ASEAN countries, received a warm reception in both Hanoi and Vientiane. By early 1978, although Laos and Vietnam still rejected the offers of membership in ASEAN, they had softened their criticism of the organization and were actively seeking a more friendly interchange with its member states.

As for U.S.-Lao relations, early in 1977 the LPDR ordered the U.S. embassy in Vientiane, composed of twenty-seven persons headed by a chargé d'affaires, to cut back to twelve persons, without a military attaché. At about the same time, the new Carter administration demonstrated a desire to normalize diplomatic relations with Vietnam and, as noted earlier, arranged for a five-person presidential commission under Leonard Woodcock to visit Hanoi to discuss this question and the related issues of accounting for Americans missing in action (MIAs) and reconstruction aid. The Foreign Ministry of the LPDR did not respond to the U.S. request that the commission be received in Vientiane until March 12, the day before its departure for Hanoi. Although the Lao government was more cordial during the actual visit (March 19–20, 1977), unlike the Vietnamese, they provided no new information or remains of MIAs. They stressed the great difficulty of finding them in their rugged mountains and insisted on a link between their efforts regarding MIAs and U.S. assistance in helping to rebuild the country. The commission concluded in its report that the Lao are less able than the Vietnamese to develop additional MIA information, "though they could produce some . . . and could gather more if they desire," adding that this would "most likely happen in the context of a general improvement of relations with Laos."[60] The LPDR's statement that no Americans were alive or prisoners in Laos was regarded as tragic but true. As for an improvement of Lao-U.S. relations, the Lao, like the Vietnamese, have maintained that the United States should fulfill Article 20 of the Paris Agreement to help "heal the wounds of war." Laos has declared its readiness to accept U.S. economic assistance "without strings" and without U.S. aid personnel within its borders. Yet until the United States and Vietnam work out their impasse over reconstruction aid, the LPDR will probably continue the "correct" relationship and basic distrust that now exists toward its former adversary. Thus, for all its inclinations toward independence, Laos will probably remain highly dependent upon the actions of its more powerful neighbor.

4
Cambodia since the Communist Victory

Although Cambodia was the last of the Indochina countries to be plunged into the war (April 1970), the Khmer communists were the first to achieve victory. On April 17, 1975, about two weeks before the Vietnamese communist troops captured Saigon, the People's Armed Forces for National Liberation of Kampuchea (PAFNLK) marched into Phnom Penh. To the bewilderment of its inhabitants, the PAFNLK, a few hours following their victorious entry, ordered a complete evacuation of the city—men, women, young, old, sick, lame, from hospitals as well as homes—all were forced to leave immediately, with only what they could carry on their backs.[1] Each urban center was similarly emptied, obviously following a predetermined plan: Ream was evacuated on April 18, Poipet on April 24, Pailin about April 27.

The emptying of the cities was the opening move of a revolution that may be the most radical of the twentieth century. The Khmer revolutionaries moved quickly to liquidate large numbers of their former enemies and initiated a total restructuring of the economy and society. Their most cherished goals were declared to be self-sufficiency and independence. They would attempt to wipe the slate clean of old values and to create a new Khmer culture and a new Khmer personality.

These developments in Cambodia aroused amazement and incredulity throughout the world. The surprise of most observers—including the few experts on Cambodia—dramatically revealed how little was known about the Cambodian communist movement, a lack of knowledge that has been only marginally remedied in the months since victory. The Khmer revolutionaries have been jealously secretive about themselves. The new rulers expelled almost all foreigners from the country. There are no foreign journalists in Cambodia, and by 1977 only nine countries (Albania, People's Republic of China, Cuba, Egypt, Laos, North Korea, Romania, Vietnam, and Yugoslavia) had reestablished diplomatic missions in Phnom Penh. Embassy personnel, except for the Chinese, are normally limited in their movement to an area within 100 yards of their embassies. Thus, few reports from outside observers emerge from within Cambodia, except for an occasional official visitor who describes a brief stay. A principal, if limited, source of information about Cambodian internal developments is Cambodian refugees. (By the beginning of 1977, some 35,000 Cambodians had fled to Thailand, and at least 50,000 had reached Vietnam.)[2] Another source is official government radio broadcasts.[3] In view of the sparse information available from Cambodia, any analysis of its internal situation must be tentative.

Origins of the Revolution

Until September 1977, the new leaders of Cambodia did not publicly acknowledge their membership in a communist party, nor did they discuss the brand of Marxism-Leninism they embrace.[4] The government radio and the revolutionary cadres transmitted orders from an anonymous authority known simply as "Angka" ("Revolutionary Organization"). Despite this secrecy, the Communist Party of Kampuchea clearly commanded the country. As in Laos, the Indochina Communist Party, founded by Ho Chi Minh in 1930, had attempted to organize resistance against the French through a committee for Cambodia, which was composed principally of Vietnamese and Chinese residents of Cambodia. In 1951, as noted earlier, the ICP was formally dissolved, and separate communist parties were established the same year in Vietnam and Cambodia and, by 1955, in Laos. The Cambodian party, led by Secretary General Sieu Heng, was called the Revolutionary Cambodian People's Party (Pracheachon); in September 1966, it became the Communist Party of Kampuchea.[5] The Cambodian party was small, smaller than the Lao Dong Party in Vietnam, and it grew only slightly during the later 1950s and the early 1960s.

Although scholars outside Cambodia paid little attention at the time, by the 1960s important social changes within the country belied the widespread image of a harmonious, prosperous, and contented society. By about 1965, class division had become sharper, and the tensions greater, between countryside and city, young and old, left and right. Much of the rural population was not far above the subsistence level, rural indebtedness was distressing in some areas, and the proportion of poor peasants was probably increasing.[6] Although this was hardly as revolutionary a situation as in China, some areas had acute suffering. In the Samlaut region of Battambang Province, there was a peasant rebellion in 1967, which the security forces of Prince Sihanouk (the chief of state) put down with extreme harshness.[7]

The leadership elements who expanded their small revolutionary organization by mobilizing this discontent in the later 1960s and achieved victory in the 1970–1975 war—were drawn from a number of sources.[8] The earliest leaders before 1954, who were linked either with the Viet Minh or were in a separate Cambodian resistance group, opposed the French and Prince Sihanouk, whom they considered a French "puppet." Some members of this group remained underground in Cambodia after the Geneva Conference in 1954, and others, variously estimated at 2,000 to 6,000 were transported by the Viet Minh to North Vietnam.[9] Those sent to North Vietnam rapidly infiltrated back into Cambodia following the U.S. and South Vietnamese incursion there in 1970, which signaled the beginning of the war. Probably the most important source of future leaders was students who had been in France, many during the 1950s. Reflecting upon the ills of their country while participating in Cambodian student politics in Paris, many Khmer students intensified their nationalism and embraced Marxism.

A few, including Khieu Samphan and Hou Youn, completed advanced degrees in France and returned in the late 1950s to posts at the French university faculties in Phnom Penh.[10] Others completed university undergraduate studies and returned in the late 1950s and early 1960s, many taking posts as teachers in the elementary and secondary schools while continuing their intense pursuit of politics. Several (including Khieu Samphan and Hou Youn) accepted invitations from Prince Sihanouk, during his attempt in the early 1960s to disarm the opposition left-wing intellectuals, to join his government in ministerial posts.[11] Others, who sensed danger from Sihanouk's police during the same period (Ieng Sary, Son Sen, and Saloth Sar), quit Phnom Penh to join forces with the maquis.[12] Following the Samlaut rebellion of March 1967, for which the Communist Party claimed credit, Sihanouk cracked down on the left-wing leaders, and many more fled to the maquis, some of whom later went to China during the Cultural Revolution.[13] As these leaders assembled in the countryside, they apparently united their efforts under the discipline of the Party.

When Lon Nol and the discontented elite associated with him ousted Prince Sihanouk in March 1970, the revolutionary movement gained a strange bedfellow. Furious at the treachery of his erstwhile associates and determined to avenge himself, the prince threw his lot in with the group he had once derisively dubbed the Khmer Rouge.[14] Though many of the Khmer Rouge leaders had fled to save themselves from his wrath[15] and were committed to extirpating his royal regime, they welcomed him to the revolutionary organization. Sihanouk's participation added legitimacy to the Khmer Rouge cause, and his endorsement brought support from many of his followers (who became known as Khmer Rumda), who would otherwise have been unwilling to accept the revolutionary leadership. The prince was a useful spokesman for the revolutionaries abroad, and the government of which he was the titular head (Gouvernement royal d'union nationale de Kampuchéa, or GRUNK) was almost successful in replacing his Phnom Penh successors at the United Nations. Although Sihanouk's participation was vital to the revolutionary organization, neither he nor his followers had a significant influence on its decisions during the war. The prince himself seemed to understand that even his public prominence would be short-lived, telling an interviewer in 1973, "When I shall no longer be useful to them [the Khmer Rouge], they'll spit me out like a cherry pit."[16]

The new leadership cites January 17, 1968, as the beginning of its renewed armed struggle. The first armed struggle was against the French colonialists, who withdrew from Cambodia in 1953 only to be replaced by the U.S. imperialists. The revolutionary leaders then launched a political struggle until 1968, during which they secretly prepared their military organization. From 1968 to 1970, in their version, they fought a "people's war" against the "enemy's counterrevolutionary, cruel, fascist internal war." In March 1970, the United States inspired the Lon Nol clique to stage a coup d'etat and later, with their "Thieu-Ky puppet clique," invaded Cambodia, transforming the conflict into an open war of aggression.[17] At the time of the U.S. and South Vietnamese incursions into Cambodia in May 1970, the Khmer communists, whose political and military organization was still weak, benefited from a security shield in the east and northeast provided by the Viet Cong and PAVN, although the Cambodian leadership does not currently acknowledge this support. The Vietnamese communists also provided armed propaganda teams, advisers, and supplies in helping to build the newly established Front unifié nationale de Kampuchéa (FUNK). FUNK could, of course, tap into the rural discontent in expanding its membership.

By about 1972, Vietnamese military support diminished, but FUNK had grown in size and military strength—largely through its own initiative, but also with Chinese and Vietnamese supplies and with the continued presence in Cambodia of Vietnamese forces that were primarily targeted against South Vietnam. By April 1975, FUNK and its army, PAFNLK, had grown significantly, and its enemy in Phnom Penh—riddled with factionalism, corruption, and decay and faced with seriously declining U.S. supplies—was badly demoralized and ineffective. Following the establishment of a stranglehold on the Mekong River supply line to Phnom Penh, bloated from the prewar population of a half million to some 2 to 3 million, government resistance collapsed, and PAFNLK marched victoriously into the city.

The Party

In September 1977, the Cambodian people were informed for the first time that the Communist Party of Kampuchea had been leading the revolution. At a rally in Phnom Penh on September 27, on the eve of his departure for an official visit to the PRC, Prime Minister Pol Pot, who was revealed as the secretary general of the Party and who, it appears, was the same person as Saloth Sar,[18] gave a five-hour speech in which he announced the seventeenth anniversary of the founding of the Party (in September 1960) and gave a rambling history of the Party, its revolutionary struggle, and an outline of its strategy. He stated, "Our party has decided to openly and officially proclaim its existence to the nation and to the international public."[19]

In bringing the Party out of secrecy, the leaders were apparently rewriting its history to remove the Vietnamese communist role in its founding and earliest years. Pol Pot did not mention that the forerunner of the Communist Party of Kampuchea was the Revolutionary Cambodian People's Party (Pracheachon), as noted above, founded in 1951 as an offshoot of the Indochina Communist Party, which the Vietnamese directed.[20] His brief allusions to the Cambodian revolutionary struggle before 1960 included an elliptical criticism of the Vietnamese, and perhaps of the Soviet Union and the PRC, for pressuring the Indochina countries to conclude the Geneva Agreement of 1954. Pol Pot noted that the Cambodian people, poor peasants in particular, had joined in the revolutionary struggle against the French, but that they did not have "a correct and clear-sighted guideline. . . . They did not know what strategy and tactics to use, which direction to follow, which goal to achieve, which forces to rely on and which form to fight in. Our people did not know how to fight on the basis of independence, initiative and self-reliance. Being without a correct guideline is like being blind." Despite the heroic struggle of the Cambodian people, he asserted, "this revolutionary struggle of our people and the war booty that was subsequently captured vanished into thin air through the 1954 Geneva Agreement." The lesson that Pol Pot drew from this costly experience was that the Cambodian people must follow a correct party line, a line that "should be based on the principles of independence, initiative, self-determination and self-reliance, which means that we must rely primarily on our own people, our own army, our own revolution and on the actual revolutionary movement of the masses in our own country."[21]

Several factors appear to have contributed to the Party's decision to reveal itself. Two and one-half years after victory, the Party leaders were now firmly in command of the country. They had dealt harshly with their enemies and launched radical measures for the restructuring of society. It was now time, they must have judged, to remove some of the mystery of the Party's role and introduce themselves to the Cambodian people. In addition, there were indications, during the Pol Pot visit to the PRC, that the Chinese had encouraged the Cambodians to proclaim the leading role of the Cambodian Communist Party. The Chinese believed it proper, it seems likely, that there be open party-to-party relations in addition to the government-to-government relations between the two countries.[22]

Leadership

Although the ruling Communist Party maintains tight secrecy and we know little about the Party Central Committee, which directs the revolutionary organization, we have information about the most important members of the Party.[23] As mentioned above, the secretary of the Party, generally the most powerful member in communist regimes, has been acknowledged to be Pol Pot, known earlier as Saloth Sar. When Pol Pot was announced as prime minister of the new government in March 1976, his name had never before been listed with the revolutionary organizations (GRUNK and FUNK), and he was unknown to Western observers. Speculation that Pol Pot was the same person as Saloth Sar was confirmed by photos of Pol Pot taken by journalists during his visit to China in September 1977, as well as by the facts of his official biography issued during his trip.[24]

Born in 1925 in Kompong Thom, Pol Pot attended a technical school in Phnom Penh, learning carpentry. At the age of twenty-one, he left for Paris to study radio electronics. Although he failed at three examinations and did not earn a diploma, he was said to be a passionate reader of French literature and began reading Marx and other political books. Returning to Phnom Penh in 1953 to work as a teacher, he joined the Pracheachon group and was active in left-wing journalist circles. As noted earlier, he fled to the maquis in 1963 and emerged during the war as one of PAFNLK's three vice-chairmen, with responsibility for the Military Directorate.

Three prominent members of the Party now holding important government posts—Ieng Sary, Khieu Samphan, and Son Sen—were also university students in France during the 1950s. Ieng Sary, an ethnic Khmer born in South Vietnam in 1930 of a well-off land-owning family, completed his baccalaureate at Lycée Sisowath in

Phnom Penh and, at the age of twenty, left for Paris to begin commercial studies, transferring in 1953 to the Institut d'Études Politiques. Active in student politics, he was elected president of the Union of Khmer Students for 1955–1956. Two tendencies were evident among Khmer students—hard-liners and moderates—and Ieng Sary was among the hard-liners along with Saloth Sar and Son Sen, who believed that Prince Sihanouk was the principal enemy of the Khmer people and must be overthrown by armed struggle. The moderates, who included Khieu Sampan, Hou Youn, Hu Nim, and Chau Seng, saw a larger danger on the world scene from U.S. imperialism and believed that they should work within the royal government, taking posts of command and accomplishing a revolution from above.[25] Returning to Phnom Penh in 1957, Ieng Sary was a teacher at the Lycée Sisowath and also at the private Lycée Kampubot, where a number of future revolutionary leaders (including Hou Youn and Saloth Sar) also taught. He fled to the maquis in 1963 and emerged with important posts in the GRUNK government during the war. He is now deputy prime minister charged with foreign affairs.

Khieu Samphan, who is chairman of the State Presidium, is the formal chief of state. He was born in 1931 and studied at Lycée Sisowath before leaving for France in 1954 to study economics.[26] He earned his doctorate from the University of Paris in 1959 and returned to Cambodia to serve as a professor of political economy at the faculty of law at Phnom Penh, as well as the director of a French-language biweekly newspaper, l'Observateur. Although subsequently harassed by government police (in 1960 they stripped him naked and photographed him in public to humiliate him for criticism of the regime), in 1962 he became secretary of state for commerce in Sihanouk's new government. Colleagues who knew him during this period in Sihanouk's government described Khieu Samphan as a thoughtful, able man of impeccable integrity.[27] Fearing arrest by Sihanouk's security forces following the Samlaut rebellion in 1967, Khieu Samphan, along with others in the government, fled. He was not heard from until he emerged during the war in vital GRUNK posts as deputy prime minister and minister of defense and later as commander in chief of PAFNLK, leading to speculation that he was GRUNK's most powerful leader.[28] His elevation in January 1976 to the chairmanship of the State Presidium raised the question whether his duties would be largely ceremonial. In September 1977, when members of the Standing Committee of the Party Central Committee were first announced during Secretary General Pol Pot's visit to the PRC, Khieu Samphan's name did not appear among them, confirming speculation that he was not among the principal decision makers of the Party.

Son Sen, an ethnic Khmer, now the deputy prime minister charged with national defense, was born in South Vietnam in 1930. After studies at a teacher's college in Phnom Penh, he left in 1950 for Paris, where he earned a diploma in letters but failed (according to one account) the entrance exam for the École Normale Supérieure. He returned to Phnom Penh in 1956.[29] Like a number of fellow revolutionaries, he taught at Lycée Sisowath in Phnom Penh and was later director of curriculum at the National Pedagogical Institute. He fled to the maquis in 1963, emerging during the war as chief of the General Staff of PAFNLK.

Hu Nim, born in 1932, earned a law degree in France in 1957 and a doctorate in law at the University of Phnom Penh in 1965. He participated in Sihanouk governments until 1967, when he fled. He later emerged as GRUNK's minister of information. He appeared to hold this post until early 1977, after which there has been no mention of him, leading to speculation that he has been purged or is ill.

As in the case of Pol Pot, it is common practice for Cambodian communists to adopt revolutionary pseudonyms. Confounding the leadership puzzle was an announcement in September 1976 that Pol Pot had taken sick leave and would be temporarily replaced as prime minister by the chairman of the Standing Committee of the People's Representative Assembly, Nuon Chea, another personality unknown to outsiders.[30] Still another high cabinet official new to outsiders was Vorn Vet, deputy prime minister charged with the economy. There were reports that these three leaders—Pol Pot, Nuon Chea, and Vorn Vet—were veterans of the anti-French resistance and that Nuon Chea and Vorn Vet had perhaps taken part in anti-Japanese resistance in the 1940s.[31] If true, there is a continuity between the earlier resistance organizations and the current leadership, which is dominated by intellectuals who were still students in France in the 1950s.[32]

Unlike the Vietnamese, and even the Lao leaders, the Cambodian leaders are young. Many were born in the late 1920s and early 1930s, too young to have been involved in anticolonial politics. Apparently, only a few former anti-French resistance fighters, as just noted, are at the top levels of leadership today. No members of the top leadership—as far as present information indicates—come from the resistance fighters who were in Vietnam from 1954 to 1970. Members of this group, though welcome to participate in the wartime struggle, were suspected for their close ties with the Vietnamese.[33] Khmer mistrust of the Vietnamese is so long-standing and deep that even fellow revolutionaries involved with the Vietnamese for so long would be required to demonstrate their Cambodian nationalist *bona fides.*

A surprising number of the Party and government leaders are related by marriage, appearing to belong to one clan. Saloth Sar is married to Khieu Ponmary, the daughter of a prominent family, a former teacher at Lycée Sisowath, and now the chairman of the Association of Democratic Women of Kamphuchea. Ieng Sary is married to her sister, Khieu Thirith, who taught at Lycée Norodom after studying English literature in Paris and is now minister of social action in the current government. Son Sen is married to another former teacher at Lycée Sisowath, Yun Yat, who is now minister of culture and education.

Despite their intellectual and middle-class background, Cambodian leaders appear to continue the austere habits they acquired during the war. Wartime life stressed self-sacrifice, egalitarianism, and rigorous discipline.[34] Cadres lived a communal life, limited in provisions, and were frequently in personal danger. All were required to work in the fields and do other manual labor. Titles of age, rank, or profession—subtly complex and important in pre-revolutionary Cambodia—were forbidden; a single form of address for everyone replaced them: *Mit/mitt* ("friend" or "comrade"). Personal traits of "liberalism" associated with the oppressor and reactionary class, excesses in eating, drinking, gambling, or sexual freedom—all were condemned. At regular meetings, criticism and self-criticism exposed deficiencies and inculcated proper revolutionary behavior. Strict secrecy about the group's activities was enforced, and cadres had to take a revolutionary name, both for security and to emphasize the importance of developing a new, revolutionary personality. Refugees suggest that the Cambodian leaders still impose these values upon themselves and others.

Secrecy and Cohesion

The Cambodian revolutionaries' obsession with secrecy went beyond even the past practices of the Vietnamese and Lao communists. This zealous Cambodian secrecy seemed to have both political and psychological roots. Governing through a mysterious organization, Angka, instilled fear. Cadres taught that Angka must be trusted because "it has as many eyes as a pineapple" and cannot make mistakes.[35] It also sees all wrongdoing. Because there are so few cadres for a country of 7.7 million—one estimate held that there were 70,000 military in the Khmer Rouge in 1975 and only 1,000 cadres[36] —fear is a useful instrument to maintain authority. Furthermore, just as the Vietnamese and Lao revolutionary leaders judged that "communism" and "Marxism-Leninism" were regarded unfavorably by their politically unsophisticated peasantry, the Cambodian rulers obviously deemed it politically desirable to hide their ideological affiliation. An anonymous ruling Angka, instead of individual leaders, also served the cause of egalitarianism and collective leadership, to which the Cambodian communists are clearly committed. The denunciation of Stalin's "cult of personality" after his death in 1953 and the criticism of Maurice Thorez, leader of the French Communist Party, for "personalism" must have made a strong impression upon the future Cambodian revolutionary leaders who were students in France during this period. Individual leaders were largely unknown to the Cambodian people, and no single leader in the Cambodian organization today could be condemned for self-glorification.

During and immediately after the war, because of the diverse makeup of the Khmer Rouge, many analysts believed there was serious factional rivalry within the leadership. Speculation focused upon assumed "pro-Hanoi" and "pro-Peking" cliques, as well as upon French-educated and veteran resistant groups. This speculation about factionalism was revived during the border disputes with Thailand and Vietnam in the summer of 1977, when frontier attacks were seen as a distraction from "convulsive seizures of sedition, factional revolts and purges within the party."[37]

There were reports of intermittent purges in the northwest

region of the country during the first half of 1977: one round is thought to have taken place in February and another in April. Certain province and district cadres were reported to have been executed, and some lower-ranking members of the army and militia to have been disarmed and sent to other regions; a shake-up of the remaining personnel followed. Although the extent and the reasons for the purge remain obscure, several explanations have been offered. One view is that these measures might have been part of a rectification campaign to flush out older cadres who were not considered sufficiently zealous in ferreting out class enemies. Another is that local cadres in provinces near Thailand, who were engaged in barter with Thai elements in the search for critical supplies, were believed by morbidly suspicious Party officials in Phnom Penh to have been engaged in subversive plots with CIA agents and their Thai collaborators, who were plotting sabotage in Cambodia. Still another hypothesis, also unconfirmed, is that a genuine coup plot may have been hatched by regional Party officials distressed by the harshness of the central leadership and concerned by the disaffection of the people in their region.[38]

A radio broadcast from North Korea carrying a message of greetings from President Kim Il-sung to Pol Pot on the KCP's seventeenth anniversary tended to corroborate the reports of earlier purges in Cambodia. The message noted that "the heroic Cambodian people have wiped out some time ago the counter-revolutionary group of spies who had committed subversive activities and sabotage, worming themselves into the revolutionary ranks for a long time at the instigation of foreign imperialists, and thus demonstrated the might of the political and ideological unity and cohesion of the country rallied close around the Central Committee of the party."[39] It is noteworthy that Phnom Penh radio, in rebroadcasting this message, omitted the paragraph cited above, reinforcing the speculation that the Cambodian Party leaders did not wish their people to hear hints of past Party purges.[40]

Another reason for speculation about purges in Cambodia is that several former prominent Khmer communist leaders have disappeared from public view. Hou Youn, former GRUNK minister of the interior, did not appear in the new government named in April 1976. The minister of information, Hu Nim, and the chairman of the Commerce Committee, Chhoeur Doeun, have not been heard from since February 1977, raising the possibility that they have been purged. When it was announced in September 1976 that Pol Pot was taking sick leave, there was speculation about a clash reaching the highest level of the Party leadership. His announced return to the prime minister's post in September 1977 and the public revelation that he is secretary of the Party dispelled the rumors of his demise, although it is still not clear whether his year-long absence was connected with the reports of factional struggles within the Party.

After the Cambodian conflict with the Vietnamese burst into public view, following the rupture of diplomatic relations by the Cambodians on December 31, 1977, Cambodian spokesmen have intermittently denounced the Vietnamese for attempts at political subversion within Cambodia. The Cambodian communist leaders' suspicion of the Vietnamese is compounded by their belief, as Pol Pot asserted, that "various spy rings working for imperialism and international reactionaries are still planted among us to carry out subversive activities against our revolution." He estimated that 1–2 percent of the population must be regarded as enemies of democratic Cambodia. "We must deal with them the same way we would with any enemy," he insisted, "by separating, educating and coopting elements that can be won over . . . neutralizing any reluctant elements . . . and isolating and eradicating only the smallest possible number of these elements who are cruel and who determinedly oppose the revolution and the people and collaborate with foreign enemies to oppose their own nation."[41]

The new regime's obsession with the threat of counterrevolutionaries throws light upon the Party leadership's initial decision to empty the cities in April 1975. Pol Pot cited this concern for security as the reason for the forced evacuation of the cities:

One of the important factors [for our success] is the evacuation of city residents to the countryside. This was decided before victory was won, that is, in February 1975, because we knew our strength was not strong enough to defend the revolutionary regime. Judging from the struggles waged from 1976 to 1977, the enemy's secret agent network lying low in our country was very massive and complicated. But when we crushed them, it was difficult for them to stage a comeback. Their forces were scattered in various cooperatives

which are in our own grip. Thus we have the initiative in our hands.
The enemy dare not attack from outside. They counted on especially
the sabotage and trouble-making by their secret agents or traitors to
our country, so as to strike together from within and without. If
there are no enemy agents among us, the enemy from outside dare
not take reckless actions.[42]

In addition to speculation about the lack of cohesion among
the revolutionary leadership, there have been frequent assertions
about lack of discipline within the ranks. The reports of widespread
Khmer Rouge cruelty during wartime[43] and the harsh forced
exodus from the cities were frequently attributed to angry young
soldiers taking revenge on their enemies and on the decadent
cities, acting without discipline or control from a central authority.
Although it is possible that some units and individuals acted spon-
taneously with violence, the bulk of the evidence points to effective planning and a disciplined organization responsive to the
authority of the central leadership.[44] Although brutal in their
methods, the Khmer communist soldiers were apparently faith-
fully carrying out the policies of the central organization.[45]

Party Organization

Only a limited picture of the ruling Party's internal organization has been pieced together from a few wartime defector reports
and radio broadcasts, which reveal certain practices common to
communist parties.[46] The Party is organized in committees that
correspond to the administrative units of the country: the center,
region, sector, district, township, and village. Collective leadership
within the committees is stressed, and the principle of democratic
centralism is invoked. The Party maintains control by assigning
its cadres to guide policymaking within the governmental agencies
and administrative units. Party cells operate within the army, and
political commissars, in principle, share command with military
officers at company level and above, although it is not clear that
Party ranks are large enough to fulfill this requirement. Party
cadres also direct the activities of a variety of front organizations.
The Party youth organization—the Alliance of Communist Youth
of Kampuchea—performs auxiliary Party functions and serves as
an important source of recruits for the Party.

Party training concentrates heavily on political indoctrination and stresses strict discipline. It insists on punctuality, secrecy, and self-abnegation. It denounces the bureaucratism of past Khmer officialdom and teaches cadres to "study from the people in order to be like the people." On the other hand, Party cadres are admonished that they "should not let the people lead them by the nose either." Criticism meetings are conducted weekly. Cadres at all levels (as the wartime leaders did) must perform agricultural tasks, and life is Spartan. Cadres customarily wear simple black dress and must not seek food rations or comforts above those of the common people.[47] Despite the slogan that cadres must "serve the people," refugees give the picture of a small number of relatively young cadres of peasant background, most of them illiterate, whose orders are feared and obeyed and who live apart from the general population.

Doctrine

The Khmer leaders draw their fundamental doctrine from several sources. Important among them, even though they hid it from public view until late 1977, have been Marxism-Leninism and Maoism. Prerevolutionary Khmer society, they believe, was engaged in a class struggle between an oppressor class, "imperialist, feudal and capitalist," and an oppressed class, the workers and peasants. The worker-peasant class (comprising 95 percent of the Cambodian nation, according to the constitution's preamble, and made up of "workers, poor farmers, middle farmers, lower-level farmers and other laborers in the countryside and in the cities") has expelled the French colonialists and defeated the American imperialists and the Cambodians who served them—the feudal landlords, reactionary capitalists, and comprador bourgeoisie. The former oppressor class will be replaced by the worker-peasant class ("the people"), which is now in command.

Along with their Marxist ideology, the Khmer leaders, as mentioned earlier, are committed to a fundamentalist belief in independent national development. They revere national self-sufficiency and independence. "What we are trying to bring about has never occurred before," declared Ieng Sary. "We are not following any model, either Chinese or Vietnamese."[48] Though the Khmer leaders' obsession with self-reliance is difficult to understand, perhaps their seething anger against Western imperialism and culture has impelled them to rid their society of the corruption brought on by colonialists and to demonstrate their ability to go it alone.

An exploration of the Khmer communists' attitude toward the cities reveals their fundamental beliefs about how they must change their society. Before Pol Pot stated in October 1977 that the cities had been evacuated because of fear of subversion, Khmer leaders had explained that the cities had been emptied to get the people rapidly into food production in the countryside because of the critical shortage of food. Phnom Penh, with its population of 2–3 million, had been almost wholly dependent upon U.S. supplies by the end of the war, and the communist leadership knew the difficulty they would confront in feeding the entire nation without calling upon outside assistance, a measure abhorrent to their rigid doctrine of self-sufficiency. An unspoken corollary was their vision of the Cambodian cities, particularly Phnom Penh, as cesspools of the old society, filled with a decadent royal court, a corrupt aristocracy, rapacious feudal landlords and comprador bourgeoisie, and an exploiting foreign mercantile class (of Vietnamese and Chinese). This oppressor class had collaborated with the U.S. imperialists, who had unleashed a savage war of aggression against the Cambodian people. Thus, immediate evacuation of the unproductive, parasitical cities would eliminate potential centers of counterrevolution, as Pol Pot pointed out, and would also hasten destruction of the old society and prepare the way for the construction of a new one. Cities and towns would play a part in the new Khmer society, but, as Ieng Sary later affirmed for his cohorts, "we merely want to reduce them to human dimensions."[49]

In contrast to Vietnam and Laos, where there have been no accounts of systematic executions, in Cambodia there were numerous accounts of executions of "enemies" of the new society until sometime in 1976, when the killings apparently tapered off. Wartime pronouncements from FUNK stated that only "seven traitors" would be executed when the revolution was victorious, and Prince Sihanouk, who frequently joined in these pronouncements, urged them to flee. Although there were widespread reports of Khmer Rouge liquidation of their enemies in areas they had captured during the war, only a few in the most vulnerable circles appear to have sufficiently feared bloody retribution to flee at the end of the war.[50] But according to refugee accounts, designated categories of enemies were executed soon after power was seized. First, the top government and military officers were summarily shot. Then, it appears, came the turn of large numbers of the officer corps of the republican army and their wives, the old bureaucracy, the "comprador" bourgeoisie who had engaged in what was considered exploitative commerce, and the educated middle class.[51]

The social doctrine of the revolutionary leadership makes an assault on Cambodia's past. The hierarchical society that emerged with the arrival of the Hindu influence in the fourth century, reinforced by kingship, Buddhism, and folk belief, is a target for change.[52] The language is being purified to eliminate references to social rank and privilege in favor of egalitarian terms, and offenders are criticized severely. Buddhism has been displaced from its central role. The pagoda is no longer the communal center, and bonzes are often stigmatized with slogans that they are "parasites who eat the rice of the people."[53] The countryside is being reorganized into "production cooperatives." The traditional practices of lavish weddings, funerals, and festivals are condemned, and mobilization for production is the rallying cry. People must learn the primary value of labor. In short, the old society must be destroyed, and a new one, and a new type of person, must be created.

The Government

The present government in Cambodia emerged from a process that brought 1,115 representatives to FUNK's Third National Congress on December 14, 1975, to approve a new constitution, which provides the framework for a radical alteration of Cambodian institutions and society (see Figure 4.1).[54] In keeping with the cherished principle of self-sufficiency, Khieu Samphan emphasized that the constitution was "not the result of any research on foreign documents, nor [was] it the fruit of any research by scholars." Rather, it was the product of the workers, peasants, and Revolutionary Army. The constitution, promulgated on January 5, 1976, proclaims all "important means of production" to be the "collective property" of the state. One effect of this provision is

Figure 4.1
DEMOCRATIC CAMBODIA
GOVERNMENT STRUCTURE

People's Representative Assembly

250 members elected for 5-year term. Last election 20 March 1976. Meets at least once a year.

of People's Representative Assembly

Standing Committee

Chairman
Nuon Chea

First Vice Chairman
Nguon Kang

Second Vice Chairman
Peou Sou

Members
Kheng Sok   Ros Preap
Mat Ly   Sor Sean
Mey Chham   Thang Si
Ros Nim, Mrs.

State Presidium

Chairman
Khieu Samphan

First Vice Chairman
So Phim

Second Vice Chairman
Nhim Ros

Judicial Committee

Kang Chap

Administration

Prime
Minister

Pol Pot

Vice Prime Minister for Foreign Affairs
Ieng Sary

Vice Prime Minister for National Defense
Son Sen

Vice Prime Minister for Economic Affairs
Vorn Vet

Committees

Agriculture
Chey Suon

Commerce
Chhoeur Doeun
Van Rit

Communications
Mey Prang

Energy
unknown

Industry
Cheng An

Rubber Plantations
unknown

Ministries

Culture and Education
Yun Yat (Mrs. Son Sen)

Information and Propaganda
Hu Nim

Public Health
Thioun Thoeunn

Public Works
Toch Phoeun

Social Affairs
Ieng Thirith (Mrs. Ieng Sary)

to abolish accumulated wealth since—according to Khieu Samphan —the collectivized "important means of production" include "fields, orchards, farm lands, factories, trains, automobiles, ships and motor boats."[55] A new "national" culture will be established: it will be "national, popular, prosperous and clean," replacing the "corrupt, reactionary culture of various oppressive classes and that of colonialism and imperialism." Two pillars of previous regimes were abolished: Buddhism as the state religion, and the monarchy. The constitution provides that every Cambodian "has the right to hold a belief" and also "to have no beliefs," but "reactionary religion," an indirect attack on Buddhism, is "absolutely forbidden." For the machinery of government, the constitution provided a 250-member People's Representative Assembly (PRA) elected every five years, consisting of 150 peasants, 50 workers, and 50 members of the Revolutionary Army. This PRA, which is to meet only once a year, selects a permanent Standing Committee to carry out the legislative functions. It also selects the nation's judges and a three-member national presidium made up of a chairman and two deputy chairmen, who constitute a "collective leadership" that, in the words of Khieu Samphan (its first chairman), is "less prone to make mistakes."

Elections to the PRA were held in March 1976, and although official summaries stated that 98 percent of 3,635,581 eligible voters voted, most refugees say they did not have the opportunity to vote.[56] Some reported that officials said that they themselves had voted on behalf of the village or cooperative.[57] In early April 1976, the royal government (GRUNK) was dissolved, and the new government was appointed.[58]

On April 4, 1976, just before the promulgation of the new government, Prince Sihanouk announced his resignation and departure from public life. Responding to queries from reporters about the fate of the former prince, from whom there had been no public utterance in months, Ieng Sary, on a trip abroad in May 1977, stated:

> He is alive, living with his wife in the former royal palace. When he resigned, he asked permission to go abroad. We made it clear to him that this would serve neither the interests of the country nor his interests. Had he left, he would not be considered a patriot; he

would have become something like a Cambodian Bao Dai [the
Vietnamese emperor deposed in 1954].[59]

There was no public word from Sihanouk until January 3, 1978,
when a message he is said to have sent to the "esteemed and be-
loved KCP Central Committee" was broadcast on Phnom Penh
radio, a message expressing his "seething indignation at the unwarranted, massive and coordinated invasion" by the "aggressor Vietnam." He was quoted as saying that "we unite with the com-
patriots around the party and Government of Democratic Cambodia in fervently and fully supporting the historic statement
and the wise, correct attitude of the KCP, the People's Assembly
and the Government of Democratic Cambodia."[60] Thus, as the
Party leaders were attempting to mobilize popular support in the
conflict with Vietnam, it was clear that they still judged Prince
Sihanouk's endorsement to be useful.

Economic Prospects

Cambodia is currently running a dead heat with Laos for the
position of poorest country in Asia. Both states are estimated to
have a per capita GNP of $70. In Cambodia there are two times
as many people and slightly less arable land per capita (1.3 acres
in 1971) than in Laos, but there are no substantial mineral resources for development. The Cambodian literacy rate is estimated
at 55 percent (only 12 percent in Laos), and the country has ten
times as many miles of highways as Laos and two major seaports.
Its economic development under France consisted of French-
owned rubber plantations and some rice production for export.
Light industries for the processing of rice, fish, and wood products
and for textile production constituted the industrial sector. The
agricultural sector contributed twice as much to Cambodia's GNP
as the small industrial sector, and 85 percent of the population
lived in rural villages practicing traditional farming techniques.[61]

The onset of heavy fighting and aerial bombardment by the
United States after March 1970 eroded the economy even more.
Agricultural production had already begun to stagnate in 1963,
and well before the PAFNLK took Phnom Penh on April 17,
1975, a U.S. airlift of food was attempting to feed a badly swollen

city whose population was variously estimated at between 2 and 3 million people (up from 0.6 million in 1969). By 1971, exports had almost completely halted, with rice production failing even to reach the Cambodian cities. By mid-1972, according to U.S. sources, the small industrial sector was operating at only half its prewar capacity, and the country's two railroad lines—to the north and to the coast from Phnom Penh—had been closed. Heavy U.S. bombing, especially from January until August 15, 1973, damaged and destroyed much of the communications system of the country. (Foreign Minister Ieng Sary told the UN General Assembly in October 1976 that it had been 60–80 percent destroyed or damaged.)[62] As early as 1971, four years before the end of the fighting, the Cambodian government estimated that more than 2 million persons (approximately a quarter of the population) had already been displaced by the war.[63]

With its foreign exchange earnings dropping to virtually zero by October 1971, Cambodia became the beneficiary of an Exchange Support Fund organized by the International Monetary Fund with an initial $35 million capitalization, to supplement bilateral foreign aid. During the last five years of the war, the United States provided $503 million in aid, plus $1.8 billion in military matériel and training.[64] The Khmer Rouge's takeover of Phnom Penh abruptly terminated not only the airlift of food, but also all other U.S. aid. Then followed an embargo on private trade by Americans with Cambodia and the bombing of the country's one oil refinery during the *Mayaguez* incident. In mid-June 1975 an intelligence memorandum from the White House was given to the press by an unattributed source (supposedly National Security Advisor Kissinger) with an estimate that "one million people are expected to die from hunger and exposure" because of inadequate food stocks. A State Department spokesman later tailored this estimate by saying that "many thousands face the threat of starvation."[65]

Thus, when the fighting ended, the country was shattered by the dislocations and destruction resulting from brutal revolutionary offensives and aerial bombardments. The communists, by their own account, suddenly took control over "almost four million newly liberated people from Phnom Penh and other provincial capitals."[66]

In three years since the end of the fighting in Cambodia, the Angka's historically unprecedented national action has taken a calamitous toll in human life. But it has restored national self-sufficiency in rice at a precariously low level of consumption, and it has resumed export trade in a few products. Despite the desperate needs at the end of the war, no outside assistance was sought or received from international organizations. The economy has been devoted overwhelmingly to "cooperative agriculture," and previously existing light industries serving the agricultural sector have been gradually restored to production. Relentless heavy labor has been organized during the dry season to attack the problem of water conservation through the construction of dikes, canals, reservoirs, and irrigation ditches. Dry season rice cultivation has been encouraged, along with the introduction of "strategic crops" that can be exported. This astounding national economic campaign has been maintained at "great leap forward" speed through intense labor, which has often continued both night and day. At the same time the leaders take pride that there has been "not a cent spent on fertilizer" since conservation of natural manure has become a national goal.[67] They have operated the economy without the use of money, private property, or mass circulation newspapers. As for education, such elementary schooling as exists is an adjunct to the agricultural cooperative and emphasizes practical knowledge. No higher education exists except in the field of medicine.[68]

The Cambodian leadership claims that it has no previous models to follow but that it is learning through experience. Its system of agricultural cooperatives began in the "liberated zones" in 1973 and has been extended throughout the entire country. The cooperatives vary in size from 50 to 2,000 families. During the dry season, brigades of workers are mobilized at various water conservation projects. The people have been "pooling their strength . . . to dig canals and reservoirs in the most seething manner, thus turning [the] countryside everywhere into work sites permanently pervaded by a festive atmosphere."[69] This enormous human labor, coming on top of what the leaders have called the "untold hardships" of the immediate postwar period, has been planned in the absence of machines. As Khieu Samphan has put it, "No, we have no machines. We do everything by mainly relying on the strength of our people. We work completely self-reliantly. This shows the overwhelming heroism of our people. This also shows the great force of our people. Though barehanded, they can do everything."[70]

Cambodia has accepted only the most meager foreign assistance since the war. A few hundred Chinese technicians have helped restore some industry and communications—the PRC was for a time the only country whose aid Cambodia accepted. Additional economic assistance is now being received from North Korea, Yugoslavia, and Romania.[71] Foreign Minister Ieng Sary told the UN General Assembly in October 1976 that his country's devotion to the principles of independence and self-reliance did "not mean living in isolation from international cooperation and refusing all foreign aid," but it did mean that economic construction efforts "must necessarily and primarily depend on the great, inexhaustible and productive strength of the people and on all of the useful resources of the nation" and that foreign aid must be "unconditional."[72]

Obviously, the productive strength of the people of Cambodia *is* exhaustible. Malaria and other diseases must have ravaged an overworked, frightened, and undernourished population during the first years after the war. Both Pol Pot and Ieng Sary said in 1976 that 80 percent of the peasants had malaria. Prime Minister Khieu Samphan, however, proudly claimed in April 1977 that malaria had been reduced by 80 percent. (The seriousness of the problem can be noted in the fact that $1.6 million worth of DDT was purchased from U.S. companies licensed by the U.S. government for shipment to Cambodia, in the only exception to the U.S. embargo.)[73] So far as nourishment is concerned, Khieu Samphan's proud claims strike a grim note by Western standards:

> a sufficient amount of 3, 2½ or 2 small cans [of rice] is allocated daily. Moreover, there is dessert. In the past, how many times did the poor or middle peasants eat sweet foods per month? Very rarely. They could afford only green guava and other fruits. Now on the average they eat dessert three times per month, which is sufficient to take care of their health and increase their weight.[74]

This incredible Spartan work camp of a nation is nonetheless reaching the point at which it will have some products to export and some imports it can purchase. As rice production has advanced sufficiently to feed the people at a subsistence level, new drives have been started to develop self-sufficiency in cotton and in "strategic crops for export" (jute, kapok, coconut, tobacco, medicinal plants). Two years after the end of the war, Cambodian sources reported that 200,000 inhabitants in Phnom Penh and 50,000 in Kompong Som were working in textile mills, food-producing plants, and factories producing economic supplies such as cement, gunnysacks, pharmaceuticals, and locomotive repairs.[75] In a trip to several South and Southeast Asian countries in April 1977, Foreign Minister Ieng Sary announced that Cambodia had 100,000 tons of rice for export, as well as rubber (probably 20,000 tons).[76] Previously the Cambodians had engaged in trade through Hong Kong, using Chinese credit and middlemen.[77] In March 1977 a major agreement was made with Japan for the shipment of rolled steel to Cambodia, with an expectation of future deliveries of machine tools and chemical materials. Cambodia planned to finance the purchase through the sale of rice, lumber, rubber, and shrimp.[78] This marks a major addition to Cambodia's tiny list of trading partners: Thailand, the PRC, and Pakistan.

Will the gradual opening up of trade relations prompt the leadership to expand its international political contact beyond the UN General Assembly and the Conference of Non-Aligned Powers? Cambodia spurns the Mekong Development Committee, notwithstanding the readiness of Laos and Vietnam to participate with Thailand in this mutually beneficial enterprise. Even though all three Indochinese countries have chosen to emphasize agriculture as the base for development (and to transfer wartime refugees from the cities to the countryside), the Cambodian approach has been unparalleled in its ruthless pace and total application. Unlike Laos, Cambodia has not temporized over collectivization. Unlike Laos and Vietnam, it has not attempted to salvage former enemies through "reeducation." Rather, it has applied a brand of agrarian totalitarianism and a subsistence communalism dictated by a recently unveiled communist party in a terrifying national pursuit of economic independence. The Spartan simplicity of their revolutionary slogans expresses the constricted economic prospect that the leadership has offered the Cambodian people: "If we have rice, we have everything. . . . Everything should serve rice production."[79]

The Suffering of the Cambodian People

A monumental tragedy has been under way in Cambodia since the start of the war in 1970. Though last to join the Indochina war, the Cambodians suffered a dislocation and devastation that soon rivaled, perhaps surpassed, that of their Lao neighbors (who had been enmeshed in the war since 1964) and the Vietnamese (who had resumed fighting in 1960). The enormous U.S. bombing and the intensity of the fighting extracted a heavy toll in lives. The wartime population loss as a result of military service or as a result of bombing, terroristic attacks, displacement, disease, and malnutrition has been estimated at 600,000 persons by the revolutionary side.[80] As for deaths in the postwar period, outsiders have not had access to Cambodia, and it is impossible to calculate with confidence the numbers who perished in the evacuation from the cities and in the subsequent transplantation of population or who perished from disease, starvation, and execution. It may nonetheless be instructive to record some of the published guesses about the death toll in Cambodia, even though they vary considerably and even though all suffer from the inability of independent observers to gain direct access to Cambodia.

François Ponchaud has written that "at the end of the year 1975, unofficial diplomatic sources put forth the figure of 800,000 deaths, those from the American Embassy 1,200,000, and those from welfare agencies installed in Bangkok 1,400,000!"[81] The authors of a recent book on Cambodia estimate that "at a minimum, 1.2 million men, women and children died in Cambodia between April 17, 1975, and December 1976."[82] *Time Magazine* estimates that 500,000 to 600,000, or one-twelfth of Cambodia's population, perished during the first year of the communist takeover.[83] Two correspondents of the *London Daily Telegraph*, reporting from Bangkok, give a figure of 800,000 deaths in the first year of communist rule.[84] In testimony before a House of Representatives subcommittee investigating human rights in Cambodia, Assistant Secretary of State Richard Holbrooke gave a cautious assessment that pointed out the lack of precise information: "Journalists and scholars, some testifying before this subcommittee, guess that between half a million and 1.2 million have died since 1975. We have no way to confirm a precise figure but the number of deaths appears to be in the tens if not hundreds of thousands."[85] Robert Shaplen, Southeast Asian correspondent for *The New Yorker,* has reported that "most observers, including diplomats, now believe the total is at least a million" who have been killed or who have starved or died of disease as a result of the forced marches, including 200,000 executed.[86]

An interview with Khieu Samphan, given at the Colombo Conference in Sri Lanka in 1976 and published in the Italian magazine *Familia Christiana,* raised press speculation as to whether Khieu Samphan was acknowledging the high rate of deaths. According to this account, Khieu Samphan stated that more than a million had died in the five years of warfare. When asked the present population of Cambodia, he replied, "five million," and in answer to a question asking the prewar population, replied, "seven million." "If one million persons died in the fighting," the interviewer then asked, "what happened to the remaining million?" Khieu Samphan's published answer was, "It's incredible how concerned you Westerners are about war criminals. In any case, if you want to make a mathematical calculation, count those Cambodians who went to live in Thailand, France, the United States and in other countries."[87] It seems unlikely that Khieu Samphan would deliberately acknowledge, even if true, losses that would imply such a deadly toll under the new regime. (U.S. government sources estimated the population at over 7 million in 1972, making a reduction to 5 million by 1976 hard to believe.) More likely, he spoke mistakenly, was not translated correctly, or was responding to an earlier question about treatment of war criminals.

An interview given by Ieng Sary on May 23, 1977, seems to reinforce this. Sary stated that according to a recent census, Cambodia had 7.76 million inhabitants. He denied that there has been an extraordinary death toll since victory, claiming "some 2,000 to 3,000 people died during the evacuation of the capital and as many again during the initial period in the paddies."[88] He refuted the charges that the new regime has massacred thousands, stating "only top criminals were sent to the Angka for trial."[89]

No fair-minded person can deny the enormous suffering of the Cambodian people both during and after the war. How many persons have died from various causes since the taking of Phnom Penh, however, will remain shrouded and subject to broad speculation.

Assessment of the Khmer Communist Methods

How can one explain the harsh imposition of work camp conditions upon an entire nation by a small group of revolutionary leaders? One obvious reason for their choice of Draconian methods is that the Khmer communists are in a hurry to make their revolution. They must feel that they need to eliminate swiftly the vestiges of the old society as they begin building a new one. As noted earlier, the Khmer rulers are rigid ideologues with a dogmatic commitment to their homegrown doctrine of self-sufficiency, they are defiant of the rest of the world, and they are single-mindedly determined to move their own nation toward their own goals. The exclusion of almost all foreign assistance (except Chinese), in view of the war's vast destruction, was bound to inflict great misery upon the Cambodian people, who were forced to substitute both a prodigious work effort and reduced consumption for the former foreign food and vital supplies. In addition, the Khmer communist organization is small in membership. Beginning with a small framework in the 1950s, the revolutionary organization grew modestly during the 1960s. Only during wartime, in the early 1970s, did it expand rapidly, largely with young, illiterate peasant boys and a few girls. By war's end, as already noted, there may have been a military force of 70,000 and only 1,000 cadres. Thus the Khmer communists did not undergo the gradual organizational growth of the Vietnamese or even of the Lao. Their plan to remold an entire society with this inexperienced organization reinforced a tendency to rely upon fear.

What role can one attribute to the elusive concept of "national character," which, as G. K. Chesterson said, is as "undefinable as a smell but as unmistakable?" In prewar years, Cambodians were widely regarded in the West as a sweet, peaceful, gentle folk, "bons enfants," living simply in an abundant Garden of Eden, practicing an otherworldly Theravada Buddhism. The wartime and postwar horrors have challenged this image and forced a reexamination of this stereotype. The horrible cruelties the Lon Nol regime inflicted upon its enemies indicate that excesses were not confined to the communist side. The massacre in 1970 of thousands of Vietnamese residents of Cambodia—either directed by the republican military forces or tolerated by them—was additional evidence of unbridled malevolence among Cambodians under non-communist leadership. These events raised the question whether Cambodian culture has a streak of aggressiveness that might be unleashed by wartime stress.

The Khmer national past contains periods of aggressive ter-ritorial expansion, especially from the ninth to the fourteenth century, when the Angkor Empire extended from the South China Sea (across the territory of southern Vietnam) to eastern Thailand. The Khmer were successively defeated by their Vietnamese and Thai neighbors from the fourteenth to the nineteenth century, and by the French in the late nineteenth century, defeats that one student of Khmer society attributes more to the negligence of its military leaders and to palace intrigue than to a diminishing spirit of the Khmer people.[90] Cambodian folklore is filled with accounts of grisly executions and mutilations of enemies.[91] In Southeast Asia, Cambodia has a reputation for vigorous soldiers. During the first Indochina war, French officers found the Cambodian soldiers the toughest of the Indochinese.[92] The U.S. military who trained Khmer Krom (ethnic Khmer born in South Vietnam) to fight against the communists in Cambodia reported a streak of ferocity in many of their recruits. Although the Buddhism of the Cam-bodians preaches kindness, serenity, and pity for the unfortunate, the Cambodian mentality sees the notion of pardon, according to one author, as a sign of weakness, even an avowal of fault. Pardon risks a "loss of face." Indeed, the enemy is more likely to be regarded as evil—to recognize virtue in him makes one his accomplice.[93]

Of course, it may be facile to pounce upon cultural traits or "national character" to simplify complex issues ex post facto—twelve years of the Hitler regime produced a contemporary stereo-type of the German as Nazi. Nevertheless, cultural traits have a bearing upon behavior, and the foregoing observations may be important in explaining the Khmer communist methods.

Another important factor is the deep-seated anger of the Khmer Rouge leaders as well as their lower-level cadres. When they were students, they blamed the Cambodian elite for becom-ing instruments of the imperialists to exploit the Cambodian people and degrade Cambodian society. Their anger became rage

during their days in the maquis, as they saw their country deci-
mated, as they struggled under great danger with short rations.
Some reports suggest that the leadership hardened its ideology and
rid itself of wavering factions during 1973, the period of maxi-
mum U.S. bombardment, and 1974.[94] Upon victory, the Khmer
Rouge released their virulence against their adversaries—one Khmer
Rouge cadre told a refugee they felt "uncontrollable hatred."[95]
It was in this mood that the early executions of Lon Nol officials
took place and the harsh evacuations were carried out.

Foreign Policy

In foreign policy, despite its communist orientation, Cambodia places itself squarely among the nonaligned Third World
Nations.[96] Foreign Secretary Ieng Sary, in his speech to the UN
General Assembly on October 15, 1976, proclaimed that Cambodia
will "show active solidarity with an unwavering support for all
movements of people's struggle for independence, freedom, democracy and social progress and against imperialism, colonialism,
neo-colonialism, racism, Zionism and all the forms of foreign
exploitation and domination."[97] He further asserted a host of
Third World–oriented positions.

After a period of self-imposed, almost total isolation in the
immediate months following the victory, in 1976 the Cambodian
leaders began to expand their diplomatic relations and to invite
selected visitors. By the year's end, nine countries had permanent
representation in Phnom Penh. In the spring of 1976, diplomatic
relations were established with Malaysia, Peru, Philippines, Burma,
Mexico, Nigeria, Ivory Coast, and Singapore, and later in the year
with Greece, Japan, the United Kingdom, Finland, and Austria.
During 1977, a Cambodian diplomatic delegation visited several
Asian countries, to whom it proclaimed its interest in establishing
relations, searched for trading partners for its limited products,
and declared itself ready to receive small amounts of unconditional
aid from friendly sources.[98] In November Cambodia accepted a
visit from Burma's Ne Win, the first chief of state to see the new
Kampuchea. The Malaysian foreign minister's December visit
provided further indications that Cambodia was cautiously opening to the world, both to find markets and to find support in its

fierce border conflict with Vietnam.

Relations between Cambodia and Thailand have fluctuated since April 1975. The Khmer revolutionaries mistrust the "feudal," monarchist regime of Thailand, their historic adversary who was allied with the Americans against them in the Indochina war. Similarly, the conservative Thai establishment, including the short-lived democratic governments of Kukrit and Seni Pramot, were appalled by the new radical communist regime on their border. Nevertheless, the Khmer leaders have an interest in stable relations with Thailand to offset the potentially strong Vietnamese influence in the region. The Thais, on their side, see the utility of peaceable relations with their neighbor. Following assiduous Thai efforts to show goodwill in 1975, relations improved, symbolized by the resumption of border trade and the establishment of liaison offices on the frontier. This was jeopardized by sporadic incidents—alleged violation of Cambodian waters by Thai fishermen and armed clashes between local frontier units. In June 1976, nevertheless, the foreign minister of the new Seni Pramot government traveled to Sisophan in Cambodia to discuss establishment of diplomatic missions. Further incidents again delayed improvement, and in October 1976, the accession to power of a new, rigidly anticommunist military government in Thailand added new strains to Cambodian-Thai relations.

Renewed border clashes took place in 1977. One Khmer attack on a Thai village killed thirty villagers, and another in August killed twenty-nine Thai soldiers and an unknown number of Khmer. These clashes resulted in part from the disagreement of both sides over the border demarcation and perhaps in part from the Khmer military's punitive raids in retaliation for being cheated by Thai smugglers with unfulfilled deliveries of scarce supplies or for adulterated medicine and watered gasoline. The Khmer military were also angry about the Cambodian refugees who infiltrate into their country from Thailand and who join in the low-level resistance that has continued in Cambodia since the communist victory. The Khmer military believe the Thai authorities supplied and encouraged these infiltrators, although the Thai government has denied any involvement. There are reports of from 300 to 700 Khmer Serai ("Free Cambodia") guerrillas, an anti-communist group trained and supplied by the CIA during the war, in a Thai refugee camp near the disputed border area. According to accounts by journalists who have interviewed refugees from the sensitive area, the Khmer military have depopulated a region along the frontier, attempting to establish a *cordon sanitaire,* a no-man's-land reinforced by military emplacements to prevent the flight of refugees and the infiltration of guerrillas. According to speculation coming from Thailand, "revolts and purges within the ranks of the army and the party" in Cambodia had created an "acute sense of vulnerability to invasion," with the dominant Khmer communist group fearing that the seditious faction in the army and Party would link up with outside forces. Simultaneous reports of tensions on the Cambodian-Vietnamese frontier have reinforced this speculation.[99] The new government of General Kriangsak Chamanand, which ousted the intensely anticommunist regime of Prime Minister Thanin Kravichien in October 1977, initiated an active search for détente with Cambodia. Negotiations to resolve the border dispute were renewed, including a four-day goodwill mission to Phnom Penh by the Thai foreign minister in February 1978. The two sides promised to continue their efforts to normalize diplomatic relations and to expand trade and economic cooperation. Despite these statements of friendly intentions from both capitals, border clashes continued throughout the early months of 1978. With more than 30 million inhabitants, Thailand is presumably stronger than its Cambodian neighbor, but a serious military attack by Thailand on Cambodia, in view of the complex involvement of other powers, would be a risky undertaking for Thailand and add tensions to the region.

Cambodia does not have diplomatic relations with the Soviet Union or its East European allies. The Soviet Union maintained diplomatic relations with the Lon Nol government until its end, a fact that clearly did not please the Khmer communist leadership; and Soviet diplomats remaining in Phnom Penh in April 1975 were forced to take refuge in the French embassy, leaving unceremoniously with the Western diplomatic corps. A more polite, if not friendly, attitude toward the Soviet Union was indicated by the Khmer publication of a Soviet message of congratulation on the first anniversary of victory, April 17, 1976, along with messages from other East European communist nations. A previous public mention of the USSR was in August 1975, when Cambodia condemned "hegemonism" at the Lima conference of nonaligned nations.

The PRC has been the closest friend of the new Democratic Kampuchea. The only outside assistance the Khmer authorities accepted in the first year after the victory came from China, and Chinese diplomats, journalists, and photographers have been permitted to travel within Cambodia. On appropriate diplomatic occasions, Cambodian officials express appreciation for Chinese support during the revolutionary struggle (which the Soviets did not provide) and characterize the Sino-Khmer relationship as one of "militant solidarity and revolutionary fraternal friendship."[100]

This close relationship was dramatized in September 1977 by an official visit to the PRC by a delegation of Cambodia's top leaders, including Pol Pot, Ieng Sary, Vorn Vet, Son Sen, and Nuon Chea. Present at the airport to meet them were China's preeminent leaders, including Hua Kuo-feng and Teng Hsiao-p'ing; according to Chinese news releases, 100,000 people gathered in Tien An Men Square to give the Cambodian delegation a warm welcome. Chinese broadcasts proclaimed that the Cambodians and Chinese were "fighting shoulder to shoulder in the struggle against imperialism, revisionism and hegemonism," an indication that the Chinese regard Cambodia as firmly in the Chinese camp in the Sino-Soviet dispute. At a banquet honoring the Cambodian delegation, Chairman Hua Kuo-feng publicly endorsed the Cambodian revolution by noting that the Cambodians "are not only good at destroying the old world but also good at building a new one."[101] In his speech at this banquet, Pol Pot was effusive in his praise of the wisdom of Mao Tse-tung, proclaiming that "we have creatively and successfully applied Mao Tse-tung thought, from the time we had only empty hands. . . . Our people and the revolutionary people of the world deeply believe that Mao Tse-tung thought is always efficacious, sharp and victorious."[102]

Owing, in part, to Chinese encouragement, the Cambodian leaders believed it would now be useful to ameliorate Cambodia's image of brutality in much of the world press. During his China visit, Pol Pot met with foreign journalists and extolled the achievements of the new regime. In view of the rising tensions and rapidly deteriorating relations with the Vietnamese, it was especially important to reinforce Chinese support for Cambodia. Moreover,

Cambodia was beginning to make efforts to develop markets in international trade and to expand its diplomatic contacts, both for purposes of commerce and to insure its access abroad to counter any initiatives the Vietnamese might take with other Southeast Asian nations. The Khmer communists undoubtedly see their friendship with the Chinese as a useful protection against potential Vietnamese and Thai threats to their independence. The Chinese, disturbed by the significant Soviet role in Vietnam and Laos, achieve some counterbalance to Soviet influence in Indochina when Cambodia plays a more active role.

Second only to China as an important ally is North Korea, with which Cambodia maintains cordial relations. Following their visit to the PRC, Pol Pot's delegation stopped in Pyongyang for an official goodwill visit, beginning on October 4. Pol Pot thanked the North Koreans for material and political support during their revolution, and he and President Kim Il-sung exchanged expressions of fraternal solidarity.[103]

As discussed in Chapter 2, the tensions between Cambodia and Vietnam have erupted into armed conflict on the frontier. The severe fighting in December 1977 and January 1978 tapered off into local clashes during February and March. It was not clear why the Cambodian leadership persisted in their refusal to meet with the Vietnamese for a discussion of a settlement. Cambodian spokesmen continued to denounce the Vietnamese in vituperative terms, terms formerly reserved only for the U.S. "imperialists." Although the Cambodian leaders were seemingly dissatisfied with the delineation of certain border areas, they did not make public their specific claims. They made frequent allusions to the "expansionist and annexationist" designs of the Vietnamese and suggested in their denunciations that the Vietnamese had been attempting to subvert the Cambodian revolution. The Vietnamese, in response, charged that the Cambodian leaders were raising the false issue of Vietnamese aggression in order to cover up their crimes against their own people. In view of the lack of access to Cambodia by journalists or other independent observers, it has been impossible to pursue the details of these charges and assess their weight. It is clear that Cambodian resentment of the Vietnamese has deep historic roots, and even if their differences are patched up, serious tensions will inevitably remain.

U.S.-Cambodian Relations

The Cambodians harbor a suspicion and hostility toward the United States that is unmatched either by their fellow Vietnamese or Lao revolutionaries. Their public pronouncements continue to hail their victory over "the U.S. imperialists and their stooges, the Lon Nol clique." The U.S. attacks during the *Mayaguez* incident confirmed their belief in the continuing, implacable hostility of the U.S. imperialists to the Cambodian revolution.

Unlike the Vietnamese and the Lao, who insist that the United States recognize its obligation to provide funds to "heal the wounds of war," the Cambodians have made no mention of such a payment. Representatives of the Select Committee on Missing Persons in Asia tried to contact the Cambodian government in 1975–1976 but were met by total rebuffs.[104] Cambodian authorities in Paris, Peking, and Hanoi refused even to acknowledge phone calls or mail from the U.S. representatives. In response to a request presented by the U.S. Liaison Office in Peking for members of the Woodcock Commission to meet somewhere with Cambodian authorities, a Phnom Penh press communiqué in March 1977 issued a flat refusal and noted, "The scars of the U.S. imperialist war of aggression are everywhere in Cambodia. The national and class anger of the Cambodian people against the United States imperialists and their running dogs of all stripes is still boiling."[105]

Thus, it appears there is no likelihood of normalization of relations with Cambodia in the near future.

5
Indochina and the United States: Problems and Prospects

As our account has shown, developments within Indochina since the communist victories have been rapid and far-reaching. The aim of this chapter is to draw some conclusions about the nature of revolutions in Indochina and to review the important internal political and economic developments and the foreign policy orientations of the Indochina states. We shall then assess current U.S. interests within the Indochina region and examine the major issues confronting U.S. policymakers as they forge new relations with the governments of Indochina.

An Assessment of the Revolutions in Indochina

Like the French, Russian, and Chinese revolutions, the revolutions of Indochina can be called "great," "grand," or "social revolutions." This type of revolution brings "rapid, fundamental and violent domestic change in the dominant values and myths of a society, in its political institutions, social structure, leadership and government activity and policies."[1] Unlike coups d'etat, rebellions, and insurrections, which produce relatively minor, often transitory, change *within* regimes, full-scale revolutions produce changes *of* regime, involving the destruction of the old society and the construction of a new one. The process of change is painful, particularly for those who were in the upper echelons of the old society, since there is characteristically a purge of the old order and repression of those groups perceived as threatening to the new one. New institutions are created, a new value system is propagated, and, in the modern socialist revolutions, a great

157

effort is made to create a new, socialist individual.

Although all of the Indochina countries have followed this pattern of revolution, each regime has differed in its pace, method, and style. In all three, the new leaders took steps to neutralize or eliminate the leading elements of the old "decadent, bourgeois" society. In Vietnam and Laos, members of the former enemy officer corps, the upper echelons of the civil service, bourgeois intellectuals, and professionals have been incarcerated in reeducation camps. There has been no evidence of systematic executions of former enemies in Vietnam or Laos. In Cambodia, by contrast, thousands of former military officers, civil servants, and middle-class intellectuals and professionals have been executed, according to credible refugee accounts, and few have been committed to reeducation camps. A new revolutionary ideology has been celebrated in all three countries. In Vietnam and Laos, it has been openly labeled as Marxist-Leninist, but in Cambodia, the Marxist-Leninist label was hidden until the fall of 1977, when the "communist" identity of Angka was first publicly revealed to the Cambodian people.[2] The communist party in each country is now the dominant political instrument, and communist-led mass organizations are the principal means for mobilizing popular participation in the tasks defined by the new order.

Although phases of revolution are not immutable, and significant differences appear between countries, there do appear to be common patterns.[3] The consolidation of control following the seizure of power—the current phase in all three Indochina countries—has characteristically been a difficult period, during which radical political and social changes are first implemented and purges are conducted. However, forces emerge that tend to wind down revolutions, and in the Indochina states, it is reasonable to expect that there will be a period of relaxation and perhaps the creation of a new equilibrium.

It must be recognized that the Indochina revolutions are conclusive and irreversible. Even though sectors of unorganized opposition and even pockets of active armed resistance remain in all three countries, the new regimes are there to stay. The leadership of Vietnam and Laos is cohesive and stable. Although we know much less about Cambodia and the reports of leadership factions are more difficult to assess, there seems little likelihood of any changes in the communist nature of the revolutionary regime. All the Indochina states have developed political and administrative institutions that enable them to maintain effective control within their countries. Their battle-hardened wartime armies have been kept intact, giving powerful military strength to the incumbent regimes.

The armed anticommunist resistance fighters who have challenged the authorities of all three countries appear destined to be crushed. In Vietnam, the dissidents, drawn especially from the highland minorities, from the Hoa Hao religious sect, and from former Saigon army elements, have harassed the government and diverted military and bureaucratic resources, but they seem to be under SRV control. The armed dissidents in Laos are a more serious threat. Recruited especially from Meo and other highland groups who were members of CIA-supported anticommunist military units, as well as from former Royal Army elements and newly disaffected peasants, the guerrillas appear to get low-level assistance in arms, ammunition, and supplies from local Thai military commanders in some regions. They are reinforced by Laotian refugees in camps in Thailand, from where they gain easy access to Laos across the 1,000-mile Mekong River border. The new Lao regime, whose military and administrative capability is limited—far below that of the SRV—is under stress from these resistance activities and has apparently relied upon the help of Vietnamese military units to contain the guerrillas. If guerrilla activities became a serious threat to the Lao regime, Vietnamese reinforcements would probably be brought in to meet the challenge, thereby increasing Lao dependence upon their Vietnamese allies. The scattered armed bands that operate within Cambodia against enormous obstacles also draw a small number of recruits from refugee camps in Thailand. The Angka has created a no-man's-land along the border—at least five kilometers wide—which is sown with land mines and patrolled by soldiers to prevent guerrillas from entering and to curb refugees from fleeing to Thailand. It has severely restricted travel within Cambodia, requiring a pass from local authorities to travel from village to village. At the agricultural communes into which the countryside has been organized, meals are provided from central kitchens, making both the acquisition of food for resistance fighters and escape to Thailand more difficult. Thus, even though the harsh measures of the new regime may breed repugnance, the prospects are slim that the resistance fighters can mount a serious threat.

Indochinese exile groups abroad will continue to entertain hopes, and collect funds, for the overthrow of the communist regimes, as the Russian, East European, and Chinese exile groups did in earlier years. The armed resistance that may continue, however, though bold and courageous, will risk death or captivity for those involved and will probably bring only an increase in repression against suspected supporters. A more serious challenge to the authorities may be a generalized despondence or recalcitrance among the population, which would hamper the regime's efforts to mobilize mass support for its goal of a great economic leap forward.

External threats to the Indochina regimes also appear unlikely. Despite an obsession, apparent in their rhetoric, that the United States continues to foment subversion against them, there is no evidence of U.S. support for hostile military activity against these states. Thailand is also perceived as a threat by Laos and Cambodia. The Indochina refugee camps, particularly since some guerrillas are recruited there, are seen as a provocation, and the armed clashes between the Thais and their Lao and Cambodian neighbors indicate the serious level of tension. Indeed, there is a constant danger that such incidents may flare up into sustained military engagements. However, there are serious limitations upon Thailand's inclination to initiate hostilities against its two communist neighbors, even though it is considerably stronger than either. Thailand's communist insurgencies in the northeast, north, and south make it especially vulnerable to outside interference; Vietnam, China, or the Soviet Union could exploit this vulnerability through aid or even direct intervention. Thus, although the Thai governments have had ideological differences, superimposed upon a history of conflict with their communist neighbors, they also have substantial reasons to search for a peaceful accommodation.

The more serious potential threat to the independence of Laos and Cambodia appears to come from Vietnam. In early 1977 Vietnam probably preferred to live amicably with its neighbors and devote its energies to its own internal socialist trans-

formation and development. The outbreak of severe border warfare with Cambodia in the autumn of 1977, however, has upset
this pattern and posed questions about the continuing viability
of Cambodia and the possibility of Chinese or Soviet intervention
in the dispute. There seems to be no real alternative to communism in Indochina, but national independence or alignment
may still be in flux.

Economic Problems and Prospects

Economically, the Indochina states are weak. Each has embarked upon development efforts that, although they differ in
method, have fundamental similarities. Even before the Indochina
war, the Indochina states ranked in the lowest third of Southeast
Asian nations in economic development. Although certain economic activities of South Vietnam and Laos spurted during the
war with the help of U.S. assistance, the overall impact of the war
was great devastation and dislocation, and relatively little permanent development. Millions were uprooted, leaving monumental
problems of resettlement. Bombing caused havoc and vast destruction throughout Indochina. Many light industrial plants and much
equipment in North Vietnam was damaged, and large segments of
the transportation and communications infrastructure were
destroyed. In South Vietnam, shrapnel and the widespread use of
defoliant and herbicide spray caused significant injury to the
countryside and forests. The end of the war, the decline in foreign
assistance, and the creation of a new economic order have generated
high unemployment in South Vietnam. Managerial skills are
pitifully low in Laos and Cambodia and inadequate in Vietnam.
These basic problems have been compounded by a severe drought
throughout the region in 1977, followed by typhoons in Vietnam,
causing critical food deficits in Vietnam and Laos.

The Indochina states have embarked upon ambitious drives
for economic growth, each placing primary emphasis on agricultural development, with the industrial sector serving and growing
out of it. Although all are constructing a socialist order, the
three development strategies are not constrained by either the
Soviet or the Chinese model. In their economically advisable
emphasis upon agriculture, both Vietnam and Cambodia have

sought to reduce their bloated urban population and increase the number tilling the land. Cambodia's method was a ruthless, almost total, evacuation of the cities, with only a restricted number permitted to return by 1978. Vietnam has transferred the city population more gradually, with the creation of New Economic Zones to be populated through a combination of persuasion and coercion.

Economists from outside banks and international agencies consider Vietnam's development plans to be realistic, and such observers are encouraging about the prospects for long-term economic growth. Laos starts from a far lower economic base, with a paucity of organizational and managerial competence, and its development will be, at best, very slow. Cambodia, because of its tightly closed society and communal productive system, remains an economic enigma. At a monumental human cost, the Cambodian leaders have acquired a small rice surplus for export. Cambodia's limited entry into the international economy since 1977 may shed greater light upon its prospects for sustained economic growth.

Foreign Policy

The Indochina communist regimes came to power in close succession, indicating how intertwined had been the three revolutions. Yet their foreign policies show sharp differences. Vietnam and Laos have been open and active in their foreign relations, assiduously seeking support for their economic development plans, not only from their friends in the socialist world, but also from Western industrialized nations and from international agencies. Cambodia, on the other hand, has been almost completely closed to the outside world during the first two years of the new order. Zealously following its doctrine of self-sufficiency and independence, it spurned all foreign assistance, except for small amounts of aid from the PRC, until 1977, when it began to accept limited help from other countries.

In relations with the Sino-Soviet powers, Cambodia has aligned its foreign policy with the PRC and has regarded the Soviet Union and its East European allies with suspicion. Vietnam and Laos, in contrast, have steered a neutral course in the Sino-Soviet conflict, although tilting toward the Soviet Union.

None of the three can be described as a "satellite" or a "puppet" of either the Soviet Union or China.

The first priority of the new leaders of the Indochina states is clearly the consolidation of their control and the economic development of their countries. They have not invested their energies in the spread of revolution abroad. Despite the great world prestige gained by the Vietnamese for their remarkable success in revolution, and despite the fact that Vietnamese spokesmen sometimes proclaim that their revolution will serve as an inspiration and example to oppressed people fighting for their own national liberation, the Vietnamese have not taken an active role in fomenting such movements. The enormous stock of U.S. arms acquired by the SRV in South Vietnam has not been routed to the communist insurgents in Thailand in any significant increase of support nor to other insurgencies in Southeast Asia.

The Indochina countries have generally had amicable relations with their ASEAN neighbors in Southeast Asia. Except for alternating hostility and accommodation vis-à-vis Thailand, they have achieved correct state-to-state relations. However, the Indochina states have regarded the ASEAN organization with suspicion, charging that it is a tool of U.S. intervention in the region. Although the ASEAN countries, particularly Thailand, have felt a sense of relief that Vietnam has not stepped up its support to Southeast Asian insurgencies, they still feel apprehensive on this score. Furthermore, they feel uneasy about the prospects that Vietnam's development effort will narrow the economic gap between them, thus augmenting Vietnam's military threat to the region and rendering the communist economic model appealing to certain groups within their societies.

Developments in the region since the end of the Indochina war indicate that the Southeast Asian countries are not dominoes that will topple once Indochina falls to communism. There were tremors in noncommunist Southeast Asia, but communist groups there have not been significantly emboldened, national leaders have not lost the will to fight them, and neither Vietnam nor China has mounted a new campaign to subvert the rest of Southeast Asia—all presumptive elements of the earlier domino theory. The domino theory was clearly too simplistic to provide a guide to the future. A complex set of factors determines a country's vulnerability to communist revolution, and the most important factors appear to be internal; the communist rise to power in Indochina and the end of U.S. military intervention are unlikely to be the critical factors in determining the political future of Southeast Asia. Furthermore, the emergence of the Sino-Soviet conflict and the differences between the communist systems within Indochina—especially the severe armed clashes between Vietnam and Cambodia—have altered the initial assumptions of the domino theory.

Relations among the Indochina states vary in their degree of tension. Though initially presenting a public facade of amicable fraternal relations, the Cambodians have felt threatened by the Vietnamese, and their relations have deteriorated into a serious border war in an area of historic territorial dispute. Although like the Cambodians, the Lao have historic reasons to be apprehensive about Vietnamese expansion, the Lao communist leaders have had long, intimate relations with their Vietnamese senior partner, have followed the Vietnamese direction in both foreign and domestic policy, and current relations continue to be close.

U.S. Interests in Indochina

After twenty-five years of deliberate efforts to exclude the communists from taking power in Indochina, the United States has had to redefine its policy and reexamine its interests in the area. The simple anticommunism of the National Security Council policy statements of the early 1950s—revealed in the "Pentagon Papers"[4]—is no longer applicable or appropriate. The following discussion will separate the question of interests into four categories: military-security, political, economic, and moral-humanitarian.

Military-Security

In the course of the U.S. withdrawal from Indochina, President Nixon enunciated a new doctrine of U.S. policy toward Asia, and after the communist victory, President Ford provided a capstone with his Pacific Doctrine. In his foreign policy report to the Congress in 1971, Nixon made clear that the United States would seek to reduce its military role in Southeast Asia and would not bear "primary responsibility" for its defense. Rather, this task should be undertaken by the countries of the region, with U.S.

"assistance."[5] President Ford, in December 1975, emphasized that the United States was a Pacific power whose position of strength throughout the area is basic to any stable balance of power and whose strategy rests on a partnership with Japan and normalized relations with China. He recognized an American "stake in stability and security in Southeast Asia," but noted that each of the countries there must protect its independence "by relying on its own national resilience and diplomacy," with continuing U.S. aid.[6] Both these pronouncements imply that the United States has an interest in preventing any one power from robbing Southeast Asian states of their independence. President Ford made no mention of the Southeast Asia Treaty Organization, which both Philippine and Thai leaders were then ready to "phase out." Rather, he pointed to the economic potential of ASEAN. On June 29, 1977, in the first major policy statement on Asia by the Carter administration, Secretary of State Cyrus Vance told the Asia Society in New York that the United States "will remain an Asian and Pacific power" and "will continue its key role in contributing to peace and stability in Asia and the Pacific."[7]

As the U.S. unwillingness in 1975 to use its military forces to prevent the final communist takeover of three Indochina states demonstrated, Washington no longer regarded this area as a "vital interest," in accordance with the falling dominoes theory. It now has more refined perceptions and expectations of the area. It would probably not regard even a consolidation of all Indochina under Vietnamese communist control (which does not seem likely in the near future) as worth fighting about. Would events in Indochina affect any vital U.S. interest of the United States?

Vietnam, as has been pointed out, has become the strongest military force in Southeast Asia, resting its strength upon a vigorous population, a continuing high level of military mobilization, years of fighting experience, and a vast windfall of weapons. This military strength could be used in a number of ways inimical to U.S. interests. As a world power, the U.S. needs access and support for its naval and air forces in the Indian Ocean, where the Diego Garcia Island base has been developed in recent years.[8] Its stopover landing rights at Takli base in Thailand and its great air and naval bases at Clark Field and Subic Bay in the Philippines are currently important in the disposition of its power. The United States could retain its military capabilities in South and Southeast Asia without the use of these bases, but their retention eases any large-scale U.S. military reentry into the region, reduces some costs, and heightens the flexibility of U.S. military operations in the area. It therefore appears that "anti-imperialist" propaganda or activities emanating from Indochina and directed at Thailand or the Philippines, to encourage their withholding military base privileges, threaten a U.S. military advantage. Yet the retention of base rights in these countries is probably not so vital in itself as to call for U.S. military intervention. Indeed, the retention of the two U.S. bases in the Philippines has not yet been settled, and some opinion within the State Department even opposes the effort.[9]

However, the significant factor would be the manner in which U.S. base rights might be threatened. If there were direct use of military force from Indochina against its personnel or installations, the United States would want to protect its credibility as a military power. On the other hand, a negotiated withdrawal of U.S. base rights, even though inspired by Indochinese communist political pressure, would be tolerable. There is also a third possibility regarding Vietnamese moves against U.S. bases in Southeast Asia: namely, harassment by local insurgents, supported and inspired by Hanoi. However, in the case of the Philippines, in view of the distance from Hanoi and the insurgents' preoccupation with their own separatist issues, it is unlikely that the SRV would be a significant support for insurgents there. In the case of Thailand, as pointed out earlier, Vietnam is a greater potential threat, but the U.S. presence in the area will probably not grow beyond the 270 military advisers permitted under the current agreement (July 16, 1976). This would reduce the likelihood that Americans might have to defend themselves against guerrilla attack.

Although it is highly unlikely, some Southeast Asian leaders fear that the Vietnamese might at some time be willing to bestow military base privileges on the Soviet Union—for example, at Cam Ranh Bay. The United States has a strong interest in preventing such a development, which would create new tensions in China, among ASEAN states, and in Japan and would generate demands for increased U.S. naval strength. Since 1969 the Soviets have also been floating a proposal for an Asian collective security system based on renunciation of force, respect for existing frontiers, noninterference in internal affairs, and economic cooperation. There has been little support for such a diplomatic scheme from China or Japan, and, as we have seen, ASEAN, which adopted its own proposal in 1971 for a neutral "zone of peace" in Southeast Asia, has shown no interest in the Soviet scheme. At the Colombo conference of nonaligned states in 1976, Laos and Vietnam prevented any consensus about the ASEAN idea by insisting on the eradication of "neocolonialism" from the region. It is unlikely that either the Soviet collective security or the ASEAN neutralization ideas will receive the support of all interested parties, but the United States does not want to be diplomatically upstaged by the Soviets nor to be considered a holdout against an Asian agreement to neutralize the region. If a solid agreement on the neutralization of Southeast Asia should emerge, the utility of any U.S. bases in the Philippines would probably diminish to the point of making their abandonment not only politically expedient but also militarily and economically sound.[10]

The Indochina states pose no direct security threat to the United States, but their commitment to the cause of "people's liberation" creates continuing problems for Thailand and potential problems for Malaysia and even Singapore, the Philippines, and Indonesia. Until the military coup d'état of October 1976 in Thailand, there was no evidence of increased Vietnamese or Lao support of the insurgent elements as a result of the communist victories in Indochina. The mutual hostility between Thailand and Laos and Vietnam—bred by the 1976 change to a military-dominated government in Thailand—threatened to increase the illicit flow of arms through Laos to Thai antigovernment elements. However, the more relaxed regime in Thailand since General Kriangsak's November 1977 coup has witnessed an attempt by all three Indochina states to improve their relations with Thailand. It is in the interest of the United States that counterinsurgency warfare not breed a brittle government in Thailand or so alienate the people as to make possible a "liberation" government quite hostile to the United States. Neither outcome would seem to threaten vital U.S. interests, but an unfriendly or politically polarized Thailand would be undesirable and might complicate U.S. access to South Asia.

Another security concern of the United States is that territorial disputes in the region not draw in great powers. As of this writing, the seriousness of Vietnamese-Cambodian border warfare has come to light, and the Soviet and Chinese support of opposing sides in a potential Indochina "quagmire," with the United States a detached outsider, presents a historical irony. Whether such long-standing national territorial grievances can be settled amicably remains very much in doubt. The Cambodian-Vietnam conflict has nonetheless alleviated some of the hostility of Indochina states toward Thailand, although intermittent skirmishes on the Cambodian-Thai border continued through early 1978.

There is still the danger that Indochinese retaliation against armed resistance elements entering Laos or Cambodia from Thailand might precipitate further armed conflicts. The United States has not abrogated the Rusk-Thanat Agreement of 1962, which promised, independent of SEATO, that the United States would protect Thailand against attack. Despite armed clashes on the Cambodian border in 1977, there seemed to be little likelihood that the disputes between Cambodia and Thailand (including offshore territory), or between Laos and Thailand, would escalate into sustained military engagements. The rival claims of Vietnam, China, and the Philippines to the Paracel Islands seem to be stabilized by the fact of partial Chinese occupation. As offshore oil prospecting proceeds, however, the potential stakes in rival claims will increase. There is no short-term likelihood, however, that any of the Southeast Asian contestants other than China will obtain nuclear weapons. The U.S. interest is to stay neutral in these nettlesome territorial disputes and to identify itself with peaceful methods of resolution in accordance with international law.[11] It was from such a territorial dispute that the *Mayaguez* incident emerged. The U.S. resort to force on that occasion, with its unfortunate exacerbation of U.S. relations with Thailand and Cambodia, resulted partly from inattention to Cambodian assertions about their territorial sea and partly from the absence of a direct U.S. diplomatic channel to the Khmer government, a situation that still exists.

In sum, the United States has no vital security interests at stake in Indochina or in the potential armed conflicts of these states with their neighbors, but it does have important secondary interests. Furthermore, in the wake of U.S. withdrawal from the Vietnam war, it is of particular interest that no new military commitment be made that cannot be fully sustained.

Political

The United States has an interest in minimizing the concentration of political power in Indochina and in preventing any single power from dominating Southeast Asia. The Socialist Republic of Vietnam is large enough and potentially strong enough economically to become a significant middle power in the region within a decade. Japan, the major American ally in Asia, has strong economic and political interests in Indochina. Any serious limitations on its economic access to the region would threaten its essential raw material imports, growing export markets, and even vital sea routes. In addition, Japan characterizes itself as playing a role, through economic aid to Indochina, in acquiring influence and preventing serious conflict between Vietnam and the ASEAN states. These states, which have been friendly toward the United States, seek reassurance as to their ability to survive and prosper in the face of the new communist states of Indochina. It would be to the United States' advantage to support efforts at "peaceful and mutually beneficial relations" with all countries in the region, including the Indochina states, which the ASEAN summit conference of August 1977 officially announced as its goal.[12]

An exclusive reliance of the three states of Indochina on either the Soviet Union or China might initially heighten the political impact of this state in the region, as a model or as an adversary. In addition, if the Vietnamese assert hegemony over Laos or Cambodia, their political weight would increase. Although a federated Indochina, especially if under Soviet influence, might provide some counterbalance to China in Southeast Asia, it might also provoke China into a preemptive occupation of a segment of northern Laos, even into collaborating politically with Thailand. Any Chinese action that would seem to require a Soviet response might increase Soviet presence in Southeast Asia, even in the role of champion of national independence, and might heighten the tensions between the PRC and USSR to dangerous levels. Such developments would threaten the states of the region, which might be caught in military cross fire, and the United States would find it hard to avoid taking sides and military involvement.

On the other hand, although the Khmer and Lao would not welcome Vietnamese rule over all of Indochina and although the United States would find it objectionable, how damaging to U.S. interests would such a unification be? Curiously, despite the U.S. obsession with the danger of Vietnamese expansion during the 1960s, the PRC is more likely to have its interests damaged than the United States. An Indochina unified by the Vietnamese would reduce Chinese influence in the region, and the United States, like the USSR, might see some advantage in a counterweight to China. U.S. influence in the Indochina states might grow if the SRV, while consolidating power in Indochina, were under pressure from China. (The case of U.S. relations with Yugoslavia under pressure from the USSR provides some interesting similarities; and Poland, which shares with Vietnam a historic fear of its powerful communist neighbor, has long been receptive to friendly relations with the United States.) But insofar as an Indochina dominated by Vietnam would threaten other countries in Southeast Asia, especially Thailand, and unduly increase Soviet influence, the United States would look with disfavor upon such a development. The Thai would fear that the Vietnamese appetite might be whetted for annexation of northeast Thailand, the Lao-Thai region where more ethnic Lao live than in Laos itself. In sum, an uncertain balance sheet emerges from considering a Vietnamese attempt at hegemony. Although the issue is not of vital interest to the United States, it appears on balance that three separate states in Indochina would be more favorable to the U.S. interest in peaceful political development in the region.

The United States has been concerned to minimize the role of Indochina states in supporting insurgent "national liberation" movements in Thailand or elsewhere. The high priority all three Indochina states now give to national economic development is desirable. It would be contrary to U.S. interests for Thailand to support or permit such harassment of Laos, through blockade or refugee incursions, that the Lao would invoke greater Vietnamese military support or undertake retaliatory operations across the

Mekong. This would only risk an engagement of U.S. equipment and even advisers in long-standing ethnic and ideological struggles of no strategic importance to the United States.

The competing models of economic development represented by the Draconian Cambodian self-reliance on the one extreme and the pluralistic enterprise of Malaysia and Singapore on the other, with their contrasting political values and institutions, pose a contest in which the United States has an interest. To the extent that economic modernization can succeed in tandem with the idea of political freedoms and limited government, the world will be more receptive to U.S. leadership and initiative. The entry of outside states and international organizations into Indochina to assist in their economic development may open these revolutionary regimes, however slightly, to noncommunist ideas. Even though the aid would foster the "socialist development" of Indochina, it might moderate their otherwise closed societies and promote some interdependency.

Economic

The United States has no substantial interest in commercial relations with the states of Indochina. The U.S. assets taken over by the revolutionary governments are not as significant to the United States as the frozen bank accounts of the South Vietnamese and Cambodian governments in the United States are to those governments. The past investments of U.S. oil companies in off-shore exploration might be recouped through future joint ventures with a Vietnamese state oil authority. There are overlapping national claims to some offshore drilling areas that U.S. companies should avoid, but enough exclusive tracts remain to be worthy of renewed exploration. To refrain from entering is to increase the likelihood that European companies will agree to contracts and take whatever profit is to be had.

With respect to the economic development of Indochina, there is scant possibility that U.S. models of enterprise and market management will prevail over socialist methods. At the same time, the United States has no real interest in seeing the communist-managed economies of Indochina fall farther behind their neighbors; mere economic stagnation would not lead to a new noncommunist regime without the help of outside intervention. Such interventions risk provoking counterintrusions, which are hard to predict and inimical to peace in the region. Therefore, the U.S. interest seems to lie in steady economic development in Indochina so as to increase the trade and contact with the West and with the other peoples of the region and gradually to improve the lot of the people. On balance, aid to Indochina states by international agencies, by Western countries, and even by the United States (were it permitted by Congress) is not inimical to U.S. interests.

The economic, social, and administrative burden of refugees from Indochina—which currently is borne by Thailand, with heavy United Nations support—is additionally a financial drain on the United States, the major donor. It is in the U.S. interest as well as Thailand's to see the flight of persons diminish and to repatriate as many refugees as might wish voluntarily to return home if there could be internationally monitored assurances that there would be no discrimination against them when they return.

Moral-Humanitarian

The American effort to maintain its security, political power, and economic capacity rests ultimately on a deep-seated belief in basic human values associated with freedom and human well-being. For all the essential pragmatism of U.S. foreign policy, an underlying moral purpose is its necessary foundation. Recently, the Carter administration has put a new emphasis upon human rights as a worldwide American concern. The conflicts that this U.S. interest raises are not readily resolved. The United Nations system has expressed both the universalistic impulse and the domestic sovereignty principle in various declarations, conventions, and resolutions over the years, and the emphasis that nations apply to these ideals at particular times certainly rests in part on political objectives, notwithstanding the moral-legal language they may use.

Nonetheless, the United States has an interest in upholding such principles as freedom of movement, freedom to dissent, humane treatment of prisoners, and equal treatment for all peoples within a country. The reports of ruthless population transfers and executions in Cambodia after April 1975 did not bring forth sustained attention from the U.S. government, even though a few news accounts gave evidence of extensive disruption of the population. Hearings before the Fraser Subcommittee of the House International Affairs Committee in May-June 1977 did focus attention briefly on the human rights question in Cambodia and Vietnam, as have a few publishers. The State Department, though professing to have no sure evidence about the number of deaths in Cambodia, made clear its condemnation of the government's ruthless policies. A verification of the extent of this human tragedy is not in prospect, and there seems to be little that outsiders might be able to do to halt it. The U.S. government cannot afford, however, to champion the cause of human rights in the Soviet Union or Argentina and ignore the reports of political persecution in Indochina. Nor can it remain indifferent to the fate of the tens of thousands of persons who, because they served in the armies and administrations sponsored by the United States, now endure hardship under revolutionary governments. Thus, the extent and conditions of political "reeducation" in Laos and Vietnam are an issue that the U.S. government has an interest in raising publicly, and privately once channels exist, both for reasons of humanity and as a symbol of U.S. concern for its friends. The fact that neither government is likely to modify its policy appreciably to meet U.S. expressions of concern, even from former antiwar activists, does not negate the importance of the issue for the United States. The Lao communists have responded to foreign interest in their camps by opening to the press a nonpolitical reeducation center for addicts and prostitutes, but the Vietnamese have seen fit to challenge the numbers alleged by Western critics to be in camps in Vietnam.

The fate of refugees from Vietnam, Laos, and Cambodia, who in 1977 were still fleeing at a rate of 1,500 per month, is a question of compassion as well as of international law. It also has a moral dimension stemming from the unsuccessful U.S. war effort that underlies the refugee flight, and from the enormous wealth of the United States, a country founded and built by refugees. With the help of the UN high commissioner for refugees, the United States has attempted to foster humane care and resettlement of refugees, in recognition of its own role in the war that caused them to flee. If the United States accepted a substantial number (of the 100,000 refugees in Thailand in early 1978), it might point the way and could more effectively persuade other countries to welcome the Indochinese refugees. If refugees' families could be reunited through arrangement of special exits from Indochina, or through voluntary repatriation of some refugees, the United States' purposes would also be served. Instead of the continuing expense and demoralizing effect of squalid refugee camps, it would be better to develop conditions in Indochina that do not induce the flight of citizens, better even to encourage some repatriation. If more would stay at home in Indochina, as a result of a more acceptable government, the U.S. interest in stability and self-reliant peoples would be fulfilled.

Problems and Recommendations

The bitter war between the United States and Indochina has left a residue of problems—U.S. servicemen still listed as missing in action, U.S. business assets overrun by the new communist governments, victors' retribution upon the United States' former friends and associates, and destruction caused by U.S. military might. It is understandable that attitudes and emotions acquired during the conflict continue to structure the thinking of many Americans who deal with these problems, but such thinking is no longer appropriate. The war is over. The revolution has taken place and is not likely to be reversed. The current issues between the Indochina states and the United States, therefore, bear not upon the outcome of a military struggle, nor even upon the vindication of the struggle, but rather upon the political and economic relationship that will exist between the countries in future years. Such questions call for the perspective not of the military or political tactician, but rather of the statesman.

U.S. policy objectives in Indochina should not be simply to seek short-term advantage, or to avoid the current discomfort of admitting that a national commitment was not fulfilled. The United States should utilize the break between itself and communist Indochina to construct a policy that projects into the international arena of the 1980s, not back to the 1950s or 1960s. What should U.S. relationships in Southeast Asia and in Indochina look like ten years from now, not ten months from now? That is what U.S. policymakers should be asking themselves.

Ten years from now, Vietnam may well arrive at a level of development that will place it among the important middle powers of Asia and the Third World. Its identification with the Third World and thus its challenge to the rich industrial powers will not diminish during its period of recovery and growth. Nor will it leave the camp of countries inspired by Marxist-Leninist ideas. Yet its sense of national independence will undoubtedly remain intense as it pursues economic modernization, and pragmatism will continue to weigh heavily in its policies. Consequently, Vietnam will want the benefits of selective trade and technology imports from the United States (and as much reconstruction aid as it can bargain for) and will wish to avoid a heavy dependence upon the Soviet Union.

Ten years from now, what will be the significance of the position the United States takes on Indochina in 1978? One need only recall the more than twenty years that U.S. relations with Communist China were locked in sterile hostility, or the fruitless diplomatic breach of more than fifteen years with Castro's Cuba, to realize the disadvantages of persisting hostility. But dismantling the habits and vested interests of broken diplomatic relations is not easy, as these cases have shown, even when the will to shift policy is clear. Thus, the initial period of relations with a new revolutionary government can be critical for many years to come. The U.S. record with new communist states appears to have been better where nationalism was encouraged through diplomatic and economic relations (as in Yugoslavia or Poland) than where the revolution was refused recognition or the settlement of economic claims was prolonged, as with the Soviet Union 1917–1933, China, and Cuba. (The case of Albania, which can be effectively ignored by the United States without consequence, is not relevant to U.S. relations with Indochina.)

Although forward thinking about the outstanding problems is critical, obligations have nonetheless been incurred as a result of the Indochina war, obligations that cannot simply be written off in order to get on with the future. Past policies make it both expedient and morally impelling for the United States to consider the questions of refugees and of human rights in Indochina with a sense of special responsibility. Thousands of Vietnamese, Lao, and Cambodians associated themselves with the side that U.S. power failed to sustain. It was their own cause as well as that of the Americans, but collaboration with the "neocolonialists" irrevocably tainted individuals and their families, who have since suffered penalties ranging from summary execution and prolonged intern-ment in reeducation camps to coercive downgrading and reloca-tion in the economy. In addition, families not identified with the losing side have found the new regime so repugnant that they have preferred the risks of flight to continued endurance of oppressive economic or political conditions. Toward them, as well, the United States cannot feel absolved of responsibility. It partially recognized this responsibility in the spring of 1975, when it offered haven to thousands who were potential targets of retribu-tion and to others who chose to flee.

A further postwar U.S. responsibility, about which Americans are far less ready to agree, goes beyond the individual human di-mension to the physical and economic consequences of U.S. military actions during the war. The enormous destruction of transportation systems, village structures, cultivable fields, irriga-tion systems, and forests by U.S. bombing and chemical warfare will take years to repair. The damage to civilians who were maimed and diseased by the indiscriminate use of U.S. firepower and the corrosion of Vietnamese society caused by the massive U.S. military presence will be a bitter reminder to many Vietnamese of the misfortune of U.S. intervention.

Vietnam's new leaders, who emerged from the Paris negotia-tions with an expectation of large-scale economic assistance, still view the U.S. obligation as proper and binding. The U.S. govern-ment, as we have seen, firmly rejects the claim of a remaining legal obligation. But the moral question remains open. Is there an American responsibility to help deal with the human tragedies and economic deprivation left behind by massive military firepower, or did such a responsibility simply end as the Paris cease-fire arrange-ments were progressively violated and turned into a dead letter? The latent moral issue, however repressed it was in the statements of U.S. officials in 1977, may yet find expression among decision makers as the memory of the war recedes and is reshaped through writings and films portraying the tragic aspects of the U.S. intervention.

With this general introduction, let us consider the outstanding questions that the United States must face in relation to Indochina.

Refugees

The dramatic air and sea lift of about 130,000 Vietnamese to the United States in conjunction with the U.S. flight from Saigon in April of 1975 brought the first wave of Indochina refugees. They joined about 15,000 Indochinese students and trainees stranded in the United States because of the fall of their governments. During the next two years, tens of thousands more reached Thailand from Laos and Cambodia, and thousands of others fled Vietnam by boat. By the end of 1976, 114,000 displaced persons from Indochina had been registered in Thailand, and only 37,000 had been resettled in third countries, despite the efforts of the UN High Commission for Refugees (UNHCR) to promote and assist the resettlement of refugees from camps in Thailand. By the end of 1977, some 100,000 refugees were officially counted in Thailand, and 10,000 boat case arrivals from Vietnam had been recorded in other East Asian countries. Some 73,000 Indochina refugees had been resettled in third countries since the U.S. airlift in 1975. The arrival of refugees in Thailand in 1977 averaged about 1,500 per month and dramatically increased in the autumn.[13]

The post-1975 wave of refugees has flowed most heavily from Laos, where the Mekong River border with Thailand permits relatively easy escape. In 1977 well over three-quarters of the camp population in Thailand had arrived from Laos, over half from the mountainous regions inhabited by the Meo and Lao Theung peoples. More than 10,000 of the camp population in Thailand had come from Cambodia, undertaking a more perilous exit from their country, often through jungle and across minefields near the border. (It was rumored that more than 60,000 other Cambodians succeeded in escaping the harshness of their regime by entering Vietnam.) The Vietnamese who wished to flee could leave only by sea, in small craft that, often as not, took them to their death, sometimes after being ignored by larger vessels on the high seas. Ship captains from many countries and immigration officials (in Taiwan, Malaysia, and Singapore especially) sometimes callously refused to involve themselves in the distress of Vietnamese boats searching for safe haven. Even in ports where boat people were deposited by rescuing ships or grudgingly allowed by local officials to land their boats, they were often stripped of their remaining possessions and held under the threat of future expulsion.[14]

The U.S. response to this human tragedy developed in installments. The immediate postwar reception of 130,000 refugees from Vietnam was followed by an additional few thousand who were expected to be entering en route to settlement elsewhere. Then followed about 3,500 Lao, who had not been eligible under the original legislation passed in 1975, which provided haven only for Vietnamese and Cambodians, in whose countries the communists had seized full power several months earlier than in Laos. Next, in spring 1976, President Ford obtained further authority to admit 11,000 emergency immigration cases under "extended parole" by the attorney general, under existing law. A few additional admissions were set aside for boat cases in early 1977. Next, in August 1977, came an executive-congressional agreement on 15,000 new "parole" entries to cover boat cases, the immediate family of previous immigrants to the United States, and former U.S. employees or close associates of U.S. programs in their homeland. In December 1977, the State Department initiated a request for an additional 7,000 entries, as the flow of "boat people" from Vietnam and the Mekong River escapes from Laos increased.

Meanwhile, other countries had taken in far fewer refugees than the 148,355 the United States admitted from May 1975 to 1977. France had taken 37,000, mainly as refugees but some under other classifications. Canada had received some 7,000 and Australia more than 4,000, and groups of 100–1,000 Indochina refugees had been resettled in West European states, the Philippines, and Hong Kong.[15] In September 1977, U.S. diplomats reported that the new program for admitting 15,000 Indochina refugees was positively affecting the attitude of other states toward the problem. Australia was preparing to receive additional numbers, as were Canada (450), New Zealand (428), Belgium (150), and Denmark (50). At the same time, Malaysia was no longer pushing refugee boat arrivals back out to sea.[16]

In addition to trying to set an example on the question of admitting refugees, the United States has given the greatest support for the UNHCR's maintenance of refugees. For the first eighteen months of the UNHCR provision of food, shelter, clothing, medical care, and implements in Thailand, the United States contributed $5.5 million, almost half the amount that was sought in an appeal to some thirty governments. Another $10.2 million was required for the resettlement and repatriation program during the same period, and many voluntary agencies helped in meeting this funding goal. For 1977, the UNHCR set a target of $14.4 million for material assistance and resettlement costs for Indochina refugees in Thailand and other countries. By the end of 1978 the United States will have contributed $31 million to the UNHCR for its Indochina peninsula operations, and through fiscal 1977 it had spent $203 million for assisting refugee resettlement in the United States.[17]

Caring for refugees has become a major, recurring responsibility of the United Nations and the wealthier states of the world over three decades of political upheaval—for example, in Eastern Europe and Germany, Palestine, Nigeria, Tibet, Cuba, and India-Pakistan. In such operations, humanitarian instincts to relieve the hardship of the homeless have clashed with the economic and social goal of stabilizing populations into productive communities. Preferably, of course, all members of a state could achieve social and economic betterment within their own societies without risking flight and dependency on international charity. But the prospects are slim for achieving such social and political satisfaction in the Indochina states in the near future. Their economic backwardness and strong drives for self-sufficiency, the ineptness and harshness of their administration, the atmosphere of uncertainty and arbitrariness, and the revolutionary downgrading of certain social and political segments will probably push out the more desperate or daring elements for many months to come.

At the same time, the very act of receiving, maintaining, and resettling such escapees tends to encourage further flight. The human hemorrhage of Indochina will have no natural staunching point so long as economic conditions deteriorate at home and hope for resettlement abroad seems plausible for those who make it abroad. No Berlin-type wall will appear along the Mekong River to block the flow of refugees. Nor will neighboring countries continue receiving Indochina refugees without financial support and resettlement programs elsewhere. Thailand, with the overwhelming number located within its territory, indicated to the UNHCR in the summer of 1977 a willingness to consider the permanent resettlement of some of the Indochina refugees, particularly the lowland Lao (Lao Loum) elements. However, it is certainly not likely to respond favorably to suggestions that Vietnamese be permanently resettled in Thailand, and it will be reluctant about the permanent resettlement of Cambodians, Meo, and Lao Theung highland minorities from Laos. In any case, to undertake any permanent resettlement of refugees, Thailand will require strong encouragement and material assistance, as well as an indication that effective international measures are taken for the absorption of refugees elsewhere as well. Thailand has delayed resettlement out of fear of attracting more escapees, whose motivation might be mere economic opportunism and whose resettlement would put further pressure on the limited private cultivable land available in Thailand. To discourage such migrants, Thailand declared in July 1977 that it would distinguish between refugees falling within the competence of the UNHCR and persons "who leave their country of nationality or habitual residence for reasons of personal convenience, for example, economic migrants, or persons who are not bona fide refugees." The latter might eventually face "voluntary repatriation" as the preferred Thai solution to their status, at which time improved economic conditions in Laos and international assistance and supervision might make the option reasonable.[18]

The United States has the moral obligation to do its best in sustaining and resettling Indochina refugees so long as they continue to flee. The U.S. immigration programs, which take into consideration the reunification of families or previous association with the U.S. government agencies, have been helpful to tens of thousands, but they are inadequate in light of the continuing problem. Forced repatriation is out of the question, and voluntary repatriation has not appealed to more than a few thousand of the earliest refugees. U.S. policy must therefore combine a readiness to set the example in both financial support and admission for resettlement and a readiness to press hard on Thailand and neighboring Asian countries, including Korea, to assimilate substantial numbers within their borders. The UNHCR will be the vital vehicle for administering these maintenance and resettlement efforts. At the same time, it is contributing to the resettlement of displaced Vietnamese and Lao within their own countries. The UNHCR's politically neutral, humanitarian approach toward displaced persons is more difficult for the United States and anticommunist governments to adopt. Yet it stands as a reminder that the ultimate solution to the refugee problem is to eliminate the motivation to flee. Thus the United States, though committing itself to the reduction of refugee camps, should also view with favor the long-run improvement of economic and social conditions within the Indochina states themselves.

Human Rights

A second barrier between the United States and the governments of Indochina is the question of human rights. In its early months, the Carter administration picked up this issue, which the Congress had been developing for many months previous, and dramatized its readiness to support, at least symbolically, the universal right of political dissent. President Carter communicated personally with several Soviet dissidents, the State Department recommended a termination of U.S. military assistance to a few governments noted for their use of detention without trial and even torture of political opponents, and U.S. delegates took an aggressive stance in the United Nations Commission on Human Rights. The new administration thereby stirred some animosity, much uncertainty, raised the hopes of many political dissidents living under authoritarian regimes, and received a modicum of praise around the world. After this first flurry in early 1977 and after subsequent speeches by high administration officials, who reiterated the commitment to human rights, the Department of State seemed to take a lower profile on the issue as the months went by. Negotiations on a new strategic arms limitation agreement prompted some retrenchment with respect to the Soviet Union. Charges of both hypocrisy and futility were leveled at the administration's policy, alleging that it had selectively withdrawn aid from delinquent states and had exposed some political dissidents who had responded to the U.S. human rights rhetoric with bolder action against increased government repression. Notwithstanding this criticism, there was evidence that authoritarian governments were sensitive to the charge that their jails permitted torture and prolonged detention without trial. When leaders in the Philippines or Haiti thought that martial law could be lifted or political prisoners reduced in number, they were not modest in publicizing their good deeds.

The question nonetheless remains whether the condition of human rights in Indochina is a legitimate concern for the United States. The answer would seem to be that the treatment of other human beings by their governments should not be a matter of indifference to the U.S. government or people. This universal concern is embodied in the words of the UN Charter as well as in a number of international covenants the United States belatedly signed in October 1977.[19] The degree to which the U.S. attempts to regulate human rights abroad, however, through public statements or economic support or denial, is a matter of political practicality. Which particular rights, of all the human rights embodied in the United Nations covenants, are to be emphasized is also a matter of politics. The U.S. tendency is to stress political and civil rights, but socialist countries emphasize social and economic rights, and Third World countries stress the evils of racial discrimination.

The postvictory conditions of political life in Vietnam, Laos, and Cambodia also raise problems of obtaining adequate information. In May and June 1977 the Fraser Subcommittee of the House Committee on International Affairs made an effort to monitor the human rights situation in Vietnam and Cambodia. The testimony on Cambodia elicited the aforementioned cautious statement by Assistant Secretary of State Holbrooke as well as other testimony with conflicting estimates of the number of deaths since 1975 and conflicting assessments of the causes of Khmer anger and brutality. The testimony on Vietnam also varied significantly in its estimates of the number of persons still detained in reeducation camps, the conditions in such centers, and the degree of religious activity allowed by the government.

Concerning Vietnam, attention was also focused upon outstanding leaders of the former "Third Force" in South Vietnam, who were imprisoned by the very communists with whom they had once tried to work toward a peaceful resolution of the war. Refugee accounts were recorded of pitiable conditions of near starvation, disease, and suicidal despair in the places of detention. Actual self-immolation by Buddhist priests and nuns was reported to have occurred since 1975 in protest against the regime. Some witnesses testified that reeducation camps would be continued for at least five more years, and some estimates put the number detained as high as 300,000. Only a few selected friends of the regime had been allowed to visit "showplace" camps, since foreign reporters were generally excluded from the country. No modern revolution, it was argued, had detained so many of its opponents for so long.[20]

A contrasting point of view was expressed by some academic Vietnam specialists, church and humanitarian relief workers who stayed in Vietnam after the communist victory, and a fraction of the leaders of the antiwar movement of the 1960s.[21] They tended to emphasize that the predicted bloodbath in Vietnam had not taken place and that even the history on which the prediction had been made was a distortion of the reality of the Viet Minh revolution. Their estimate of detainees in reeducation camps ranged as low as 50,000, and the problem of nutrition in such centers was said to be a function of the national food shortage produced by the withdrawal of U.S. assistance, a severe drought in 1977, and wartime damage to agriculture. Some witnesses even linked the human rights question to the call for amnesty for U.S. draft evaders and deserters. It was also pointed out that the International Covenant on Civil and Political Rights provides in Article 4 for measures taken "in time of public emergency which threaten the life of a nation which may derogate from their normal obligations under the Covenant." The reconstruction of the war-torn society, it was argued, should be left to the new Vietnamese leaders, who will not in any case take U.S. protestations very seriously, and whose record thus far does not merit as much attention as do some other regimes, such as Indonesia.[22]

Notwithstanding this considerable gap in viewpoints, it seems reasonable for American groups to speak out against the unlimited detention in camps, without trial, of Vietnamese who had served the Saigon government or cooperated with the Americans. It is reasonable to suggest that even from a Vietnamese communist perspective, their "reeducation" ought by now to be accomplished. American spokesmen for human rights might usefully focus attention upon known political leaders (including "Third Force" personalities who had also been persecuted by the Thieu government), calling for their release from detention and exit visas for them. Continuing appeals to Vietnamese authorities on behalf of reunification of families abroad are also warranted. Substantial American assistance to refugees is a form of human rights activity

in the most basic sense. Assistance to the victims of the war within
Vietnam, Laos, and eventually Cambodia, would also demonstrate
a concern for human rights. In such matters as artificial limbs,
medicines, and treatment for burn victims, agricultural aid to cope
with defoliated forests, and mine and ordnance deactivating equipment, U.S. assistance could greatly benefit the war's surviving
victims. It would not be easy to link the offering of such aid directly to the treatment of political prisoners, but skillful diplomacy
might convey the message, and the atmosphere created by such
moves might lessen the feeling that an "emergency" exists, a
feeling that partly underlies the maintenance of reeducation camps.

With respect to Cambodia, considerable time will pass before
the new government is likely to be responsive to any U.S. statements about its treatment of its own people. It is remotely possible
that the United States could influence the Cambodian regime
through representations to the PRC, the external power that
carries the most weight in Cambodia. However, the PRC has
shown no inclination, at least publicly, to pressure the Cambodian
leaders to soften their harsh internal policies. The United States
should nonetheless continue to seek the facts about the internal
situation of Cambodia and support the efforts of the world press
to enter the country and report the situation. If some years from
now diplomatic relations can be restored with Cambodia, the
American condemnation of summary executions and ruthless
displacement of populations should be clearly on record, and the
importance of free access to outside journalists should be stressed
in the new negotiations.

Normalized Relations

The ultimate question in the current U.S.-Indochina relationship is whether diplomatic relations, and thereby commercial
relations, can be normalized. The Carter administration has taken
the position that in an interdependent world it is important for
the United States to be able to communicate easily with other
peoples in order to promote U.S. interests, avoid misunderstand-
ings, and build new, common bonds.[23] For this reason, the Department of State has tried to shorten the list of countries with
whom the United States has never established, or has broken,
diplomatic relations, a list that includes the People's Republic of

China, Mongolia, North Korea, Vietnam, Cuba, and a few Arab and African states. Halfway arrangements, without formal diplomatic relations, have been used in the case of China and Cuba,[24] but this approach appears unattractive to both sides in the case of Vietnam or Cambodia. In Laos a U.S. embassy has been maintained since 1975, but without an ambassador.

As already mentioned, the two direct meetings in Paris between U.S. and Vietnamese negotiators in May and June 1977 aired the opposing conditions set for any normalization of relations and left the talks at an impasse without any fixed date for renewal. In December, another meeting in Paris took place without significant movement by either side. The United States seemed willing to wait on the development of Vietnam's economic situation and allow the president to concentrate on other foreign policy questions of greater magnitude for world peace and stability. It would have been imprudent for the president to expend significant political capital on the Vietnam issue at the same time that he was pushing the unpopular Panama Canal Treaty through the Senate, wrestling with a possible peace conference on Israel, and exploring new relationships with China and arms limitations with the Soviet Union. In September 1977, nonetheless, the administration was willing to institute status reviews of military personnel listed as missing in action (which had been suspended under the Ford administration). With the federal courts acquiescing in this move, the way was clear to reduce the number of Americans listed as missing in action by making a presumption of death while still allowing next of kin to oppose such determinations. This action followed logically upon the Woodcock Commission's attempts to put the MIA question into proper proportion and thereby to reduce it as a barrier to normal relations.

With formal talks suspended between the United States and Vietnam, the issues dividing the two parties seemed clear. Both sides were willing to develop normal diplomatic relations with exchange of ambassadors. The United States had abandoned its objection to the entry of Vietnam into the United Nations. The Vietnamese had committed themselves to more systematic efforts to provide information on MIAs. The Vietnamese wanted the U.S. trade embargo lifted before an embassy could be established in Hanoi, but the United States wanted an embassy first. Finally,

the Vietnamese insisted upon some acknowledgment and fulfillment of the U.S. obligation "to heal the wounds of war," but the
United States avoided any specific commitment of reconstruction
aid that might imply a legal obligation or set a target beyond the
willingness of Congress to appropriate. The Vietnamese apparently
wanted to see normalization accomplished in three phases: first,
a stepped-up search for American MIAs; second, a U.S. contribution to Vietnamese reconstruction with further efforts to find the
missing in action; and third, the establishment of normal diplomatic
relations. The United States, by contrast, preferred the establishment of an embassy in Hanoi without conceding a specific level of
economic assistance, and with a lifting of the trade embargo following the exchange of ambassadors.

Negotiations in late 1977 had reached the delicate bargaining
stage. The U.S. government could reasonably conclude that
further concessions toward the Vietnamese would lose more than
they might gain. The State Department might also assume that in
view of Congress's hostility toward economic assistance, the U.S.
government could not satisfy the minimal demands of the Vietnamese. U.S. negotiators might reason that mounting economic
difficulties within Vietnam would eventually induce the SRV to
soften their demands for reconstruction aid in order to open the
door to trade, technological transfer, and perhaps later economic
concessions. The critical question was how much the Vietnamese
leaders considered reconstruction aid a matter of deep principle
rather than a bargaining position that might be modified in the
face of U.S. firmness. Since the Carter administration was invest-
ing its foreign policy efforts in more critical areas in late 1977,
the initiative for breaking the impasse seemed to lie with the
Vietnamese.

Whether the United States' passive stance was detrimental to
its own interests depends upon the possible costs and benefits of
normal diplomatic relations with Vietnam. The major arguments
for an exchange of diplomatic missions are the following. First,
the United States would obtain a listening post in Hanoi, the
better to monitor and possibly influence the Sino-Soviet competition for Vietnamese attention and support. A cynical estimate of
this advantage might be that there is little to listen to in Hanoi
and that Vietnamese independence from both of the communist

giants will probably be maintained. In any case, however, the ability of the United States to exert influence will be minimal.

Second, the United States would gain a regular diplomatic channel through which to pursue the questions of MIAs and U.S. business assets left behind in 1975. Such a channel would, of course, not assure a satisfactory solution of either issue. In addition, as mentioned above, the United States might press through diplomatic channels for exit visas for those Vietnamese whose families had become separated through flight to the United States, and for exit visas, or at least release from detention, for prominent "Third Force" personalities whom the new government has treated as politically hostile.

Third, the United States would obtain access to Vietnamese exports such as coal, timber, and minerals, and U.S. oil companies would be able to renegotiate contracts for exploration and a share in the exploitation of offshore oil. Some American investors might also wish to enter into joint ventures in Vietnam or other investments under the ten-to-fifteen-year guarantee against nationalization. Such possible trade developments might include the opening of air routes to Vietnam by U.S. carriers. The dollar value of such commercial and financial opportunities for private American investors would not be significant for the U.S. economy. Nonetheless, trade and investment relationships with the United States might temper the Vietnamese commitment to Soviet technology and methods of organization, and might even affect the Vietnamese ideological and policy outlook.

Finally, the United States would obtain a more direct means of reminding the Vietnamese of the value of a stabilized Southeast Asia—in which disputes with Thailand or other neighbors (even Cambodia) over disputed borders or islands should be worked out without resort to force or subversion. The United States has an interest, along with its major Asian ally, Japan, in encouraging economic and social development in Southeast Asia without the conflict and tensions that have in the past drawn in major outside powers. The ASEAN friends of the United States would benefit from any U.S. leverage on Indochina that might inhibit Vietnamese encouragement of insurgency in Southeast Asia. The degree to which U.S. diplomatic encouragement might restrain the Vietnamese leaders is of course subject to their own cost-benefit analyses. In any case, for the immediate future, their internal development seems likely to receive priority over foreign adventures.

The major costs of seeking normal diplomatic relations under the bargaining impasse previously described would be the following. The United States would probably have to acknowledge an obligation to contribute significant reconstruction aid, notwithstanding the North Vietnamese violations of the Paris Agreement. Thus, the administration would have to press Congress again, against its inclinations, to finance such aid.[25] The ASEAN states would look with envy and possible resentment upon substantial U.S. economic assistance to Indochina. Furthermore, criticism from certain segments of American opinion would be voiced when their expectations of MIA information were not fulfilled after diplomatic recognition of Vietnam. Each of these costs might be reduced through careful preparation of the constituencies involved and proper presentation of the benefits at stake. The level of economic and humanitarian assistance that would be manageable both in Congress and in relation to ASEAN would certainly be much less than the several billion dollars in reconstruction aid anticipated by North Vietnam in 1973 and probably considerably less than $1 billion.

Even if the United States should continue a strategy of waiting for the Vietnamese to increase their self-proclaimed "flexibility" to the point of dropping their insistence upon identifiable reconstruction aid, it should take certain positive steps to indicate its readiness to normalize relations. The work of the Montgomery Committee and the Woodcock Commission in establishing reasonable expectations for MIA recovery should be further publicized and endorsed by the administration. Misinformation on surviving MIAs should be officially refuted, and the public should be educated to expect only a few future identifications of servicemen from remote burial spots in Indochina. The administration should also remain alert to thwart efforts in Congress to restrict American contributions to international organizations in support of humanitarian and economic aid in Indochina.[26] This source of American funds, which amounted to $34 million worth of aid in 1977, could provide an important indirect means to meet the Vietnamese demand for reconstruction assistance. At the same time, if natural adversity such as severe drought or typhoons should create dramatically desperate food shortages in Indochina, the president might not only support private humanitarian assistance efforts but also request a modest humanitarian aid package, consisting primarily of emergency food aid, from the Congress. In addition, the administration might ask Congress to provide for medical supplies and electronic sensors for locating unexploded military ordnance. The State Department might let it be known, if it has not already done so, that the U.S. lifting of the trade embargo and the establishment of diplomatic missions would be timed in a flexible manner.

Thus, the U.S. stance would indicate a readiness to establish normal, friendly relations, to engage in commerce and communication on a mutually advantageous basis, and to contribute in a voluntary but modest fashion to the humanitarian and economic needs created by a long and brutal war. One might then hope that the Vietnamese could adapt their insistence upon the principle of reconstruction assistance to the forward-looking stance of U.S. policy with its goal of peace and development in the region. If this could be achieved, relations with Laos would quickly improve, to the benefit of that severely impoverished state. And the long, dark aftermath of revolution in Cambodia might gradually let in the light of international assistance and visitors from the outside world to brighten the outlook of its tragically isolated people.

Notes

Chapter 1

1. This position was most clearly expressed by Secretary of State Kissinger in press conferences and speeches in Minneapolis, July 15, 1975, and Detroit, November 24, 1975, and by President Ford in his "Pacific Doctrine" speech in Honolulu, December 7, 1975.

2. S. Barber, "Vietnam: Carter's Men Disagree," *Far Eastern Economic Review* (hereafter *FEER*), February 11, 1977, p. 31.

3. Laos and Cambodia were UN members since attaining independence from France, but Vietnam, being a divided country, had not been admitted.

4. A week later, the United States abstained on the membership application of Angola, which it had previously vetoed in June 1976, in the second departure from a thirty-year U.S. policy of favoring universal membership in the UN. Ambassador Scranton warned Washington that another U.S. veto would have an adverse effect on our relations in Africa, notwithstanding our charges that Angola lacked control over its people and was dependent on Cuban armed forces.

5. The House Select Committee on Missing Persons in Southeast Asia issued a final report on December 13, 1976, which provides the most authoritative data available on this thorny subject.

6. As quoted in *Nhan Dan* (Hanoi), April 16, 1976. Cf. U.S., Congress, House of Representatives, *Americans Missing in Southeast Asia: Hearings before the Select Committee on Missing Persons in Southeast Asia*, 94th Cong., 2d Sess., pt. 5, 1976, pp. 131, 186. The State Department provided only a summary of the letter, despite the Select Committee's request for the exact text.

7. Ibid., pp. 47-48.

8. Ibid., pt. 3, "Chronology of the FPJMT, 1973-75," pp. 229-232; and *Final Report*, December 13, 1976, pp. 117-120.

9. *New York Times*, November 13 and 14, 1976.

10. Press conference by Secretary of State Kissinger, Washington, D.C., April 22, 1976. On a subsequent occasion he called for a "wholly satisfactory accounting." Address by Hon. H. A. Kissinger, Seattle, Wash., July 22, 1976.

11. Apparently President Ford was incensed by the fact that U.S. records showed that two of the twelve had died in prison during the war. Douglas Pike, U.S. Department of State, Policy Planning, interview with the authors, November 3, 1976.

12. *Americans Missing in Southeast Asia: Final Report,* pp. 238, 242. Since visiting Hanoi a second time (as well as Laos) in March 1977, Chairman Montgomery seems to have reduced his own estimate of a realistic expectation to fewer than 100. Interview with the authors, June 29, 1977.

13. "Report of the Presidential Commission's Trip to Vietnam and Laos, March 16-20, 1977," *U.S. Department of State Bulletin,* April 18, 1977.

14. Ibid., p. 3.

15. Ibid., p. 6.

16. A list of voluntary agencies that contributed approximately $3 million in licensed shipments of humanitarian supplies to Vietnam in the first year after the fall of Saigon, but after often "inexcusable delays," is found in U.S., Congress, Senate, Committee on the Judiciary, Subcommittee to Investigate Problems Connected with Refugees and Escapees, *Aftermath of the War: Humanitarian Problems of Southeast Asia: Staff Report,* 94th Cong., 2d sess., May 17, 1976, pp. 23-25. Under President Carter, $5 million worth of private shipments were licensed in the first four months. *New York Times,* May 3, 1977.

17. U.S., Congress, House of Representatives, Committee on International Relations, *U.S. Embargo of Trade with South Vietnam and Cambodia: Hearing before the Subcommittee on International Trade and Commerce,* 94th Cong., 1st sess., June 4, 1975, p. 3. See also *FEER,* May 20, 1977, p. 17.

18. French, Canadian, Japanese, Australian, Algerian, Indonesian, and Norwegian oil specialists have apparently been in contact with the Vietnamese during 1976. Soviet technology is not being sought for the offshore fields, though it is apparently acceptable for inland exploration.

19. Secretary of State Kissinger, speech before the Upper Midwest Council, Minneapolis, Minnesota, July 15, 1975.

20. President Ford's Pacific Doctrine, Honolulu, Hawaii, December 7, 1975.

21. U.S. note of March 26, 1976, in *Americans Missing in Southeast Asia,* pt. 5, pp. 180-182.

22. *Christian Science Monitor,* August 9, 1976.

23. "Report of the Presidential Commission's trip to Vietnam and Laos, March 16-20, 1977." The State Department eventually articulated a coherent

policy of normalizing diplomatic relations wherever feasible and particularly with China and Cuba. *Speech by Deputy Secretary Warren Christopher at Occidental College,* June 11, 1977, Department of State, Bureau of Public Affairs.

24. *New York Times,* May 5, 1977.

25. *U.S. Foreign Policy for the 1970s: The Emerging Structure of Peace,* The President's Report to Congress, February 9, 1972.

26. *Americans Missing in Southeast Asia: Final Report,* pp. 249-253; and U.S., Senate, Committee on Foreign Relations, *Vietnam: 1976: Report by Senator George McGovern,* 94th Cong., 2d sess., March 1976, pp. 14-17.

27. *Americans Missing in Southeast Asia: Final Report,* pp. 114-116.

28. Gareth Porter, *A Peace Denied: The United States, Vietnam, and the Paris Agreement* (Bloomington: Indiana University Press, 1975), pp. 148, 153, 200-201, 231. Porter points out that negotiators at Paris had tried without success to include in the agreement a provision for cease-fires in Laos and Cambodia, and though the DRV gave a private assurance to use its influence in Laos, it consistently refused such an understanding regarding Cambodia. The North Vietnamese had far less influence there, although the U.S. government may not have perceived this at the time.

29. *Vietnam: 1976,* pp. 9-15.

30. *New York Times,* May 20, 1977.

31. Porter, *A Peace Denied,* p. 201. It appears that North Vietnam did limit the flow of weapons to the Khmer Rouge in 1973 and early 1974, but this did not end the fighting. W. Shawcross, "Cambodia When the Bombing Finally Stopped," *FEER,* January 14, 1977, pp. 32, 34.

32. *Vietnam: 1976,* p. 17. In April 1976, the Hanoi newspaper *Nhan Dan* published excerpts from the Nixon letter of February 1, 1973; *Foreign Broadcast Information Service (FBIS),* April 16, 1976, K1.

33. *Aftermath of the War: Humanitarian Problems of Southeast Asia,* p. 47.

34. Ibid., p. 9.

35. *Congressional Record,* May 4, 1977, p. H4008; *New York Times,* May 5, 1977.

36. *New York Times,* May 20, 1977.

37. Ibid.

38. Ibid., June 3, 1977.

39. Ibid., June 23, 1977.

40. *Congressional Quarterly,* August 13, 1977, pp. 3-4, and September 24, 1977, p. 6.

41. *Americans Missing in Southeast Asia: Final Report,* p. 235; and Clyde Farnsworth, *New York Times,* June 26, 1977.

42. Dr. V. Umbricht, "Multilateral Aid to Vietnam; Second Five-Year

Plan Period 1976-1980," *Third Progress Report on Assistance to Vietnam*, to the secretary general of the United Nations, May 1977, Annex to Chapter 2. The International Red Cross has also played a major role in providing medical supplies and equipment.

Chapter 2

1. Rupert Emerson has pointed out that Vietnam, unlike most Third World countries, is endowed with the qualities out of which the classic definition of a nation—in the European context—was developed: a people with a unique culture, a long history as a nation, a well-defined territory, and a language of their own. Rupert Emerson, *Empire to Nation* (Cambridge, Mass.: Harvard University Press, 1960).

2. A Hanoi intellectual, Dr. Nguyen Khac Vien, claims that there are "at least 150 thousand tons of unexploded bombs and shells which are daily causing loss of life; several million acres of rice fields, gardens and forests destroyed by bombs and chemicals; permanent threat of epidemic (malaria, plague, cholera, typhoid)." *New York Times,* December 15, 1976.

3. From *Congressional Record,* May 10, 1972, pp. 16761-16762. Quoted in David W. P. Elliott, "North Vietnam since Ho," *Problems of Communism* 24, no. 4 (July-August 1975): 42.

4. An excellent analysis of the Fourth Party Congress is contained in William S. Turley, "Vietnam since Reunification," *Problems of Communism* 26, no. 2 (March-April 1977): 36-54.

5. Douglas Pike, "Year End Report: Vietnam during the Year 1976" Washington, D.C., January 1977, p. 9.

6. Ibid., p. 11.

7. Turley, "Vietnam since Reunification," p. 40.

8. For the most complete assessment of the role of the North in the southern revolution from 1954 to 1959, see Carlyle Thayer, "The Origins of the National Front for Liberation of South Vietnam" (Ph.D. diss., The Australian National University, February 1977). See also Joseph J. Zasloff, "The Role of North Vietnam in the Southern Insurgency," The Rand Corporation, RM 4140-PR, July 1964; Senior General Van Tien Dung, "Great Spring Victory," *FBIS,* June 7, 1976, July 7, 1976 supplements.

9. Pike, "Vietnam 1976," p. 26.

10. See Turley, "Vietnam since Reunification," p. 36.

11. Ho Chi Minh City radio broadcast, December 21, 1976, in *FBIS,* December 29, 1976.

12. *Thirty Years of Struggle of the Party* (Hanoi, 1960), p. 27.

13. Le Duan, "All Unite to Build the United Socialist Fatherland of Vietnam," *Hoc Tap* (Hanoi), July 1976, p. 28, cited in Turley, "Vietnam since Reunification," p. 38.

14. Le Duc Tho's Address to Fourth Party Congress, cited in Turley, "Vietnam since Reunification," p. 44.

15. Both Turley, "Vietnam since Reunification," p. 44, and Pike, "Vietnam 1976," p. 20, give the figure of 1,553,500 as "official membership figures." Turley cites *Hoc Tap*, June 1966.

16. Turley, "Vietnam since Reunification," p. 43, cites Radio Hanoi, September 14-19, 23, 25, 29, 1976, in *FBIS*, September 17, 20, 21, 23, 28-30, October 1 and 4, 1976.

17. Hanoi, VNA in English, December 16, 1976.

18. Turley, "Vietnam since Reunification," p. 44. According to Turley, "the Vietnamese have never followed the Maoist example of viewing the peasantry as a legitimate, sufficient basis for the revolution, even though a majority of the Party's members are from rural, often middle peasant backgrounds."

19. Radio Hanoi, December 17, 1976, in *FBIS*, January 17, 1977.

20. Turley, "Vietnam since Reunification," cites Radio Hanoi of November 11, 12, 20, and 23, 1976, and Radio Ho Chi Minh City of November 12, 1976, *FBIS*, November 19, 23, and 26, 1976.

21. Turley, "Vietnam since Reunification," p. 43.

22. See VWP Central Committee Political Report, Hanoi, VNA in English, in *FBIS*, December 27, 1976, p. 99. The Central Committee report warned, "Particular caution must be exercised against the reactionaries and spies who try to infiltrate the Party."

23. Turley, "Vietnam since Reunification," pp. 57-58.

24. General Resolution of the Fourth Party Congress, Hanoi, VNA in English, December 24, 1976, in *FBIS*, December 28, 1976, K30-31. Political report of the political consultative conference on national reunification, read by Chairman Troung Chinh, VNA in English, November 17, 1975, in *FBIS*, December 11, 1975, supplement, p. 9.

25. According to William J. Duiker, "Ideology and Nation-Building in the Democratic Republic of Vietnam," *Asian Survey* 27, no. 5 (May 1977): 421-422, the communists believed that Thieu's "land to the tiller" program had decreased the power of the feudal forces in rural areas in the South. He cites Chieng Thang (pseudonym), "The Last Stage of Anti-U.S. National Salvation Resistance," *Nhan Dan*, December 1, 1975.

26. *FBIS*, December 11, 1975, supplement, p. 12.

27. Since the formation of the DRV in 1945, there have been five national assembly elections in the North: 1946, 1960, 1964, 1971, and 1975. See Tai Sung An, "The All-Vietnam National Assembly: Significant Developments," *Asian Survey* 18, no. 5 (May 1977): 432-439.

28. Pike notes that all the top echelon Party and governmental leaders received more than 95 percent of the vote. Pike, "Vietnam 1976," p. 74.

29. Nguyen Huu Tho Report, Saigon Domestic Service in Vietnamese, May 13, 1976, in *FBIS*, May 17, 1976.

30. Pike, "Vietnam 1976," p. 81.

31. Ibid., pp. 80-82.

32. *World Bank Atlas, 1976* (Washington, D.C., 1976).

33. Citibank, Hong Kong, *Vietnam: An Economic Study,* September 1976, p. 14.

34. *Report of the United Nations Mission to North and South Vietnam,* March 1976, p. 16.

35. Citibank, *Vietnam,* p. 10.

36. *Report of the United Nations Mission,* p. 4.

37. Citibank, *Vietnam,* p. 41.

38. Ibid., p. 46.

39. *Report of the United Nations Mission,* pp. 5-6.

40. Ibid., pp. 19, 22. Four main reasons were cited in favor of the policy: the availability of virgin land or wasteland; the human capabilities to be re-settled; the need for increased production to meet the needs of the population; the possibility of carrying out social structuring with a view to relieving congestion in the urban centers.

41. Pike, "Vietnam 1976," p. 66.

42. Umbricht, *Third Progress Report.*

43. Ibid., Annex to Chapter 2; and *FEER,* May 20, 1977, p. 77.

44. Le Duan's Political Report to the Fourth Party Congress, Hanoi, VNA in English, December 16, 1976, in *FBIS,* December 22, 1976 ("Material on Fourth Vietnam Workers' Party Congress," Vol. 1), p. 31.

45. Ibid., pp. 14, 21.

46. Ibid., p. 31.

47. Ibid., p. 15. The official line opaquely expresses the relationship: "Rational priority is given to the development of heavy industry on the basis of the development of agriculture and light industry."

48. Quoted from Vietnamese press, in Leo Goodstadt, "Looking Abroad for Inner Relief," *Insight,* February 1977, p. 7.

49. Le Duan's report, *FBIS,* December 22, 1976, p. 33.

50. Ibid., p. 48.

51. Umbricht, *Third Progress Report,* p. 7. Other estimates by foreign banks have put the external financing requirement at over 50 percent and conclude that Vietnam will have to resort to substantial foreign borrowing on commercial terms.

52. Citibank, Hong Kong, Economics Department, "Notes on Vietnam," May 1977.

53. A North American bank estimated in May 1977 that the prospects for "particularly strong growth in coal, fish products, timber and wood products, tea and coffee were quite favorable."

54. World Bank assistance might run as much as $400 million for a three-year period.

55. Cf. Umbricht, *Third Progress Report.*

56. "Material on Fourth Vietnam Workers' Party Congress," vol. 6, *FBIS,* January 31, 1977, p. 11.

57. Pike, "Vietnam 1976," p. 58.

58. Bank of America, Asia Representative Office, Hong Kong, "Indochina Spotlight," July 1977. An early, outsider's assessment of the Party's plan for southern agriculture concluded, "South Vietnam is moving quite rapidly toward collective agriculture." Edwin E. Moise, "Land Reform and Land Reform Errors in North Vietnam," *Pacific Affairs* 49, no. 1 (Spring 1976): 92.

59. Turley, "Vietnam since Reunification," p. 50.

60. For a discussion of the pragmatism of the Vietnamese communists, see Alexander Woodside, "Progress, Stability and Peace in Mainland Southeast Asia," in *Southern Asia: The Politics of Poverty and Peace, Critical Choices for Americans,* ed. Donald C. Hellman, vol. 13 (Lexington, Mass.: Lexington Books, 1976), pp. 139-189.

61. See VWP CC Report by Le Duan, Hanoi VNA in English, December 16, 1976, in *FBIS,* December 27, 1976, supplement, vol. 2, p. 89. See also speech on Vietnamese foreign policy by Foreign Minister Nguyen Duy Trinh, Hanoi VNA in English, December 19, 1976, in *FBIS,* December 20, 1976.

62. VWP CC Report, p. 9. See also Hanoi broadcast quoting *Nhan Dan,* using similar language, February 28, 1976, in *FBIS,* March 1, 1976. For the reaction of Southeast Asian countries, see Ellen Hammer, "Indochina: Communist But Non-Aligned," *Problems of Communism* 25, no. 3 (May-June 1976): 13-16.

63. See Paul F. Langer and Joseph J. Zasloff, *North Vietnam and the Pathet Lao: Partners in the Struggle for Laos* (Cambridge, Mass.: Harvard University Press, 1970).

64. Vientiane KPL in English, March 23, 1976, in *FBIS,* March 24, 1976.

65. See *New York Times,* July 20, 1977; *Washington Post,* July 19 and 21, 1977; *FEER,* July 29, 1977.

66. For accounts of the founding of the communist party in Cambodia, see *Communist Party Power in Kampuchea (Cambodia); Documents and Discussion,* compiled and edited with an introduction by Timothy Michael Carney, Cornell University, Southeast Asia Program, no. 106 (Ithaca, N.Y., 1977); Wilfred Burchett, *Second Indochina War* (New York: International Publishers, 1970), p. 51; and Charles Meyer, *Derrière le Sourire khmer* (Paris: Plon, 1971), p. 186.

67. See David E. Brown, "Exporting Insurgency: The Communists in Cambodia," in *Indochina in Conflict,* ed. Joseph J. Zasloff and Allan E. Goodman (Lexington, Mass.: Lexington Books, 1972); J.L.S. Girling, "The

Resistance in Cambodia," *Asian Survey* 12, no. 7 (July 1972): 552-555;
Roger Kershaw, "Cambodian National Union—a Milestone in Popular Front
Technique," *World Today* 32, no. 2 (February 1976): 61-63.

68. Dispatch by René Flipo, broadcast by Agence France-Press, Hong
Kong, in *FBIS*, June 23, 1975.

69. See Allan W. Cameron, *Indochina: Prospects after the End* (Washington, D.C.: American Enterprise Institute, April 1976), p. 23; and Carlyle A.
Thayer, "Foreign Policy Orientation of the SRV," *Southeast Asian Affairs*
(1977), pp. 317-318.

70. Phnom Penh Domestic Service in Cambodian, December 31, 1977,
in *FBIS*, June 3, 1978.

71. Ibid.

72. *FEER*, January 13, 1978.

73. *New York Times*, January 4, 1978.

74. Phnom Penh Domestic Service in Cambodian, January 26, 1978,
in *FBIS*, January 27, 1978.

75. Ibid.

76. *FBIS*, January 24, 27, 30, 1978.

77. *New York Times*, February 9, 10, 1978.

78. *FEER*, January 13, 1978.

79. Hanoi International Service in English, January 27, 1978, in *FBIS*,
January 30, 1978.

80. See John F. Cady, *Southeast Asia: Its Historical Development* (New
York: McGraw-Hill, 1964), p. 419; Dennis J. Duncanson, *Government and
Revolution in Vietnam* (New York: Oxford University Press, 1968), p. 5;
John T. McAlister, Jr., "The Possibilities for Diplomacy in Southeast Asia,"
World Politics 29, no. 2 (January 1967): 265.

81. "Chinh phu lien ban cong hoa dan chu Dong duong." The Seventh
Plenum Resolution is described in Tran Huy Lier, *Lich au Tam Muoi nam
chong Phap* [Eighty years of history fighting france], vol. 2, book 2 (Hanoi:
Ban nghien cuu van su dia, 1958), p. 48.

82. We are indebted to William Turley for the citation of the Seventh
Plenum, above, and the statements by VWP cadres. Personal communication.

83. The recent SRV decision to terminate the autonomous zones in
which their highland minorities of the North live is consistent with a pattern
of the last decade to accelerate assimilation, or at least integration, and to
tighten the administrative network in these areas.

84. Up to December 1955, the government reported 5,200 such "bandits" and over 4,000 firearms had been seized. See Le Chuong, "Thanh tich
hon mot nam cua quan doi nhan dan" [Over 100 years of achievement on our
army], *Nhan Dan*, January 3, 1956.

85. Woodside, "Progress, Stability and Peace," p. 172.

86. Aware of this concern within southern Asia, the Lao government has publicly denied any intention to annex "the 16 northeast provinces of Thailand." See, for example, the broadcast in English by the Pathet Lao News Agency, January 7, 1976, and the broadcast in Lao, January 15, 1976.

87. Radio Hanoi, February 28, 1976, in *FBIS,* March 1, 1976.

88. Dispatch from Manila by Henry Kamm, *New York Times,* February 24, 1977.

89. *FEER,* May 7, 1976.

90. Ibid., July 16, 1976.

91. Both statements quoted in Lau Teik Soon, "ASEAN and Bali Summit," *Pacific Community,* July 1976, pp. 542-543.

92. Ibid., p. 545.

93. *FEER,* September 10, 1976.

94. Ibid., July 29, 1977, p. 14.

95. A *New York Times* dispatch by Bernard Weintraub from Washington, citing State Department and Pentagon sources, notes that the Vietnamese "quietly turned down offers from several African and Asian nations" and had "declined to supply guerrilla movements in Thailand, Malaysia and the Philippines." Vietnam's refusal to sell arms from this huge stockpile was attributed, in part, to a desire to cement economic links with the West, including the United States, and reluctance to being labeled an "exporter of revolution." *New York Times,* April 30, 1977.

96. A *New York Times* editorial of July 25, 1977, alludes to the possibility of low-level support to the insurgency in Malaysia, although State Department and Pentagon sources, as the previous note shows, do not corroborate such provision of arms.

97. The Manila Treaty, signed by the United States, Great Britain, France, Australia, New Zealand, and Pakistan to create SEATO, still technically persists, although France and Pakistan dissociated themselves from the organization years ago, and Great Britain has no significant military presence east of Suez.

98. See Hugh Toye, *Laos: Buffer State or Battleground* (New York: Oxford University Press, 1968), for a discussion of these historic Vietnamese-Thai tensions and their impact upon Laos.

99. For a summary of SRV ties with the Third World, see Thayer, "Foreign Policy Orientation."

100. For information on these activities, see Hanoi, VNA, December 15, 1976, in *FBIS,* December 16, 1976; *FBIS,* June 1, 1976; and Turley, "Vietnam since Reunification," p. 50.

101. For a discussion of Soviet Asian strategy, see Arnold L. Horelick, "Soviet Policy Dilemmas in Asia," *Asian Survey* 17, no. 6 (June 1977): 499-512.

102. Hanoi, VNA in English, July 31, 1975, in *FBIS*, August 1, 1975.
103. See Thayer, "Foreign Policy Orientation," p. 310.
104. Ibid.
105. See Sheldon Simon, "Peking and Indochina: The Perplexity of Victory," *Asian Survey* 16, no. 5 (May 1976): 401-410.
106. See Douglas Pike, "North Vietnam's Future Foreign Relations" (unpublished, Washington, D.C., July 1975), pp. 54-56.
107. Thayer, "Vietnamese Foreign Policy Orientation," p. 316.

Chapter 3

1. *Neo Lao Hak Sat* (NLHS) in the Lao language. The term *Pathet Lao* (PL) is commonly applied to the movement represented by the Lao Patriotic Front, which is controlled by the Lao People's Revolutionary Party (LPRP).

2. Prince Souphanouvong, the half brother of Souvanna Phouma, joined political forces with Ho Chi Minh against the French in 1945 and subsequently became the foremost public leader of the Lao Patriotic Front (the Pathet Lao).

3. Third Resolution of the Party Central Committee, *Joint Publications Research Service* (JPRS), translations in Southeast Asia, no. 657, August 16, 1976.

4. U.S. personnel had numbered over 800 earlier in the year. *New York Times*, May 10, 1976.

5. *Lao Presse*, December 17, 1975.

6. Pike, "North Vietnam: Future Foreign Relations."

7. Only one leader of some prominence, Sot Petrasy—and he does not appear to have been a Central Committee member—was not reappointed to a high government position in the LPDR after the reshuffling of posts with the toppling of the PGNU. There were rumors that his colleagues considered Sot to be too bourgeoisified by his tenure as the PL liaison officer in the RLG, living the soft life in Vientiane from 1964 through 1975.

8. Vientiane Service in Lao, May 2, 1977, in *FBIS*, May 2, 1977.

9. See John Everingham, *FEER*, May 27, 1977.

10. See Robert Melson and Howard Wolpe, "Modernization and the Politics of Communalism: A Theoretical Perspective," *American Political Science Review* 64, no. 4 (December 1970): 1112-1130.

11. According to an LPRP official history, "after a period of preparation, at the Congress of Representatives of the former members of the ICP, on March 22, 1955, the three hundred member LPP [Lao People's Party, formerly the designation of the LPRP] was formally founded." Vientiane KPL in English, March 23, 1976, in *FBIS*, March 24, 1976.

12. Ibid.

13. Since the LPRP has not made public a list of Central Committee and Politburo members, these bodies may have a larger membership than cited above. However, members of these two bodies are publicly identified at official functions, and membership lists have been compiled from such designations in the Lao press and radio.

14. Joseph J. Zasloff, *The Pathet Lao: Leadership and Organization* (Lexington, Mass.: Lexington Books, 1973), p. 30.

15. Broadcast greetings from fraternal communist parties abroad contained several apparently inadvertent references to the Lao People's Party, including a message from the Japanese Communist Party in 1966, the Vietnamese Workers' Party in 1967, the Bulgarian Communist Party in 1967, the East German Communist Party in 1968, the Albanian Communist Party in 1968, and the East German Communist Party in 1969.

16. Pathet Lao News Agency in English, October 5, 1970.

17. Interview with the authors in Vientiane, July 1974.

18. Third resolution of Party Central Committee, May 14-19, 1976, *JPRS.*

19. Prime Minister Kaysone's report to the SPC-cabinet meeting, *FBIS,* April 11, 1977, supplement, p. 9. Lao authorities expelled an Australian journalist in July 1977, charging that he was in possession of a history of the LPRP plus other documents about the Lao Party.

20. The SPC held a joint meeting with the cabinet from February 18 to 28, 1977, where general secretary of the Party, Kaysone, read a fifty-five-page political report evaluating the first year of the LPDR and laying out the tasks for the future. Kaysone's report was read to the Lao public by radio almost a month after the close of the meeting. Vientiane Domestic Service in Lao, March 17-20, 1977, in *FBIS,* April 11, 1977, supplement.

21. Hanoi, VNA in English, June 25, 1976, in *FBIS,* June 29, 1976.

22. Third resolution of the Party Central Committee, May 14-19, 1976, *JPRS.*

23. In May 1976, the authorities also rounded up 1,200 to 1,300 of Vientiane's "prostitutes, addicts, gamblers, hippies, thieves, and lost children" and shipped them off to "reeducation" camps. See John Everingham, "The Not So Gentle Revolution," *FEER,* May 7, 1976; ibid., September 10, 1976; the series on Laos by Patrice de Beer in *Le Monde,* December 1-6, 1976; and the *New York Times,* December 13, 1976.

24. See *FEER,* April 9, 1976; Robert Shaplen, "Letter from Laos," *New Yorker,* August 2, 1976, pp. 64-76; David A. Andelman, "Laos after the Takeover," *New York Times Magazine,* October 24, 1976; and the *New York Times,* September 7, 1976.

25. *FBIS,* April 11, 1977, supplement, p. 22.

26. Nayan Chanda, "Laos Gears up for Rural Progress," *FEER,* April 8,

1977, pp. 124-126. "To show their anger," the minister said, "some peasants have even cut down their fruit trees."

27. See John Everingham, "The New Communist Laos: Repression and Persistence," *Washington Post,* July 10, 1977.

28. Ibid.

29. "Lao Premier's Political Report at February 18-28 SPC-Cabinet Meeting," *FBIS,* supplement, April 11, 1977, p. 15.

30. *New York Times,* September 9, 1976. Basic economic data has been derived from Donald P. Whitaker et al., *Area Handbook for Laos* (Washington, D.C.: U.S. Government Printing Office, 1972); and Dr. Pane Rassavong, commissioner general of planning, "Briefing on the Economy of Laos," Vientiane, July 18, 1974.

31. Whitaker et al., *Area Handbook for Laos,* pp. 235-237.

32. The abandonment of cultivable land, its disruption by bomb craters and unexploded ordnance, the tremendous loss of buffalo for pulling plows, and the loss of farm tools were, of course, serious destructive consequences of the bombing, even in the mountainous eastern areas of the country.

33. J. Everingham, *FEER,* June 3, 1977, p. 19.

34. Embassy of the U.S.A., U.S. AID Mission to Laos, *Facts on Foreign Aid to Laos,* 2d ed., July 1973, pp. 21, 106.

35. Non-U.S. assistance to Laos amounted to $18.3 million in 1973. Less than a quarter of U.S. economic assistance, however, in FY 1973 was available for development; ibid., pp. 15, 132.

36. *New York Times,* May 15, 1977.

37. Rassavong, "Briefing on the Economy of Laos."

38. "Lao Premier's Political Report at February 18-28 SPC-Cabinet Meeting," *FBIS,* April 11, 1977, supplement, p. 4; *FEER,* April 8, 1977, p. 126, August 26, 1977, pp. 44-48, and December 16, 1977.

39. "Lao Premier's Political Report at February 18-28 SPC-Cabinet Meeting," *FBIS,* April 11, 1977, supplement, p. 24.

40. Vientiane Domestic Service in Lao, May 5, 1977, in *FBIS,* May 11, 1977.

41. *FBIS,* April 11, 1977.

42. *FEER,* April 8, 1977. p. 124.

43. Vientiane Domestic Service in Lao, December 21, 1976, in *FBIS,* January 3, 1977.

44. Vientiane Domestic Service in Lao, June 14, 1976, in *FBIS,* June 23, 1976.

45. *Facts on Foreign Aid to Laos,* July 1973, Table 27.

46. Vientiane Domestic Service in Lao, December 21, 1976, in *FBIS,* January 3, 1977.

47. Bank of America, Asia Representative Office, Hong Kong, *Indochina Spotlight,* May 1977.

48. Domestic Service in Lao, June 14, 1976, in *FBIS*, June 23, 1976.

49. Foreign aid to the Royal Government averaged $74.4 million from 1968-1973. Interview by the authors at the World Bank, Washington, D.C., December 29, 1977.

50. Vientiane Domestic Service in Lao, June 14, 1976, in *FBIS*, June 23, 1976.

51. *FEER*, June 3, 1977, p. 20.

52. Ibid., April 8, 1977. A summary of all the foreign economic assistance to Laos in 1976 was given by Vientiane Domestic Service, November 29, 1976, in *FBIS*, December 3, 1976.

53. Phnom Penh Domestic Service in Cambodia, December 16, 1977, in *FBIS*, December 19, 1977.

54. Vientiane KPL in English, December 19, 1977, in *FBIS*, December 19, 1977.

55. Hanoi, VNA in English, December 26, 1977, in *FBIS*, December 27, 1977.

56. Article by Kaysone Phomvihan in *Pravda*, December 2, 1976; see also *FBIS*, Laos, December 7, 1976.

57. *FBIS*, December 8, 1976, Laos, and November 29, 1976, Laos, quoting *Siang Pasason*.

58. Ibid., December 2, 1976, Laos.

59. *FEER*, September 10, 1976, p. 11.

60. "Report of the Presidential Commission's Trip to Vietnam and Laos, March 16-20, 1977," *Department of State Bulletin*, April 18, 1977.

Chapter 4

1. For a description of this evacuation, see Pulitzer Prize–winning articles by Sidney H. Schanberg, *New York Times*, May 9-13, 1975; also Jon Swain, *The Sunday Times* (London), May 11, 1975; François Ponchaud, *Cambodge Année Zéro* (Paris, 1977), Chapters 1-4.

2. Ponchaud, *Cambodge Année Zéro*, p. 216. *Newsweek*, September 19, 1977, p. 63, stated that 60,000 Cambodians had fled to Vietnam. See also Horst Faas, "Hanoi Discriminates against Cambodian Refugees," *The Nation Review* (Bangkok), October 17, 1977.

3. Broadcasts by Radio Phnom Penh are sent daily from 6 to 7 A.M., 11 to 12 A.M., and 8 to 10 P.M. local time. Translations of selected broadcasts are found in the *Foreign Broadcast Information Service (FBIS)*, Asia and Pacific Series (APA).

4. A Cambodian spokesman, in a public eulogy to Chairman Mao Tse-tung that was perhaps broadcast inadvertently, stated that the Cambodian people joined in mourning with the "fraternal Chinese Communist Party, government and people." *FBIS*, September 10, 1976. Perhaps also inadver-

tently, Kaysone Phomvihan, the general secretary of the Lao People's Revolutionary Party, sent a telegram in April 1976 addressed to Pol Pot, "Secretary-General of the Central Committee of the Communist Party of Kampuchea," *FBIS,* April 19, 1976. Some months earlier, Vientiane had published the text of congratulations from the Cambodian Communist Party Central Committee to the Lao People's Revolutionary Party Central Committee on the thirtieth anniversary of the Lao proclamation of independence, *FBIS,* October 16, 1975.

5. See Carney, *Communist Party Power in Kampuchea.* See also Wilfred Burchett, *Second Indochina War* (London: Lorrimer Publishing Co., 1970), p. 39.

6. See Milton Osborne, "Reflections on the Cambodian Tragedy," *Pacific Community* 8, no. 1 (October 1976): 2-3.

7. A British aide to Prince Sihanouk at the time writes of the military response to the present protest: "The purification of the disturbed region was undertaken with the rude vigor peculiar to soldiery who had been promised a monetary reward for each severed head they might forward to military headquarters in Phnom Penh. Villages were given over to the flames, while the surviving inhabitants fled for their lives to the shelter of the hills." Donald Lancaster, "The Decline of Prince Sihanouk's Regime," in Zasloff and Goodman, *Indochina in Conflict,* p. 52.

8. For analyses of the composition of the Khmer Rouge see Elizabeth Becker, "Who Are the Khmer Rouge," *Washington Post,* March 10, 1974; David Brown, "Exporting Insurgency: The Communists in Cambodia," in Zasloff and Goodman, *Indochina in Conflict,* pp. 125-135; Richard Dudman, *Forty Days with the Enemy* (New York: Liverright Press, 1971); J.L.S. Girling, "The Resistance in Cambodia," *Asian Survey* 12, no. 7 (July 1972): 549-563; Kenneth M. Quinn, "Political Change in Wartime: The Khmer Krahom Revolution in Southern Cambodia, 1970-1974," *Naval War College Review* 28, no. 4 (Spring 1976): 3-31; Carney, *Communist Party Power in Kampuchea;* Patrice de Beer, "Who Rules in Cambodia?" *Le Monde,* May 10, 1975; Ponchaud, *Cambodge Année Zéro,* Chapter 10.

9. For discussion of this group, see Spencer Davis, *FEER,* March 28, 1975, p. 11; Jacques Decornoy, *Le Monde,* April 16, 1975; Ponchaud, *Cambodge Année Zéro,* p. 190. Ponchaud states that there were 5,000 military effectives among this anti-French resistance, about half of whom left for Hanoi and the other half disappeared into the underground in Cambodia.

10. Hou Youn's doctoral dissertation in economics, defended in 1955, was entitled, "The Peasantry of Cambodia and Its Prospects for Modernization." Khieu Samphan, who also earned a doctorate in economics, in 1959, defended his dissertation, "The Economy of Cambodia and Its Problems of Industrialization."

11. In 1962, Khieu Samphan was named secretary of state for commerce, Hou Youn was secretary of state at the Plan, and Chau Seng successively directed the ministries of Education, Agriculture, and Economy.

12. In 1963, Ieng Sary, then a lycée teacher, Son Sen, director of curriculum at the National Pedagogical Institute until mid-1962, and Saloth Sar, a teacher active in left-wing journalism circles, fled to the maquis in apparent fear of Sihanouk's repression. See Carney, *Communist Party Power in Kampuchea;* Ponchaud, *Cambodge Année Zéro,* p. 193; Burchett, *Second Indochina War,* p. 53.

13. Among those who fled in 1967 were Tiv Ol and Koy Thuon, teachers; on April 24, 1967, Hou Youn and Khieu Samphan disappeared; Hu Nim and Poc Deuskom left soon afterward. All emerged with important positions in the Party. See Carney, *Communist Party Power in Kampuchea;* and Ponchaud, *Cambodge Année Zéro,* p. 196.

14. For a quotation from Sihanouk revealing his outrage at the humiliation inflicted upon him by his enemies on the right and his determination to seek revenge, see Charles Meyer, *Derrière le Sourire khmer* (Paris, 1971), p. 371.

15. Three Khmer Rouge leaders, Hou Youn, Hu Nim, and Khieu Samphan, who were rumored to have been executed by Sihanouk when they disappeared from Phnom Penh in 1967, appeared in a jovial mood with Prince Sihanouk in a photo taken during his visit to the "liberated" territory in 1973.

16. Interview by Oriana Fallaci, *New York Times Magazine,* August 12, 1973.

17. See *History of the Revolutionary Struggle,* broadcast on Phnom Penh Domestic Service in Cambodian, April 14, 1977, in *FBIS,* April 28, 1977.

18. Phnom Penh Domestic Service in Cambodian, September 24, 1977, in *FBIS,* September 26, 1977. Ponchaud, *Cambodge Année Zéro,* p. 213, cites an AP news release of October 10, 1976, stating that Saloth Sar has been secretary general of the Khmer Communist Party since September 30, 1972. See Chapter 4, note 24, for further references.

19. Phnom Penh Domestic Service in Cambodian, September 28, 1977, in *FBIS,* October 4, 1977, H-1 to H-38.

20. An article in *FBIS* reported the remarks of Sim Son, the Cambodian ambassador to North Korea, on the occasion of a banquet he gave in Pyongyang to celebrate the seventeenth anniversary of the founding of the Communist Party of Cambodia. "[He said that] although the Cambodian Party has a 26-year history since its founding in 1951, it is seventeen years old since its formal advent as the Communist Party of Cambodia. He said that from the day of its founding, the party organized and mobilized all the Cambodian people including workers, peasants and the masses of stooges, landlords and capitalists,

and that as a result the rascals had to leave Cambodia in 1954." Pyongyang Domestic Service in Korean, October 1, 1977, in *FBIS,* October 4, 1977.

21. See Chapter 4, note 19, H 7-8.

22. See: Nayan Chanda, "The Pieces Begin to Fit," *FEER,* October 21, 1977; Fox Butterfield, dispatches from Hong Kong in *New York Times,* September 29, 30, 1977; Lewis M. Simons, dispatches from Bangkok, *Washington Post,* September 29, 30, 1977.

23. Biographical sketches of five Party leaders are found in Carney, *Communist Party Power in Kampuchea.* A Khmer defector, a helicopter pilot who flew communist leaders about the country until his defection to Thailand in April 1976, provided a few observations on the ruling elite. See *Washington Post,* May 4, 1976; and *New York Times,* May 26, 1976. See also Ponchaud, *Cambodge Année Zéro,* Chapter 10; Peter Poole, *"Cambodia,"* *Yearbook on International Communist Affairs,* vols. for 1976 and 1977; Kenneth Quinn, "Cambodia 1976: Internal Consolidation and External Expansion," *Asian Survey* 17, no. 1 (January 1977): 43-54.

24. See *Washington Post,* September 29 and 30, 1977; *New York Times,* September 30, 1977; *FEER,* October 21, 1977. For earlier speculation that Pol Pot was Saloth Sar, see Quinn, "Cambodia 1976," p. 46. The speculation had been reinforced by a congratulatory telegram sent by Kaysone Phomvihan, general secretary of the Lao People's Revolutionary Party, to the new Prime Minister Pol Pot, addressing him as "Secretary-General of the Central Committee of the Communist Party of Kampuchea," a post believed to be held by Saloth Sar. See *FBIS,* April 19, 1976. Doubt was cast upon the theory that Pol Pot and Saloth Sar were the same person by the Cambodian helicopter pilot who defected in May 1976. Drawing upon his experience in flying leaders about the country, he claimed to have seen both Pol Pot and Saloth Sar. See *FEER,* October 29, 1976. (Presumed photos of both Pol Pot and Saloth Sar were included in this issue as well as one of Non Suon, also mentioned as the same person as Pol Pot. Non Suon was a former secretary of the Pracheachon Party, arrested in 1962 and released by the Lon Nol government in 1970.) By September 1977, however, most observers believed that Pol Pot and Saloth Sar were the same person. A biography of Pol Pot was broadcast on Pyongyang radio just before his official visit to North Korea. See Pyongyang Domestic Service in Korean, October 3, 1977, in *FBIS,* October 4, 1977.

25. Ponchaud, *Cambodge Année Zéro,* pp. 190-191.

26. Carney, *Communist Party Power in Kampuchea.* According to Ponchaud, Khieu Samphan was born in 1929 of a Cambodian father and Chinese mother, *Cambodge Année Zéro,* pp. 184-185.

27. Interviews in Phnom Penh in August 1974 by one of the authors.

28. See Chapter 4, note 15.

29. Ponchaud, *Cambodge Année Zéro*, pp. 187-188. According to Carney, *Communist Party Power in Kampuchea*, Son Sen lost his scholarship because he had been a sponsor of the August 1955 Khmer student political meeting in Paris.

30. *FBIS*, September 27, 1976.

31. See Edith Lenart, "Leaders from the Ranks," *FEER*, June 25, 1976; also Ponchaud, *Cambodge Année Zéro*, pp. 212-213.

32. It is possible that there are other members of the commanding Standing Committee of the Central Committee of the KCP who have not yet been identified. A possible addition is Phoung.

33. See Carney, *Communist Party Power in Kampuchea*.

34. See translation of Ith Sarin, "Regrets for the Khmer Soul," in ibid. Ith Sarin, an inspector of primary education who spent most of 1972 with the communist movement as a candidate member of the Party, describes, in a personal memoir, life in the Bureau of Information and Culture of a region near Phnom Penh.

35. Ibid.

36. William Shawcross, "Cambodia under Its New Rulers," *New York Review of Books*, March 4, 1976.

37. Richard Nations, "Inside the Bitter Border," *FEER*, August 19, 1977, pp. 9-12.

38. A *Wall Street Journal* reporter who interviewed several former Khmer communist cadres in Thailand reported that one, a village chief in Siem Riep Province, claimed that in February 1977, approximately fifty province officials were ordered to Phnom Penh. Two weeks later, word came back from Angka that all of these officials had been removed because they were "CIA agents" who had "killed many people so that the people wouldn't like Angka." Sometime in April, the same village chief said, the new province leaders began telling each village leader that "the chief wants to see you." The leaders went, he said, and never returned.

Another former communist cadre, an artillery unit commander, claimed that between April and July about 800 Khmer communist officers and men were "caught" in Oddar Meanchey Province along the Thai border. He said that "simple soldiers were led away with their hands tied behind their backs. Officers weren't tied up until they reached Siem Reap." Asked why they were arrested, he said that he did not "know the big story but they told us the old Khmer Rouge wanted to make a 'new revolution.' " Barry Kramer, "Cambodia's Communist Regime Begins to Purge Its Own Ranks While Continuing a Crack-Down," *Wall Street Journal*, October 19, 1977.

39. Pyongyang KCNA in English, September 29, 1977, in *FBIS*, September 30, 1977.

40. Cf. *FBIS*, October 3, 1977, H-6.

41. Phnom Penh Domestic Service in Cambodian, September 28, 1977, in *FBIS*, October 4, 1977.

42. Pol Pot press conference in Peking. Peking, NCNA in English, October 3, 1977, in *FBIS*, October 3, 1977.

43. See, for example, Donald Kirk, "Revolution and Political Violence in Cambodia, 1970-1974," in *Communism in Indochina*, ed. Joseph J. Zasloff and MacAlister Brown (Lexington, Mass.: Lexington Books, D. C. Heath and Co., 1975), pp. 215-230.

44. See Kershaw, "Cambodian National Union," p. 62.

45. See testimony of Charles Twining, U.S., Congress, House of Representatives, Committee on International Relations, *Hearings on Human Rights in Cambodia*, 95th Cong., 1st sess., July 26, 1977.

46. Carney, *Communist Party Power in Kampuchea*, brings together the limited information about the Party in an analytic essay and includes translations of several Party documents. See also Quinn, "The Khmer Krahom Revolution in Southern Cambodia, 1970-1974," pp. 3-31.

47. Ith Sarin, "Regrets for the Khmer Soul," in Carney, *Communist Party Power in Kampuchea*.

48. Tiziano Terzani interview with Ieng Sary, *Rome l'Espresso*, May 8, 1977, in *FBIS*, May 23, 1977.

49. Ibid.

50. See Kershaw, "Cambodian National Union," pp. 63-66.

51. For accounts of these executions see Nayan Chanda, "When the Killing Had to Stop," *FEER*, October 29, 1976, pp. 20-23. Lewis M. Simons, in a dispatch from Bangkok, reported: "Most observers here believe that Khmer Rouge are continuing to kill large numbers of Cambodians whom they believe oppose Communist rule. However, recent information indicates the killing is now limited largely to the former middle class and specifically to those with education." *Washington Post*, April 13, 1976. See also *Washington Post*, May 4, 1976; Ponchaud, *Cambodge Année Zéro*, Chapters 1-4; Shawcross, "Cambodia under Its New Rulers"; Kershaw, "Cambodian National Union"; testimony of Charles Twining, *Hearings on Human Rights in Cambodia*; John Barron and Anthony Paul, *Murder of a Gentle Land* (New York: Reader's Digest Press, distributed by Thomas Y. Crowell Co., 1977).

52. David P. Chandler, "The Constitution of Democratic Kamphuchea (Cambodia): The Semantics of Revolutionary Change," *Pacific Affairs* 49, no. 3 (Fall 1976): 506-515.

53. François Ponchaud, "Cambodia under the Lash," *Atlas World Press Review* (excerpted from *Le Monde*), May 1976, p. 19.

54. A translation of the constitution is found in *FBIS*, January 5, 1976. A thoughtful analysis of the constitution is given by Chandler, "The Constitution of Democratic Kamphuchea."

55. Ibid., p. 509.

56. Phnom Penh Domestic Service in Cambodian, March 21, 1976, in *FBIS*, March 22, 1976.

57. See Quinn, "Cambodia 1976," p. 45; and testimony of Richard C. Holbrooke, assistant secretary of state for Far East and Pacific affairs, Department of State, in *Hearing on Human Rights in Cambodia*, July 26, 1977.

58. The members of the royal government (GRUNK), which was dissolved in April 1976, were as follows:

Leaders of Government

Chief of State	Norodom Sihanouk (Prince)
Prime Minister	Khieu Samphan
Minister of Information and Propaganda	Hou Nim
Vice-Premier in Charge of Foreign Affairs	Ieng Sary
Vice-Premier in Charge of National Defense	Son Sen
Minister of Justice	Phurissara (Prince)
Deputy Foreign Minister	Ros Chet Thor
Minister of Public Health	Thiounn Thoeunn
Minister of Education	Kieu Thirith
Minister of Public Works	Toch Phoeun
Minister of Religions and Social Affairs	Chou Chet
Minister of Economy	Koy Thuon
Minister of Armament	Men San
Deputy Minister of Security	Sok Thouk
Deputy Minister of Information	Kong Sophal
Deputy Minister of Foreign Affairs	Van Piny
Politburo Secretary	Keat Chhon

Source: U.S. Embassy in Phnom Penh, 1975

The leaders of the Revolutionary Army of Kampuchea were as follows:

		Date
Commander in Chief	Khieu Samphan	1971
High Command:		
President	Khieu Samphan	1/72
Vice-President		
Chief of the Military Directorate	Saloth Sar	1/72
Vice-President		
Chief of the Political Directorate	Nuon Chea	1/72
Vice-President		
Deputy Chief of the Military Directorate	So Vanna	1/72

		Date
Member		
Chief of the Directorate of		
Military Matériel	Thieun Chhith	1/72
Member		
Chief of the General Staff	Son Sen	1/72
General Staff:		
Chief	Son Sen	1/72
Members	Cheat Chhe	8/76

Army founded: "Early 1968": (FBIS-APA-77-3, January 5, 1977, H7)
"January 17, 1968": (FBIS-APA-77-11 of January 17, 1977, H2)
A list of the current command of the Revolutionary Army is not available.

59. Hamburg, *Der Spiegel,* May 9, 1977, in *FBIS,* May 11, 1977.

60. Phnom Penh Domestic Service in Cambodian, January 3, 1978, in *FBIS,* January 4, 1978.

61. Donald P. Whitaker et al., eds., *Area Handbook for the Khmer Republic (Cambodia)* (Washington, D.C.: U.S. Government Printing Office, 1973), Chapter 12.

62. Ieng Sary, Address to UN General Assembly, October 5, 1976, in *FBIS,* October 15, 1976.

63. Whitaker et al., *Area Handbook for the Khmer Republic,* p. 8.

64. U.S., Department of State, Publication 7747, *Background Notes: Cambodia* (Washington, D.C.: Government Printing Office, 1977).

65. Jack Anderson, *Washington Post,* June 23, 1975; *FEER,* July 25, 1975; George C. Hildebrand and G. Porter, *Cambodia: Starvation and Revolution* (New York: Monthly Review Press, 1976), p. 59.

66. Phnom Penh Domestic Service in Cambodian, May 19, 1977, in *FBIS,* May 24, 1977, H3.

67. *FBIS,* April 18, 1977.

68. Tiziano Terzani interview with Ieng Sary, May 8, 1977.

69. Phnom Penh Domestic Service in Cambodian, March 17, 1977, in *FBIS,* March 21, 1977, H3; speech by Khieu Samphan, *FBIS,* April 18, 1977.

70. Khieu Samphan, in *FBIS,* April 18, 1977, H5.

71. *Background Notes: Cambodia.*

72. *FBIS,* October 15, 1976, H10.

73. Bank of America, Asia Representative Office, Hong Kong, *Indochina Spotlight,* March 1977.

74. Khieu Samphan, *FBIS,* April 18, 1977, H5.

75. *FBIS,* May 23, 1977, H1. The Danish ambassador to the PRC, Kjeed Mortensen, after a visit to Cambodia in January 1978 along with other

diplomats, was quoted by journalists as having said that Phnom Penh resembled a "ghost city." According to the *New York Times* account, he and his colleagues were told that the "present population was 20,000 [sic], but it appeared to be much less, he said." *New York Times,* January 23, 1978. See also *Washington Post,* January 23, 1978, and Agence France Presse dispatch from Hong Kong, January 23, 1978, in *FBIS,* January 23, 1978, for similar accounts of the diplomatic visit to Phnom Penh.

    76. *FEER,* April 29, 1977.

    77. Ibid., December 10, 1976, pp. 49-50.

    78. Tokyo KYODO in English, February 28, 1977, in *FBIS,* March 2, 1977.

    79. *FBIS,* January 12 and April 20, 1977.

    80. Foreign Minister Ieng Sary said, "During the war, we lost at least 600,000 people, not counting the wounded and maimed." Interview with Tiziano Terzani, May 8, 1977. He had previously told the UN General Assembly, "more than one million of our people, or almost 13% of the Cambodian population were killed or wounded" in attaining the victory of April 17, 1975. Phnom Penh Domestic Service in Cambodian, October 8, 1976, in *FBIS,* October 15, 1976.

    81. Ponchaud, *Cambodge Année Zéro,* p. 97.

    82. Barron and Paul, *Murder of a Gentle Land.* In testimony before a House of Representatives subcommittee in May 1977, Mr. Barron stated that he now believed that the estimate of 1.2 million deaths was low. *Hearing on Human Rights in Cambodia,* May 3, 1977, p. 16. Barron and Paul's estimates (p. 206) of the numbers dead are based on the following assumptions concerning the population:

Driven from cities and government-controlled villages in April 1975	4,000,000
Perished in forced marches to new living areas (10%)	400,000
Died in June-September famine (12%)	430,000
Died in second famine 1976 (8%)	250,000
Others executed in military/government purge	100,000
Killed during escape attempts	20,000
Total dead	1,200,000

    83. *Time Magazine,* April 19, 1976, p. 65. A first anniversary of the Indochina Resource Center, celebrating the first anniversary of peace, denounced these media "horror" stories, particularly *Time Magazine*'s, as fabrications "which obviously originated with U.S. officials, for whom they served the useful purpose of deflecting attention from, and ultimately justifying, the American war against Cambodia." *Time Magazine*'s estimates of 500,000 to 600,000 deaths, it mentioned, "just happen to approximate the number of

Cambodians who the Cambodian government believes were killed during the war by the American bombing." *U.S./Indochina Report,* April 30, 1976.

84. *London Daily Telegraph,* April 8 and August 15, 1976.

85. *Hearing on Human Rights in Cambodia,* July 26, 1977.

86. Robert Shaplen, "A Reporter at Large (Indo-China Refugees)," *The New Yorker,* September 5, 1977, pp. 33-66.

87. Rome ANSA in English, September 24, 1976, in *FBIS,* September 28, 1976.

88. Tiziano Terzani interview with Ieng Sary, May 8, 1977. The World Bank in its *World Tables 1976* gives population estimates only up to 1973, at 7.566 million.

89. Ibid.

90. Ponchaud, *Cambodge Année Zéro,* p. 171.

91. Osborne, "Reflections on the Cambodian Tragedy," p. 5.

92. Ponchaud, *Cambodge Année Zéro,* p. 171.

93. Ibid., p. 172.

94. David P. Chandler, "Transformation in Cambodia," *Commonweal* 104, no. 7, April 1, 1977.

95. David P. Chandler with Ben Kiernan and Muy Hong Lim, "The Early Phases of Liberation in Northwest Cambodia: Conversations with Peang Sophi," Working Paper Series, no. 10, November 1976, Monash University, Australia.

96. See Hammer, "Indochina: Communist But Non-Aligned," pp. 1-17.

97. Phnom Penh Domestic Service, October 8, 1976; *FBIS,* October 15, 1976, H-1.

98. Nayan Chanda, "Cambodia Looks for Friends," *FEER,* April 29, 1977, pp. 11-12.

99. On Cambodian-Thai border problems, see *London Daily Telegraph,* February 17, 1977; *FEER,* August 5, 12, and 19, 1977; *New York Times,* August 20, 1977. On Cambodian-Vietnamese border tensions, see *New York Times,* August 9, 1977; *FEER,* August 19, 1977.

100. Speech by deputy prime minister for economy, Vorn Vet, Phnom Penh Domestic Service in Cambodian, January 3, 1977, in *FBIS,* January 5, 1977.

101. Peking NCNA in English, September 28, 1977, in *FBIS,* September 29, 1977.

102. Ibid.

103. See *FBIS,* North Korea, October 5 and 7, 1977.

104. *Americans Missing in Southeast Asia: Final Report,* pp. 14-16.

105. Phnom Penh Domestic Service in Cambodian, March 18, 1977, *FBIS,* March 21, 1977.

Chapter 5

1. Samuel T. Huntington, *Political Order in Changing Societies* (New Haven: Yale University Press, 1968), p. 264.

2. *New York Times*, September 29, 30, 1977.

3. See Mark N. Hagopian, *The Phenomenon of Revolution* (New York: Dodd, Mead and Co., 1975), pp. 194-250.

4. For example, "Objective: 1. To prevent the countries of Southeast Asia from passing into the communist orbit, and to assist them to develop will and ability to resist communism from within and without and to contribute to the strengthening of the free world." 1952 Statement of Policy of the NSC, *The Pentagon Papers* (New York: Bantam Books, 1971), p. 27.

5. "Address by Marshall Green, Assistant Secretary for East Asian and Pacific Affairs, on the Nixon Doctrine," *Department of State Bulletin*, February 8, 1971, pp. 161-165.

6. President Ford's Pacific Doctrine, Honolulu, Hawaii, December 7, 1975.

7. Secretary of State Cyrus Vance, "United States and Asia," speech before the Asia Society, New York, June 29, 1977.

8. The United States engaged in what President Carter called "serious negotiations" with the Soviet Union in 1977 to reach an agreement on stabilizing the military situation in the region to prevent an escalating arms competition. Speech by President Carter, "U.S.-Soviet Relations," July 21, 1977, Charleston, South Carolina.

9. The U.S. ambassador to Malaysia, Francis T. Underhill, Jr., wrote a confidential personal estimate of the Philippine bases question in 1976, arguing carefully against U.S. retention. This memorandum was "leaked" to the press in March 1977, as negotiations over the question remained in a stall. Whether this leak was intended to encourage American opponents of base retention or to make the Philippine government less demanding in its proposal for rental is not clear.

10. A. Doak Barnett, *China Policy: Old Problems and New Challenges* (Washington, D.C.: The Brookings Institution, 1977), pp. 114-115, argues that genuine military neutralization of Southeast Asia should be in the interest of all the major as well as local powers, but that Sino-Soviet hostility makes it unlikely.

11. A minor border disagreement between Cambodia and Thailand was actually settled in 1962 by the International Court of Justice, which carefully examined the tangled, French-imposed boundary demarcations (Temple of Preah Vihaer case). Similar areas of dispute seem to underlie skirmishes on the Thai-Cambodian border in the summer of 1977 as well as on the

Cambodia-Vietnam border. See *New York Times,* September 1, 1977.

12. *FEER,* August 26 and September 2, 1977.

13. U.S., Congress, Senate, Committee on the Judiciary, *Humanitarian Problems of Southeast Asia, 1977: A Study Mission Report,* 95th Cong., 1st sess., December 1977, Tables 1 and 2, and pp. 14, 16. See also assistant secretary for East Asian and Pacific affairs, Richard C. Holbrooke, Remarks before the Subcommittee on Immigration, Citizenship and International Law, Committee on the Judiciary, U.S. House of Representatives, August 4, 1977.

14. See various heartrending accounts by Henry Kamm in the *New York Times,* June 17, 21, July 4, August 22, September 9, 16, 20, 1977.

15. *Humanitarian Problems of Southeast Asia, 1977,* Table 2.

16. *Herald American* (Boston), September 5, 1977.

17. *Humanitarian Problems of Southeast Asia, 1977,* pp. 44-45.

18. Ibid., pp. 29-35.

19. On the occasion of his address to the UN General Assembly on October 5, 1977, President Carter signed the Covenant on Civil and Political Rights and the Covenant on Economic, Social and Cultural Rights.

20. See testimony of Theodore Jacqueney, Reverend André Gelinas, Nguyen Van Coi, and Nguyen Cong Hoan in U.S., Congress, House of Representatives, Committee on International Relations, Subcommittee on International Organizations, *Hearings on Human Rights in Vietnam,* 91st Cong., 1st sess.; and T. Jacqueney, "They Are Us, Were We Vietnamese," *World View,* April 1977.

21. A petition sent to Hanoi in protest over human rights violations split the old antiwar coalition of leaders but did produce an official response denying its allegations.

22. *Human Rights in Vietnam,* testimony of Julia Forsythe, William S. Turley, Paul F. McCleary, Don Luce, and Margaret A. Meinertz.

23. "Normalization of Relations," Deputy Secretary of State Warren Christopher, at Occidental College, June 11, 1977.

24. Tabulation of over 50,000 "opinion ballots" received by the Foreign Policy Association in its Great Decisions '77 program showed 51 percent willing to give full recognition to the PRC once it promised peaceful means in resolving the Taiwan issue, and 41 percent ready to resume full diplomatic and trade relations with Cuba.

25. Nonetheless, a public opinion poll organized by the *New York Times* and CBS News in July 1977 indicated that 66 percent of Americans were in favor of sending food or medical assistance to Vietnam, and 49 percent approved of industrial and farm equipment aid.

26. Regrettably, President Carter mortgaged this possibility for 1978

by promising, as an inducement to the Congress to drop its restrictive amendments on the use of funds by international financial institutions, to instruct U.S. delegates to vote against loans to the Indochina states and to three other states previously singled out by Congress. *New York Times,* October 19, 1977.

Index

Afro-Asian Solidarity Committee, 96-97
AID, 109; offices occupied, 89
Alliance of Communist Youth of Kampuchea, 136
"Angka," 124, 133, 144, 148, 158, 159
Angkor Empire, 150
Angola, 4, 81
ARVN, 31
ASEAN, 4-5, 163, 166-167, 187, 188; member nations, 72; relations with Laos, 118-120; relations with the Soviet Union, 81; relations with Vietnam, 72-79, 86
Ashbrook Amendment (1977), 24-25
"Asia Forum," 75-76
Asian Development Bank, 17, 26, 52, 56, 75, 85, 86, 114
Asia Society, 165
Association of Democratic Women of Kamphuchea, 132

Bingham Amendment (1976), 16-17, 18

Cambodia, agriculture, 144; Buddhism in, 139, 141; economy, 142-146; education, 144; export crops, 146; foreigners expelled, 124; foreign policy, 151-156; GNP, 142; GRUNK leaders, 209 (n58) [see also Khmer Rouge]; hostilities with Vietnam, 12, 65, 66-67, 135, 155, 168; industry, 146; literacy rate, 142; malaria in, 145; and MIAs, 14; population, 71, 133; refugees from, 124, 180; relations with China, 68, 69,

71, 145, 154-155; relations with North Korea, 155; relations with the Soviet Union, 68, 69; relations with Thailand, 152-153; relations with the United States, 156; relations with Vietnam, 65-69; United States trade embargo on, 16-17; war devastation, 147-148
Cam Ranh Bay naval base, 81, 166
Cao Dai, 30-31
Carter, Jimmy, 14, 181
Chhoeur Doeun, 135
Children's Defense League, 14
China. See Cambodia; Laos; Vietnam
Chinh, Truong, 41, 42-43, 44, 45
Christmas bombing, 20
CIA support, 159
Clark Field, 166
CMEA, 81
Cochin China, 68
Colombo Conference of Non-Aligned States, 18, 77, 148
Committee for the Support of the Reunification of Korea, 96-97
Communist insurgency in Southeast Asia, 73-74
Communist Party of Kampuchea. See Pracheachon
Communist Party of Laos, 87. See also LPRP
Comprador capitalist class, 42, 102
Conference on Non-Aligned Powers, 146
Congress and executive policy, 2-4
Cong, Vo Chi, 44-45
"Cult of personality," 133